Romanians in Western Europe

Romanians in Western Europe

Migration, Status Dilemmas, and Transnational Connections

Remus Gabriel Anghel

LEXINGTON BOOKS
Lanham • Boulder • New York • Toronto • Plymouth, UK

Published by Lexington Books
A wholly owned subsidiary of The Rowman & Littlefield Publishing Group, Inc.
4501 Forbes Boulevard, Suite 200, Lanham, Maryland 20706
www.rowman.com

10 Thornbury Road, Plymouth PL6 7PP, United Kingdom

British Library Cataloguing in Publication Information Available

Library of Congress Cataloging-in-Publication Data

Anghel, Remus Gabriel.
Romanians in Western Europe : migration, status dilemmas, and transnational connections / Remus Gabriel Anghel.
pages cm
Includes bibliographical references.
ISBN 978-0-7391-7888-1 (cloth : alk. paper) — ISBN 978-0-7391-7889-8 (electronic)
1. Romanians—Germany—Nuremberg—Social conditions. 2. Romanians—Italy—Milan—Social conditions. 3. Romanians—Legal status, laws, etc.—Germany. 4. Romanians—Legal status, laws, etc.—Italy. 5. Nuremberg (Germany)—Emigration and immigration. 6. Milan (Italy)—Emigration and immigration. 7. Timisoara (Romania)—Emigration and immigration. 8. Borsa (Cluj, Romania)—Emigration and immigration. 9. Emigrant remittances—Romania—Timisoara. 10. Emigrant remittancez—Romania—Borsa (Cluj) I. Title.
DD901.N92A64 2013
305.85'9104—dc23
2013017726

∞™ The paper used in this publication meets the minimum requirements of American National Standard for Information Sciences Permanence of Paper for Printed Library Materials, ANSI/NISO Z39.48-1992.

Printed in the United States of America

For Alina and Sofia

Contents

Acknowledgments

This book has taken a number of years to complete. I would first like to express my gratitude to my professors at the University of Bielefeld, who actively encouraged me to conduct the research: Professors Joanna Pfaff-Czarnecka, Jörg Bergmann, and Thomas Faist. I also thank the International Graduate School in Sociology and the Institute for World Society Studies at the Bielefeld University for accepting me as a member in the DFG doctoral research group 844, "Making and Representing the Global."

Over the years I have also received encouragement and helpful comments from colleagues and friends in Bielefeld and Cluj, among whom I mention in particular Ştefan Dorondel and Istvan Horváth. A Marie Curie scholarship at Fieri, Turin, within the network TOM, "Transnationality of Migrants," allowed me to write a large part of the manuscript. I thank Professor Michael Eve and Pietro Cingolani for their constructive comments. I worked further on the book during my postdoctoral fellowship at the Romanian Academy in Cluj within the project POSDRU 89/1.5/S/60189, "Postdoctoral Programs for Sustainable Development in a Knowledge Based Society," co-financed by the European Social Fund. I completed the manuscript while being involved in the project "Recasting Migrants' Voices: Local Perspectives on Migration, Development and Social Change in Romania" — CNCS PNII-ID-PCE-2011-3-0602. For support in completing the book I am grateful to Ovidiu Oltean for his support, Frank Schaer for proofreading the book, and Amy King and the persons involved in reviewing my work at Lexington Books.

Above all, I thank the migrants who allowed my intrusion into their lives: Andy Altmann-Papy, Mircea Crăciun, Gaga, the Ştețco family, Ion-Neamţu, and Dan from Rona. I also thank the Romanian organizations in Nuremberg, Turin, and Milan with which I carried out interviews. Mioara Bolboacă assisted me during my research in Romania.

Introduction

November 2007, Rome. Romulus Mailat, a Romanian citizen residing without regular papers in the suburbs of Rome, was accused of robbing, raping, and savagely murdering Giovanna Regianni, a forty-seven-year-old Italian woman, wife of an Italian military official. This regrettable event made the front page of the main Italian media and had wide European coverage. It brought about unprecedented debates in Italy concerning the situation of Romanian irregular migrants.[1] This event was not a unique occurrence, inasmuch as Romanians were the largest and among the most visible migrant groups in Italy. On different occasions, Romanians had been accused of acts of theft, begging, or organized prostitution, but were also noted for their high degree of poverty and marginality. After the episode in Rome, riots flared in some Italian cities and anti-migrant attitudes intensified.[2] The Italian media took up the issue of the supposed delinquency of the Romanians. The police and the local municipality in Rome demolished the improvised shelters and migrants' camps around the city, where many irregular migrants lived. Soon after, the Prodi government issued a "security package" meant to discourage the allegedly high criminality among migrants. Debates about the irregularity of Romanian migrants took both radical and tolerant positions. Radicals complained about migrants' lack of civic virtues, whereas many Italian intellectuals and non-governmental organization (NGO) activists took a firm stance against the criminalization of irregular migrants in their country.

The arrival of many East Europeans, with Romanians among the largest migrant groups, rejuvenated public concerns on immigration in a number of West European countries. Following the liberalization of border controls and the massive economic and political changes in Eastern Europe, human mobility increased and became a permanent feature of post–Cold War Europe. The changes brought about by the European Union (EU) enlargement process increased East–West mobility to unprecedented levels. A massive flow of migrant workers to the newly united Europe posed new challenges for both East and West European states. Romanian migration has been one of the most rapidly growing in Europe in the past years. It was also often considered one of the most socially problematic, as migrants from this new EU country were often considered troublemakers by national authorities and the mass media. In Italy, it stirred up concern that uncontrolled mass migration posed problems

1

that authorities had difficulty in dealing with (Colombo and Sciortino 2003). For the first time EU citizens, in this case Romanians, were deported from the country for security and public safety reasons. Yet, as EU citizens, Romanians enjoyed special rights, including freedom of movement within the EU as well as political and welfare benefits, which rendered the expulsions and migration control measures wearing but ultimately futile. However, it was not only in Italy that debates about irregular migration stirred up concerns about who should be entitled to come and settle in the country and who should not. In Europe, securitization against unwanted immigration—the so-called Fortress Europe position— is premised on the assumption that only some, and not all, migrants should be allowed in. And clearly, there are views that these migrants, usually the desired and legal ones, do provide net benefits, and such ones are warmly welcomed by their new states and societies. Besides, there is a fundamental argument that migrants should be provided with civic, political, and economic rights, because only by possessing such rights can migrants be expected to share social responsibility and incorporate successfully into the host society.

In this book I intend to challenge the commonly held assumptions that artificially divide migrants into clear-cut categories of winners and losers of international migration based on the conditions set out for them in the receiving countries. In order to explore these issues, I compare two processes of migration and look at how migrants from Romania constructed their social status transnationally. The first is made of ethnic Germans who migrated legally from Timişoara, in Romania, to Nuremberg, Germany. The second is made of migrants who migrated irregularly from Borşa, Romania, to Milan, Italy. The analysis will unfold a puzzling situation. Irregular Romanian migrants in Milan had fewer rights and opportunities, but in migration they gained prestige and came to feel a sense of success. Migrants receiving more rights, here the Germans migrating from Timişoara to Nuremberg, perceived a loss of social prestige, despite extensive state support and full access to the rich German labor market and welfare system. The social and political understanding of migration widely differed in the two cases I analyze, as Italy and Germany had quite different ways of dealing with migration. Such differences played out in the ways in which migrants considered themselves entitled to obtain certain rights, social recognition, and a certain status in the destination countries. In 1990, when ethnic Germans started to migrate en masse to Germany, the country had a quite substantial experience of migration and a structured approach to handling it. The ethnic Germans' migration was meant to compensate for the sufferings and expulsions of East European Germans after the Second World War and to serve as a means to bring them back into the fold of their "Fatherland." In this process state institutions supported the German newcomers, giving them right of entry to the country, accommodation, and easy access to the labor market and welfare benefits. Thus for the Romanian Germans from Timişoara, Germany did everything possible to support their incorporation. These German brethren were received with open arms "as Germans among Germans" (Oltmer 2006; Schuck and Münz 1998, 182). In Romania on the other hand, this ethnic migration was bemoaned as the end of the centuries-old existence of the German community, and an important loss of human capital; the ethnic Germans had been highly valued for their industriousness and their organized spirit that had promoted modernization and economic development at the margins of Europe.

In contrast, Italy's migration policy was unstructured and public institutions were tolerant towards the massive flow of irregular migrants (Zincone 2006b). If Germany adopted a differential-exclusionist (Castles 1995) model of migration and an integration policy which provided equal juridical rights for their German co-ethnics, Italy adopted a laissez-faire approach. Instead of recruiting the labor force according to the needs of the economy, the state kept its hands off control of migration and instead pursued mass legalization campaigns whenever the number of irregular migrants became too high. Only after 2000, when irregular migration boomed, did major concerns emerge, and the country started to structure its policy (Colombo and Sciortino 2003; Zincone 2006a). A few years later, Romanians were already considered "a security problem." Migrants from Borşa arriving irregularly in Milan had to find ways to adapt to harsh living and working conditions, without any institutions to support their incorporation.

The puzzle outlined above suggests that in the course of migration, social status may change in contradicting ways. Migrants may start to climb the social ladder "from the bottom up," as in the case of migrants employed in unskilled jobs. Obviously, the situation is different when migrants' professional skills are valued in the labor market, like the young Romanians who could get entry to better jobs abroad compared to what awaited them in Romania (Bleahu 2004a; Csedö 2005; 2008; Moroşanu 2011). Likewise, asylum seekers could gain significant access to jobs upon receiving asylum recognition and educational certificates: Eastern European migrants up to 1989 (Fijalkowski 1993) are a case in point. A utility approach to migrants' incorporation would suggest that the more opportunities and rights migrants possess, the better their migration prospects are likely to be, and that economic success and economic models of migration and migrants' incorporation may provide insight into migrants' socioeconomic attainments and sense of success. But such an approach still fails to explain the dilemma outlined above. Therefore, I intend to explore here the various and often contradicting ways in which migrants from Romania in Nuremberg and Milan have sought to construct and value their social status. The analysis thus provides a framework for analyzing social status in transnational migration. It looks at how states' differing migration policies, migrants' incorporation, and migrant transnationalism impact on migrants' lives, taking into consideration broader social, political, and economic changes affecting Europe at the present time.

* * *

In recent years Romania has become one of the main source-countries for migration to Western Europe. Two momentous events account for the rapid expansion of this migration: the collapse of state socialism, followed by the liberalization of international travel from Romania after 1989, and the Romanians' gaining freedom of movement within the EU from 2002 onwards. After decades of coercive control of mobility exerted by the Romanian socialist state, Romanians after 1989 became "crazy to travel" (Diminescu 2003). But for more than ten years, the mobility of Romanians was severely restricted by West European states, until the position changed in 2002 and they were able to travel freely in the EU. Over these years there were major shifts in Romanian migration patterns: tight migration control during state socialism, easier but restricted migration in the 1990s, strong irregular migration between 2002 and 2007, and unrestricted migration after 2007 when Romania became officially an EU member state.

In the first two years after the fall of the communist regime, the destination for Romanian citizens was Germany, where the bulk of ethnic Germans still living in Romania had migrated *en masse*, together with an increasing number of Romanians. Ethnic Germans, the so-called *Aussiedler*, were very favorably received in Germany during the years of Romanian socialism and afterwards.

After 1989, fears of a huge mass migration from Eastern Europe grew in Western Europe. It was estimated that between twenty-five and fifty million potential migrants could descend on the West overnight (Tränhardt 1996, 228). It came as no surprise that during the first years after 1989 West European governments undertook serious measures to limit significantly the number of migrants from Eastern Europe. For many East Europeans a forty-year policy of open doors maintained by West European states had come to a halt.

Germany was particularly anxious over the scenario of mass migration, feeling there was reason to believe that East European migrants were targeting Germany in particular. And indeed, during the first years after 1989 Germany was the most important receiver of the East–West migration (Dietz 2003). Its migration policies started to change shortly after 1990, when firm steps were taken towards a more restrictive policy. The shrinking benefits and a more selective admission of ethnic Germans coincided with a marked decrease in the pool of ethnic Germans in Eastern Europe. Migration pressure remained high in several areas of the former Soviet Union (Groenendijk 1997), but after 1993 Germany started to selectively turn down applications from *Aussiedler*[3] (idem). Yet for Romanian Germans these new procedures did not apply. They migrated on a massive scale immediately after 1990 and in just a few years a small community of some 60,000 people remained in Romania[4] out of about 350,000 living there in 1977. These were persons too old or simply unwilling to migrate. This wave of ethnic migration brought to Germany a significant number of non-Germans as family members.[5] Meanwhile, some of those who migrated after 1989 maintained their ties to their origin communities. Ethnic organizations in Romania such as the German Democratic Forum of Romania, German high schools, and social ties to the origin communities perpetuated relations between the ethnic Germans and their places of origin (Michalon 2003b; 2004). In this sense Michalon (2003a) shows how after 1990 the migration of Germans was not only a "return migration" to Germany, but also a migration having a certain degree of circularity and involvement in the country of origin through family visits to Romania. Migration between Romania and Germany led to the establishment of a number of networks of temporary labor migration, and access to the networks of ethnic Germans mediated access to temporary labor in Germany (Michalon 2003a, 21) even many years after 1990 (Câmpeanu 2011).

In the first years after 1989 there was also a strong wave of Romanian citizens requesting political asylum, predominantly in Germany. These asylum seekers were the second largest category of migrants from Romania between 1990 and 1994. From the beginning of the 1990s Romanians moved to Germany either irregularly, crossing the borders between Poland, Czech Republic, and Germany (Reyniers 2003, 57),[6] or received invitations from Romanian Germans (Diminescu 2003, 16). Once in Germany, they submitted requests for political asylum. But after 1990 Germany's policy towards asylum seekers started to change, even though the number of potential applicants seeking to come to Germany was on the rise. Legal procedures were complicated, and some authors calculate that in the end 60 to 70 percent of applicants were allowed to stay and work indefinitely (Fijalkowski 1993; Kurthen 1995, 926). The result was that political asylum came to be used as an immigration strategy. During that period, about 240,000 Romanian citizens applied for asylum in Western Europe (Fassmann and Münz 1994, 532–33) out of which Germany received the largest numbers: there were about 60,000 applicants in 1992 and more than 140,000 applicants in 1993.[7] By 1993 Romania was considered a safe country and further applications were denied (Weber et al. 2003). Germany signed a bilateral repatriation agreement with Romania in September 1992. Romania agreed to take back 100,000 Romanian citizens, while Germany agreed to cover the transport costs (Kurthen 1995, 928). Nevertheless, a large number of asylum seekers disappeared from the statistics.[8]

Germany represented at the beginning of the 1990s the main target-country of Romanian migration, comprising both Romanian Germans and Romanian asylum seekers. In the years following 1993 Romanian migration to Germany continued but at a much slower pace, consisting mainly of marriage migrants, some limited labor migration, and a tiny brain drain.[9] Due to the large number of migrants who arrived in Germany between 1980 and 1993, the country remained the main entry point for Romanians migrating to Europe throughout the 1990s: about 500,000 migrants from Romania settled in Germany, and the number of tourist visas issued to Romania from Germany (180,000 visas a year) far exceeded the number granted by all other European countries together[10] (Diminescu 2003). Romanians receiving these invitations afterwards went to other European destinations (Diminescu 2003, 16).

After 1993 Romanian migration to Europe displayed a high degree of diversification. It became mostly irregular, with migrants starting to move towards different European countries. Data emerging from a number of case studies highlight migrants' attempts to adapt to different labor markets in Western Europe and to find permissive contexts. The research on Romanian migration to Europe suggests that migration was in the main not caused by supply factors in the country of origin but rather by a complex combination of demand and supply, with labor demand factors playing an increasingly important role.[11] This argument is less clear in the case of Romanian migration to Germany, where political factors and state institutions were important in accepting those regarded as *Aussiedler* while sending back a large number of asylum seekers. But migration persisted when there was a strong demand in other European markets for labor.

Other forms of international mobility were now emerging, such as petty trade with the countries of former Yugoslavia, Turkey, Poland, and Hungary. Petty traders were among the first who looked internationally for alternative economic niches. Their practices subsequently expanded, and many became the pioneers of the migration process (Diminescu 2003). Other pioneers of migration towards Western Europe came from among the labor migrants who were recruited before 1989 by the agencies of the socialist state to work abroad in countries such as Libya, Iran, Iraq, Syria, and Egypt (Șerban and Grigoraș 2000). For many Romanians this phase represented the first chance of a way out of Romania, a country which had severely restricted the exit of its citizens towards Europe for about 50 years (Diminescu, Ohlinger, and Rey 2003). The migration of these pioneers led to the gradual establishing of migration routes (Anghel 2008; Cingolani and Piperno 2006; Stan 2005b).

A new stage in the development of Romanian migration was from 1993 to 1996. Migration was here low in numbers but diversified: there were seasonal migrants, circular (shuttle) migrants, brain drain migrants (mostly students), ethnic migrants, marriage migrants, disguised tourists, and so on. After 1997 Romanian migration attained a certain level of development. The decisive factor was the process of de-industrialization in Romania, culminating in a stark impoverishment of the population

(Horváth 2007). Under state socialism, the process of socialist industrialization had created all over Romania a class of commuters, peasant-workers who were employed in industry but resided in villages. They had double employment, in industry and also in small-scale agricultural activities (Verdery 1996). "Because dairy products, vegetables, fruits, and good quality meat [were] often difficult to [purchase] in towns, access to them [strengthened] ties between new urban migrants and kin left behind in villages" (Chirot 1978, 479). De-industrialization reversed this relation between villages and cities, since commuters were among the first who lost their jobs in many post-socialist societies (Hann 1995, 2002). This situation put rural households under strong pressure and created a class of potential migrants (Anghel 2008; Cingolani 2009; Horváth 2008). De-industrialization also massively affected the urban population in towns and cities where industry had collapsed. In such areas most of the people lost their jobs, and incentives for migration grew. This massive restructuring partially explains the development of migration after 1997 at the national level. In order to get a sense of this dramatic change, I would note that from a total of 9.5 million jobs in 1990 only 4.5 million remained active in 1999 (Horváth and Anghel 2009) and 4.1 million in 2010 (Stănculescu and Stoiciu 2012). Unemployment and impoverishment were seeing a dramatic increase. Since then, Romanian migration has continued growing. Through this firm increase, some clearer patterns of migration developed which became more obvious afterwards, and could be seen to differ from the previous period when irregular migration was only exploratory and unstructured. Despite the control measures undertaken by West European governments to limit the migration from Eastern Europe, people had multiple opportunities to move abroad (Stan 2005b; Bleahu 2004b; Cingolani 2009).

This came about also because in the 1990s, despite fifty years of programmatic state control over population movement, Romanians had developed many ties to Europe through various channels—through Romania's ethnic minorities (including its small communities of Italians, Greeks, Turks, or Croatians), European small-scale investments, mobility schemes for students and professionals, tourism (Nagy 2008), religious networks (Catholic, neo-Protestant), recruitment agencies, migration brokers, and so on. These ties created diversified and expanding structures of opportunities for potential migrants, and migrants would often choose one among a number of possible migration destinations. This development was further sustained by the increasing demand for labor in the countries of Southern Europe, particularly Italy and Spain. In Italy, migration had started already in the 1980s, but emerged as an important subject of public concern and policy debates mainly when substantial inflows arrived in the country in a general context where there was a solid demand for labor. The Romanian migration to Italy developed further in the 1990s, driven by migrant networks based on kinship and friendship (Alexandru 2006; Anghel 2008; Bleahu 2007; Cingolani and Piperno 2006; Sandu 2006; Vlase 2008). In some cases religious networks among Catholic or Protestant believers helped organize migration (Cingolani 2008; Stan 2005b).

Furthermore, some authors consider Romanian migration to Italy circular, with migrants shuttling between Romania and Western Europe (Constantin 2004; Sandu et al. 2004). Similar to the thesis of the incomplete migration of Polish migrants to Western Europe and of Ukrainian migrants to Poland (Kaczmarczyk and Okólski 2005; Okólski 1996), Romanian migration entailed a high level of circularity and the maintenance of ties to the country of origin. It was a movement back and forth, a "settling into mobility" (Diminescu 1998). The destination countries were seen as countries where money was made, not as countries of settlement (Stan 2005b). Until 2000 to 2002, there were not many legal Romanians residing in Italy. But as migrants acquired more rights and social ties in their country of destination their migration projects changed. Long residence abroad was followed by family reunion and settlement plans (Schmidt 2006).

From 2000 to 2002, a series of institutional changes impacted on Romanian migration. In February 2000 Romania was invited to join the EU and the visa regime for Romanian citizens started to normalize (Diminescu 2003). After 2002 Romanians were granted freedom of movement within the EU. As a consequence there was mass migration towards Italy and Spain. Italy soon became the West European country with the largest Romanian migrant community (Ban 2009). Already in 2008 Pittau, Ricci, and Silj (2008) advanced a figure of over one million Romanians living in the Italian peninsula. Migration became easier and less costly. If before 2002 migration from poorer areas was less intense, after 2002 emigration spread all over Romania. After January 1, 2007, Romania joined the EU and Romanian migrants started to acquire more economic, social, and political rights given their status as European citizens.

In public and political debates, Romanian migrants often faced negative stereotypes (McMahon 2012) inasmuch as Romanian migrants in Italy displayed a certain degree of marginality and precariousness. This issue came to the fore in the European media in recent years with reports on poor Romanian Roma migrants settling in camps in different Italian cities. The precariousness of the Romanian migration was revealed in many studies showing that irregular migrants had no clear sleeping or working arrangements (Bleahu 2007; Cingolani 2011). Research also highlighted cases of migrants' marginal activities in different Italian cities, such as begging, prostitution, and pick-pocketing (Alexandru 2006; Lăzăroiu 2000; Marcu 2010, 2011; Tesar 2011). The high visibility of Romanian migration in Italy was also a consequence of its quick development, as it reached about one million people in less than a decade in a context where institutional support was lacking. In spite of this quick development, migrants adapted without too much difficulty to the market, as they arrived in a context where there was a solid demand for labor (MMT and ASG 2007).

After 2008 a last phase in the Romanian migration developed along with the current world economic crisis. If before 2008 Romanians started to settle in the West, shuttle migration developed in the period afterwards. As far as both Romania and the Southern European countries were affected by the crisis, it became increasingly difficult for Romanians to have assured and sufficient earnings either at home or abroad. At the same time, return was not a viable option, in a context when more than 20 percent of jobs in the Romanian labor market vanished in a few years (Stănculescu and Stoiciu 2012). Economic concerns aside, returning migrants do not necessarily adapt well to the society of origin upon their return (Vlase 2013). Thus, various studies undertaken in the last years tend to describe the current migratory patterns of Romanians again as forms of shuttle migration between Romania and Western Europe (Anghel 2012b; Câmpeanu 2011; Marcu 2012; Meeus 2012; Troc 2012). This migration would thus differ from the migration of Romanian citizens before 2008 when a clear process of settlement in the West was on track.

All through the development of Romanian migration after 1989, Germany and Italy were among the prime destinations of Romanian citizens. Germany was the main destination at the beginning of the 1990s, and the main entry point in Europe for more than a decade. After 2002 Italy started to emerge as the main destination of migrants. The two countries offered quite opposed opportunities to migrants from Romania. The present book will thus not only describe the different ways people migrating under contrasting conditions would construct their social status in transnational migration. It will also offer an account on how two major population movements unfolded in contemporary Europe.

CONSTRUCTING STATUS IN TRANSNATIONAL MIGRATION

The Romanian migration evolved in the context of dramatic changes in Europe, where Romanian migrants, yesterday's irregular migrants, and today's fellow Europeans are able to move freely as they adapt to different labor markets and destination states. The dilemmas this migration has raised, such as the one I put forward in the beginning of this chapter, have made us reflect on the meanings of the status and personhood of people who despite being migrants often have the rights or claims of the ordinary citizens. Besides, I suggest that there are multiple ways in which migrants' social statuses *at home* may influence their sense of status *abroad*. Following Luhmann (1997), who notes that the concept of society is not to be defined in terms of membership within some idealized state, I contend that migrants' social status needs to be recast in a transnational perspective. My argument thus unfolds in line with the literature on migrant transnationalism and the critique of methodological nationalism (Wimmer and Glick-Schiller 2002), on the assumption that societies cannot be conceived of as only included in the "container" of nation-states.

Migrant transnationalism introduces a crucial dimension of international migration by bringing to the foreground the cross-border agency of migrants: migrants as bearers of new ideologies, or increasingly, as assertive claimants of rights and agency due to their transnational involvements. Rather than seeing migrants as simply inserted into their societies of destination, and subject to the policies and practices of the destination states, migrants are depicted as social agents involved in multiple locations. Thus, migrants create new forms of transnational connections and subjectivities, generating what is called "communities without propinquity" between their origin and destination societies. In today's global world, migrants play a major role in transmitting money, goods, values, normative frameworks, and systems of practices from the developed to developing countries (Levitt 2001a, b; Levitt and Lamba-Nieves 2011). Yet, as opposed to globalization, where the diffusions of norms, values, and ideas are worldwide (Castells 1996, 1997; Hannerz 2000; Meyer 2005; Sassen 1991, 1998), migrants sustain transnational flows of ideas, norms, and money between specific locales and countries.

In the initial phase, migrant transnationalism was defined as the *processes* through which migrants sustain simultaneous and multi-stranded social relations linking origin and destination societies (Basch, Glick-Schiller, and Szanton Blanc 1994). This formula, however, attached the notion of "transnational" to potentially all migrants and was attacked for its lack of conceptual clarity. Therefore, Portes, Guarnizo, and Landolt (1999) suggested that the term *transnationalism* in reference to migrants should be confined to those migrants who maintain *occupations and activities* between their origin and destination societies. Economic globalization, in Portes's view, creates new economic niches that are exploited by migrants, like those Latin Americans who developed businesses in the small-scale transport industry that transported migrants between their origin countries and the United States (Portes 1996; Portes, Guarnizo, and Landolt 1999). Again, Vertovec (1999) used transnationalism to refer to the *ties* migrants maintain to their locales of origin and to a form of *consciousness* whereby migrants' express a feeling of being *simultaneously* (Levitt and Glick-Schiller 2006) at home and abroad. Accordingly, two defining criteria seem to circumscribe migrant transnationalism: the *simultaneity* of migrants' social relations and the *linkages* or *connections* (Mazzucato 2008 a; b) migrants maintain between their contexts of origin and destination. Research on status, I contend, would rely on this understanding of migrant transnationalism in terms of simultaneity and linkages.

Two opposing tendencies emerged from the outset and continue to mark debates on migrant transnationalism (Rogers 2005). The first tendency, where I locate my research, is the expansion of the agenda of migrant transnationalism to incorporate an increasing number of genuinely non-transnational phenomena. The second is the narrowing down of this same agenda to encompass only those phenomena linked to migrants' *regular* involvements in the social contexts of origin and destination (Portes 2003; Waldinger 2008). The distinction between migrants and transmigrants delineates this second approach. Many migrants attach meanings to their places of origin and maintain contacts back home via internet, telephone, and yearly visits. But only a minority, made up of those who sustain *regular* transnational relations over time, are transmigrants, that is, "persons . . . who live their lives across borders participating simultaneously in social relations that embed them in more than one nation-state" (Glick-Schiller 2003, 105, in Waldinger 2008; see also Soehl and Waldinger 2010; Waldinger 2008).

In contrast, the expansion of the migrant transnationalism agenda claims that migrants sustain transnational social spaces or fields that incorporate both migrants and non-migrants, social actors, social ties, networks, positions in networks, and organizations that cut across state borders (Faist 1999, 2000b, 2004). Some are only by-products of migration, but others are long-lasting (Faist 2000a; Portes, Guarnizo, and Landolt 1999), such as the case of Indian migrants in Australia (Voigt-Graf 2004, 2005), or of Moroccan migrants in Europe (Collyer et al. 2009).[12] This perspective stresses that migrants' continuous and longstanding cross-border activities are able to alter the relationships between states, citizens, and non-citizens (Bauböck 2003; Gamlen 2008; Levitt and de la Dehesa 2003) in an enduring manner. By their linkages and practices they finally change the understanding of social space beyond being confined to one national territory alone.

As people have family members, relatives, and friends living in other countries, they exchange money and goods, along with information about being *here* and *there*, and the experiences and aspirations they have in both places. Migrants' social status is thus essential in explaining migrants' transnational practices and subjectivities, as migrants are involved in simultaneous processes of constructing social status *at home* and *abroad*.

By social status I refer here to the position of a person or a group within the stratification system of a society, as well as the prestige or honor a person possesses due to their position in the society or a group (Bourdieu 1984).[13] In migration studies, scholars of the Manchester School were among the first to analyze migrants' different social statuses in the contexts of origin and destination (Epstein 1967).[14] But their initiative of inquiring into migration and migrants' socioeconomic status attainments in these contexts was not continued until the 1990s, as mean-

while migration studies focused rather on analyzing migration in societies of destination (Penninx 2006). The situation has changed during the
past fifteen years with new inquiries into migrants' social positions and
prestige claims (Goldring 1998; Glick-Schiller and Fouron 1999; Nieswand 2011). Besides the multiplicity of migrants' involvements in the
contexts of origin and destination, authors identify prestige as an essential resource migrants commonly rely on.

Max Weber (1964) considered that social prestige is social status, that
prestige is essential in determining one's position in society and power
relations. This is similar to how Bourdieu (1984) understood prestige or
symbolic capital as a source of power and a principle of social differentiation. In this book, I analyze how social prestige, as symbolic capital, is
actively constructed by migrants in a continuous process of repositioning
in their origin and destination societies. Social prestige could be negotiated at the level of a given community in terms of reputation, where it is
constructed according to the social values of a given group or community
(Wilson 1969). For instance, in the Caribbean Islands, men's reputation
was based on virility or masculinity, where they had to provide for their
families and to confront aggressively challenges to their manhood (Wilson 1969, 72). As part of the value-system of a given group or community,
reputation is marked by a system of signs, codes, and names, as in the
cases of fathers who give their names to their offspring, or of Moroccan
migrants who need to reinscribe their roles within their origin communities, differentiating themselves from those left home by the prominent
display of an ostentatious lifestyle (Salih 2002; Smith 1956, 137). But people's sense of social prestige also derives from general social values and
ideologies, something which Wilson understands under the term *respectability* (1969). This scalar distinction addresses a second meaning of social
prestige, where individuals relate to more general social norms, such as
obeying the laws, or internalizing more general ideologies. Here, social
prestige could be seen as "a value derived from conformity to the ideals
of the total society" (Wilson 1969, 78). In this respect, migrants react to
different ideologies in destination states when they are meant to comply
with the model of desirability enshrined in policies. Or they may follow
local understandings of civility and social order set up by the local population (Wimmer 2004).

The literature on transnationalism recognizes that migrants tend to
capitalize on symbolic status and gain reputation at home whenever they
may feel status downgraded abroad. Goldring (1998), for example,
touches on this issue when she identifies discrimination as an important
factor influencing migrant transnationalism. She discusses the case of
Mexican migrants who face exclusion and marginality in the United
States as they are positioned at the bottom of a racialized hierarchy. Yet
they succeed in fulfilling their status claims by maintaining transnational
relations to their communities of origin: in Goldring's words, "transna-

tional social communities are . . . communities of meaning in which status claims are interpreted based on shared histories and understandings of practices, rituals, goods, and other status markers" (Goldring 1998, 167). A similar mechanism for compensating status loss has been described in the case of Haitian migrants, who find themselves trapped in the racial category of Black Americans in the United States, but they are highly regarded in Haiti (Glick-Schiller and Fouron 1999); similarly in Europe is the case of the Ghanaian migrants in Germany (Nieswand 2006) and of Moroccan migrants in Italy (Salih 2002).

This process in which labor migrants gain social prestige in their societies of origin is often documented in migration literature when migrants sustain transnational relations with their origin communities (Massey 1987; Massey et al. 1993). Such prestige gain reflects migrants' home community-orientation, where the existence of a *back home* is essential. If the relationships between transmigrants and their home communities are often addressed in the research on migration and migrant transnationalism, one would need also to inquire into how social status in the origin societies influences migrants who *do not* maintain regular transnational relations back home. Equally important, we shall consider what migrants do at destination, looking at migrants' quest for respectability and equal status and their compliance with community social norms and values in the contexts of reception.

NATION STATES, MIGRANTS' INCORPORATION, AND SOCIAL STATUS

Countries in Western Europe have experienced much international migration in the past twenty years. Issues like immigration, ethnic and religious diversity, and nationhood and citizenship occupy center stage in political and public life. It is common for TV shows, newspapers, and even debates among neighbors and relatives to target immigration and the newly arriving immigrants. In such contexts, state policies play a central role in setting up categories of desirable and undesirable immigrants, apart from offering migrants certain rights and integration pathways. In public debate, too, policies and the effects of policies are reflected and discussed. In spite of the many voices arguing that states have a more limited capacity and leverage over international migration (Levitt and Lamba-Neves 2011), the fact is that states still have the ultimate say in allowing or restricting the entry of the immigrants and in tailoring policies for integration and citizenship acquisition. In the EU, despite the Europeanization of migration policies (Faist and Ette 2007) and policy convergence in certain fields (Joppke 2007) such as the free movement of people inside the Union, states adopt different policy approaches to increasing diversity, be they assimilationist, pluralist, or differential-exclusionist (Castles 1995). Such policies can come from a longer historical understanding of nationhood and citizenship (Brubaker 1992) or from more recent public philosophies derived from current arguments on the issues of immigration and immigrant integration that are addressed in the public space (Favell 2003).

To migrants, states offer rights and structures of opportunities during incorporation processes and generate ideologies in relation to which migrants position themselves. Irrespective of how we term them—whether "models" (Bader 2007), "configurations of citizenship" (Koopmans et al. 2005), or "philosophies of integration" (Favell 2001; 2003; Michalowski and Finotelli 2012)—it is legitimate to ask how different policies affect migrants' incorporation. What are the specific structures of opportunities available to migrants and what ideologies of integration are created? How do migrants act in such different contexts of reception?

In Western Europe, a divide exists not just between different policies in Germany, UK, Sweden, France, or the Netherlands, but also between the older and newer countries of immigration. In southern European countries such as Spain or Italy, migration was largely a development of post-1990. Migrants became a sizable share of the resident population, quickly reaching the ratio of foreign-born population to total resident population that is typical in older countries of immigration, such as Germany or France. But in contrast to other European countries, migration policies in Italy were unstructured or laissez-faire, and until recently the regularization (or legalization) of irregular migrants functioned *de facto* as the main policy of migration and integration. In contrast, Germany had a differential-exclusionist structured migration policy, clearly defining migrant categories and setting up specific avenues for incorporation. In the light of such a difference, this book seeks to answer the question of how such policies influence migrants' lives, their sense of selfhood, and their prospects for incorporation. How do migrants attain a certain social status given different contexts of reception? How do migrants internalize and interpret different ideologies of migration?

Migrants adapt to receiving societies (Glick-Schiller et al. 2005) in a continuous process of interaction between migrants, state institutions, and the resident population (Castles 2010). Their capacity to follow certain incorporation pathways—upward mobility, integration, or downward assimilation—depends to a very great extent on migrants' social, cultural, and economic capital (Bourdieu 1984) and the inequalities they encounter. Next to migration policies and the different types of contexts of reception that fundamentally shape migrants' lives in the receiving contexts, migrants' capacity to act, measured as the quality and quantity of economic, cultural, and social resources accumulated in migrants' ties, goes far in explaining migrants' differing socioeconomic statuses (Faist 2000a; Portes and Böröcz 1989). In this respect, it is argued that social resources have an alleged effect on status attainment (Lin 1999, 468).

Additionally, status attainment is influenced by achieved status, such as level of education (Lin 1999), as is the case, for instance, with highly qualified Korean migrants in the United States (Alba and Nee 1997), or Romanian migrants in Canada (Culic 2010), who attain average socioeconomic status in a short time after their arrival in the receiving contexts. Migrants possessing high economic capital are able to set up new businesses and so achieve success (Portes and Böröcz 1989). For the first generation of migrants, social status in the origin country can thus play a role in determining status in the contexts of reception. As it has been shown in a variety of cases, migrants' incorporation occurs through social networks (Eve 2010; Elrick 2009; Guilmoto and Sandron 2001; Krissman 2005; Massey, Goldring, and Durand 1994), enabling the mobilization of resources in migrants' social ties. Access to jobs, to housing, to different groups of friendships, and even to marriage is a result of who people socialize with.

Case studies in Europe for different countries demonstrate that migrant networks facilitate migration when first movers are able to help the newcomers during the process of incorporation (Bleahu 2004b; Düvell 2005; Jordan and Düvell 2002; Kindler 2008), but the analysis of such networks displays much diversity in different contexts (Engbersen 2001). For example, Germany is a country with strict internal control and regulations (Çağlar 2001), and the problems migrants have during incorporation arise mainly after their arrival in the country (Düvell 2005). The UK is a country where the entry is very difficult, but once people are in, then informal work is available to them. The uses to which such networks are put also differ: in the UK, Poles investigated by Jordan and Düvell (2002) were able to move upward when they separated themselves from their ethnic networks, whereas Turks rarely move away from their co-ethnics and do not experience much upward mobility. Some other European countries, for example Italy, have a sort of "bazaar economy" for labor (Düvell 2005, 15), where migrants with uncertain legal status find labor in places like street corners, where they meet contractors and employers (Colombo 1996; Düvell 2005, 15).

Similarly, networks helped Romanians' incorporation in Italy and Spain (Bleahu 2007; Castagnone and Petrillo 2007; Cingolani 2009; Cingolani and Piperno 2006; Elrick and Ciobanu 2009; Eve 2008; Vlase 2006); but migrants' tended to rely less on their social ties after adapting to the Spanish labor market and society (Şerban and Voicu 2010). As Bommes and Tacke (2010) note, access to the labor market cannot be explained solely in terms of access to co-ethnic networks in functionally diversified societies. In countries where migrants are able to obtain jobs in a variety of domains, especially if they have different educational and socioeconomic backgrounds, access to jobs may be less mediated by networks of co-ethnics and more commonly by more formal recruitment mechanisms or more diverse (and non-ethnic) types of social networking.

Therefore, when I analyze migrants' labor market participation I look at the structures of opportunities available for them, paying attention to the main characteristics of the labor markets in Germany and Italy. In doing so I analyze migrants' agency and migrant networks in relation to other social actors and institutions, such as labor agencies, local companies, trade unions, police, and agencies dealing with migration management.

One criticism of the network approach is that the migrant network perspective has the tendency to ethnicize migrants' sociality. As some authors mention, migrants create multiple ties to those who are not co-ethnics, as networks of co-ethnics are but one among their possible sources of support and relatedness (Glick-Schiller, Çağlar, and Buldbrandsen 2008). Even in the case of irregular migrants, who may be more dependent on their ties to co-ethnic networks, it is clearly documented that such persons establish numerous social ties with the local populations despite their marginal position in society. The number of those knowing about, profiting from, or supporting irregular migrants is several times higher than the number of irregular migrants itself (Düvell 2005). Migrants' sociality is thus developed at multiple levels: families, villages, regions, nations, religious groups, and social affiliations (Faist 2007, 4).

I will conceive migrant networks as embedded in and in turn creating the local realities of migrants' lives, as embodied in the fact that people's ideas, values, norms, and expectations are created, maintained, and reproduced in local social contexts. In migration scholarship it is widely acknowledged that people appropriate a space of their own in their new contexts of reception, set up local social relations, and provide meanings to this new social space (Appadurai 1995; Beaverstock 2005; Vertovec 1999). Locality, as a phenomenological and relational quality of individuals to relate to each other, create a worldview, and valorize people and objects, is thus multifaceted (Pfaff-Czarnecka 2005). It is both a representation, and a space of identity formation and interpersonal relations. In research conducted in urban neighborhoods in Switzerland, Wimmer (2004) shows that social relations between newcomers and older residents were not organized on an ethnic basis, but as processes of accommodation to established social norms.

The literature on migrant transnationalism thus centers the analysis on migrants' actions, their sustained cross-border linkages, and their forms of relatedness. The focus on migrants' social status (socioeconomic attainment and social prestige) helps us to better grasp the relationship between their agency and their positioning vis-à-vis the social structures and contexts of reception in a transnationalized world. I will look at three dimensions of analysis. On the one hand, migration policies shape specific contexts of reception, offering migrants opportunities and certain specific ideologies of migration and integration. Then, migrants' social status is influenced by migrants' social ties and networks that help them in accommodating themselves to contexts of reception, in incorporating into the labor market, and in establishing new social ties. And finally, migrants' social status is influenced by migrants' transnational practices, linkages, and forms of in-betweenness. Migrants' home orientation can further allow migrants to compare their status at home and abroad. It can also provide social and emotional support, and indeed prestige, whenever migrants have someone "at home" to relate to. I will formulate and refine the relationship between these three dimensions by reference to comparative research between two migrant groups from Romania, the one in Germany and the second in Italy.

FIELDWORK ENCOUNTERS: MIGRANTS AND MOBILITIES IN THE HEART OF EUROPE

Looking from afar, *Milano Centrale*, the Milan Central Station, impresses with the grandeur of its main building stretching over a few hundred meters and dominating the large square in front of it. The station was considered to be a great achievement in 1931, the year it was inaugurated. On the opposite side of *Centrale*, Via Pisani goes towards *Piazza della Republica* and the city center. Milan Central Station is the largest railroad station in northern Italy and one of the main railroad stations of Europe. More than 300,000 passengers use the train station daily,[15] making it one of the most crowded places in Milan. During the day passengers teem in front of *Centrale*, hurrying from station to the subway, to the buses going to the airports of *Malpensa, Linate*, and *Orio al Serio*, and to the city center. Moving closer to the station, the image changes. Especially on the weekends there are indeed a great deal of people on the move. But there are also many people standing for hours. These are migrants. In 2004 and 2005 when I did my fieldwork this was my first image of *Centrale*. It was an important place in these migrants' lives, where the Romanians gathered, along with migrants from other parts of the world. At *Centrale*, they could find new friends, labor and housing opportunities, ties of solidarity, and romance. People gathered around cups of *Vecchia Romagna*, an Italian brandy preferred by Romanians, telling stories about "home" and their new life in Milan.

I happened to start my fieldwork close to railroad stations. In Italy I started at *Milano Centrale*, where I could meet irregular Romanian migrants. In Germany, I visited several times a Romanian disco called *Centro*, which was located in a building in the vicinity of the railroad station in Fürth, close to Nuremberg.[16] When I conducted the fieldwork, the *Centro* used to host Romanian, Russian, and Turkish weekend parties. I used to go there to conduct participant observation with a group of Romanian *Aussiedler*.

Railroad stations are not meant primarily to be places of socialization. In both cases, though, this was where migrants looked to find their peers. Both stations became powerful images guiding my research, as in both places this was where the fieldwork problématique unfolded. These two research locations reminded me that the literature on transnationalism has yielded different interpretations of the relationships between place and mobility. In the classical anthropological and sociological tradition, "communities" and "social spaces" were understood as rooted in confined territories or places. But the current literature on migration, transnationalism, and globalization stresses that under globalized conditions social relations and subjectivity are becoming deterritorialized (Kearney 1995), "that territory and social relations no longer need to coincide directly" (Kennedy and Roudoumetof 2002, 11). In this globalized context, migrants are often seen as traveling between different locales, as free individuals in a world of flexible membership. When I started my fieldwork, both railroad stations were strategic research locations for participant observation. At *Centrale,* I observed how irregular migrants sought solidarity, new social ties, and labor opportunities. In the *Centro* disco, migrants from Romania, including ethnic Germans, partied to Romanian music, seeking fun and love affairs. I thereby obtained an entry point and contacts to migrants from Romania. As time went by, I started to meet and talk to many more migrants from Romania in the two cities.

I did not select Milan and Nuremberg randomly. I chose the two locales because of the high number of migrants from Romania residing there, amounting to several tens of thousands in both cities. In Germany, Ricky, a German friend from Timişoara, helped me obtain access to the field. When I arrived in Nuremberg he put me up for a while and introduced me to his group of friends. He was the first migrant from Timişoara I interviewed in Nuremberg, and access to his group of friends was unrestricted thereafter. I partied with them, we went out together, and I had the opportunity for casual talks. I also conducted a large number of interviews with migrants from Romania, members of Romanian associations, and Romanian students. My focus was primarily on migrants from Timişoara. I also analyzed Ricky's network and another network made up of Ricky's less close acquaintances.

I approached my research in Milan differently. I started first by going to the Romanian church and hanging around the open places where the Romanian migrants gathered in search of jobs and shelter. As with the research in Nuremberg, I didn't focus on a specific group in the beginning. That choice came later, when after a series of interviews the Romanian migrants told me that migrants from Borşa were among the most successful within the Romanian "community." Unlike in Nuremberg, where I introduced myself as a sociologist, in Milan I had to pursue a different strategy. I went almost daily to the Romanians' meeting places, such as *Centrale*, where I could just observe them without approaching them for interviews.

The quality of data I gathered in Germany and Italy differed significantly: in Germany I was able to collect rich empirical material, but in Milan the empirical information was less revealing, and I recorded a limited number of life stories. In Milan many migrants would not believe I was a researcher, fearing that I had something to do with the police or other migrants spying on them. Such access difficulties have been recorded by other scholars in different situations. Stoller (1996) mentions race relations and the colonial past as the main obstacle for him to conduct his research; he therefore needed several years to complete his research among West African migrants in New York. Parallel to my case, some African migrants were mistrustful and took him for an undercover police officer (Stoller 1997, 90). In another Romanian study, Bleahu (2006) encountered difficulties when conducting interviews with irregular migrants in Rome. She was able to overcome these access difficulties because she was related to some of the migrants she interviewed. Due to the different access to the field, in Milan I started by doing interviews with Romanian associations, and in so doing I gained access to migrants who would allow me to interview them. In contrast to Nuremberg, I had no prior contacts in Milan to migrants from Borşa. Access to these people was not easy, and it took a while until I could get in contact with more migrants. I started my fieldwork in a place on the periphery of Milan, helped by a newly set up Romanian organization. There was a small park where Romanian migrants used to meet. I went there regularly and spent most of my time in conversations. During the weekends I had the opportunity to hang out with some of them in places like *Centrale* or the city parks. After living for a while in Milan in this environment of Romanian migrants, I succeeded in forming new friendships and I even worked a few days with some of them. Furthermore, my research in Borşa, Romania, the hometown of migrants whom I studied in Milan, provided insights into individuals' migration history. Thanks to the collaboration of my research assistant who had relatives in Borşa, access was no longer an issue. The data I gathered through participant observation in Milan supplemented the rich empirical information that I collected in Borşa about migrants' life histories.

Accordingly, I applied a combination of multi-sited ethnography (Marcus 1995) and the extended case study method (Burawoy 2000), focusing more intensively on a number of individual cases I researched over the space of a few years. This involved ethnographical analysis into migrants' origin and destination locales, as migrants' construction of social selves was no longer contained within "envelopes of space and time . . . no matter how we call them, localities, communities, cultures, or even societies" (Appadurai 1997, 116). I replaced the classical extensive fieldwork "in one place" with several research periods and short visits that took place between 2004 and 2007 in Milan, Borşa, and Nuremberg. Most interviews were conducted between September 2004 and April 2006. In 2007 I conducted further fieldwork with participant observation in Borşa and Nuremberg. I was also able to obtain insights into migrants' sense of transnationality by traveling with them and looking at how they changed their attitudes "at home" and "abroad" over the years. I had thus to become myself "an ethnographic nomad" (Smith and Guarnizo 1998), traveling between the research sites: in Nuremberg, Milan, and Borşa; in Bielefeld, Germany, where I gathered my field notes; in Turin, Italy, where I spent seven months writing; and in Cluj, Romania, where I completed the research. I carried out fourteen months of research, and conducted eighty interviews in Nuremberg and thirty-seven in Borşa and Milan, mostly in Romanian. In addition, I had a very large number of informal talks and unrecorded interviews. I conducted interviews and discussions with members of Italian and German NGOs and research centers. In both places I became closely acquainted with particular migrants and remained in contact with them over the years. In both I researched migration in its historical evolution. Life narrative interviews with migrants were used as the main method of data collection.

In this research I compare two groups having different socioeconomic status and seek to determine why migrants with better socioeconomic status perceived they had suffered a loss in the course of migration, whereas those with lower status perceived they had gained. In the first case, migrants from Timişoara obtained their education mostly in Germany and had a variety of jobs. I interviewed forty of them. Eighteen had white-collar jobs: engineers, IT specialists, and managers. Twelve had received a university education. Nine had blue-collar jobs: technicians, administrators, and call center agents. Five were unemployed, and two were pensioners. All had at least a high school education and most had pursued specialization courses afterwards. I had no information on jobs or education from six of my subjects. In Milan, in contrast, most migrants were employed in so-called 3D jobs, that is, in construction and care: twenty-seven out of the thirty-seven persons I focused on. Six had white-collar jobs: these were entrepreneurs who had previously worked as construction workers. There were four persons working in industry. All migrants had high school diplomas obtained in Romania, and two had university degrees from there.

Given the wide difference in migrants' professional statuses, my interviews focused on their migration history, their socioeconomic attainment, and their social prestige. I triangulated the information (Flick 2004) with information from other interviews and information obtained from participant observation. Policies also play an important role in migrants' social incorporation. Both in Nuremberg and Milan, local institutions and labor opportunities influenced migrants' economic and social incorporation, and in both cases I looked at how migrants used their networks for social and economic incorporation. In addition, information on the processes of migration and on the migrants' locales of origin helped me appreciate how social prestige was constructed over a longer time frame.

I consider that in both cases migration and migrants' transnational practices were "embodied in specific social relations established between specific people, situated in unequivocal localities, at historically determined times" (Smith and Guarnizo 1998, 11). Following this line of inquiry into migration and migrant transnationalism, some authors (Smith 2001, 15) emphasize the role of localities in conceptualizing transnationalism and transnational spaces. Locality is a property of social life and an ideology of a situated community (Vertovec 1999), and the production of locality is realized within neighborhoods as social formations (Appadurai 1995). I look at localities first as sets of social relations and second as a process of place-making where migrants appropriate a place of their own and where sociality is displayed, such as *Centrale* in Milan and the *Centro* disco in Fürth. There, the social construction of "a place" is "a process of local meaning-making, territorial specificity, juridical control, and economic development" (Smith and Guarnizo 1998). I see localities not as bounded and stable entities, but rather as dynamic, complex, and contingent on social and political processes (Smith 2001, 112). Such a theoretical framework was used in the study of Turkish immigrants in Duisburg, Germany. According to Ehrkamp (2005), Turks made Marxloh their quarter through teahouses, satellite dishes, and real estate ownership, while transnational ties were constitutive of the process of production of their locality. In the same way, Indian migrants in Auckland constructed their locality by changing the ethnic geography and through the emerging ethnic retail businesses (Friesen, Murphy, and Kearns 2005). In the case of Lebanese traders and businessmen in West Africa (Peleikis 2000), migrants maintained ties with their village of origin through Arabic TV and video documentation of social events back home. They made their locality in Africa part of a transnational space between Africa and their village of origin in Lebanon. I also consider that such processes of localization occurred even in the case of highly mobile persons, like the British transnational elites in New York (Beaverstock 2005) who were embedded in the local context by social networking in their place of residence. Given all these, I seek to analyze migrants' social ties and forms of relatedness at destination, where social relations were often visible in specific ethnicized places. I also seek to show how place-making was realized in Nuremberg through small-scale ethnic retail businesses (butcheries, discos, and so on) and in Milan via the specific places of the city where migrants met, socialized, and found work. Finally I pay attention to how the migrants' city of origin changed due to migrants' transnational practices.

The book is divided into two parts in which I describe two migration processes, from origin to destination, continuing with the migrants' incorporation, and ending up with their transnationalism. In the first part of the book I analyze migration from Timişoara to Nuremberg, while in the second one I deal with migration from Borşa to Milan. I ask how people migrated from Timişoara and Borşa, what structures of opportunities were available to migrants, how they interacted with institutions in Germany and Italy, and how they incorporated economically and socially. I finally analyze how migrants related transnationally to their locales of origin, examining how they attained and negotiated their socioeconomic status and how they reflected upon it. Both parts have a similar structure. In chapters 1 and 3, I analyze migration from Romania to Germany and Italy. In chapters 2 and 5, I describe migrants' incorporation and socioeconomic attainment in Nuremberg and Milan, looking at how migrant networks functioned in both contexts and what status claims these migrants had. In chapters 3 and 6, I analyze migrant transnationalism and how this influenced migrants' status and prestige claims.

In the concluding chapter I summarize the argument of the book, separating the different dimensions of social status construction and how migrants actually seek status and social prestige at home and abroad. In doing so, I reveal how major changes affecting Europe as a whole have influenced the lives of people migrating from Romania to Western Europe, and how they construct a sense of self in a changing European social, political, and economic reality.

NOTES

1. Here I use the term *irregular migrants* or *irregular migration* and not *illegal migrants*, as their migration is not necessarily an illegal act. According to Ghosh, "nonnationals are generally considered to be in an irregular situation (i) when they have not complied with the required formalities, or have not obtained the authorization required by law, for admission or stay or for their activity during such stay in a country; or (ii) when they cease to meet the conditions to which their stay or activity is subject" (Ghosh 1998, 3-4). He also distinguishes between different types of irregularity: irregular entry, irregular residence, and irregular activity or employment.

2. Notably, in Rome and Verona.

3. Refusals increased to 14 percent.

4. See www.dri.gov.ro/index.html?page=date_statistice , last accessed on June 17, 2012, 17:32.

5. It is difficult to estimate the exact ratio of non-Germans who arrived in Germany with *Aussiedler* status in the Romanian case. However, information from fieldwork in Nuremberg and from other Romanian localities (Sighişoara, Sibiu) supports the argument that in the 1980s there was a high ratio of intermarriage. In cities like Sighişoara, for instance, not less than 50 percent of Germans had married Romanians. See also Poledna (1998), Verdery (1985).

6. For example, in 1991, 8,500 Romanian citizens were apprehended at the German-Polish border and another 4,500 between January 1 and March 15, 1992. About 12,450 Romanian citizens tried to enter Germany in the first six months of 1992 (Reyniers 2003, 58).

7. The number of Romanian applicants for political asylum evolved accordingly: 11,191 in 1990, 27,089 in 1991, 57,464 in 1992, 146,738 in 1993, 21,424 in 1994, 10,274 in

1995, 3,186 in 1996, 1,672 in 1997, and 917 in 1998. The number of applicants will further decrease. Source: Interview BAMF.

8. From qualitative information obtained during my fieldwork in Nuremberg, I found out that many asylum seekers remained in Germany, others migrated towards other European countries, and some returned to Romania.

9. For instance, throughout the 1990s, migrant workers and IT green card holders from Romania grew more important (Dietz 2003; 2006).

10. In comparison, there were only 40,000 visas a year from France, the second country to grant visas to Romanian citizens (Diminescu 2003, 15).

11. For a similar general conclusion concerning the East–West migration in Europe, see Favell (2008).

12. Thus, Voigt-Graf (2005) shows how kinship organized Indians' transnationalism over a longer period of time. Collyer et al. (2009) also shows how Moroccans continued remitting to Morocco at the second and third generation.

13. Migrants' status attainment is a process through which individuals attain positions in the stratified systems of the origin and receiving societies (Treiman 2000, 3042). Research on social status usually points to income, education, and jobs as the main indicators of socioeconomic attainment. Status attainment can be realized on the basis of inborn characteristics and native advantage, such as family inheritance (ascribed status), or on personal efforts, such as investing in education in order to attain a better socioeconomic status (status attainment).

14. They were also pioneers in using the concept of migrant network, applied to the analysis of the rural-urban migration in Africa (Epstein 1967; Mardsen 2000; Pfaff-Czarnecka 2008).

15. See http://www.parkingstazione.it/stazione/milano-centrale/parcheggio/ parcheggio-stazione-milano-centrale.html, last accessed January 23, 2013.

16. A few articles have already resulted from this fieldwork: Anghel (2008; 2011; 2012a).

Part I

Romanian Germans in Germany

ONE

Germans Moving "Home"

From Timişoara to Nuremberg

Freidorf, now one of Timişoara's suburbs, was merely a village a hundred years ago. It was later incorporated into the city but retained its German population until 1989, when most of them left for Germany. I first went there with Ricky[1] during one of his trips back to Romania. In 2007 he was thirty-eight but had left Romania in 1990 after finishing high school. Ricky's house belonged to Oma, his grandmother, who used to shuttle between Freiburg, where she migrated after 1989, and Freidorf, where she spent her summers. Oma was in her sixties when she left Romania, and although she never worked a day in Germany she still qualified for a pension there. She moved to Freiburg for good, and yet she kept very much alive her relations to her Romanian neighbors and the household in Freidorf. In autumn Oma would take the bus for Germany and would make the round trip as soon as the warm welcoming weather set in in Romania. Whenever she or Ricky came home, Layla, the dog, would get frantic, barking with joy and running madly through the courtyard. For the rest of the year Oma's friends would take care of Layla.

Ricky's room retained much of his teenager memories: Depeche Mode posters on the walls, LP discs with pop music from the 1980s. He lived there in his adolescence and so far not much has changed in the neighborhood. Houses have remained the same as before: big houses constructed by Germans in the 1950s and 1960s. The former communist name of the street still stood on the wall of the house: The Proletarian. Time seemed to stand still on the street, but once we started walking towards the city center new constructions appeared: a new restaurant at the corner, some new petrol stations on the way. Every time he came home, Ricky had his ritual walk all the way from Freidorf towards the center of Timişoara, only five kilometers away. We passed through the neighborhood and reached Iosefin, a quarter named after the Austrian Emperor Franz Josef, during whose reign the city prospered and urbanized with the incorporation of the new quarters of Iosefin and Elisabetin (named after the Empress Elisabeth). Although Freidorf was nearby, it was included in the city only in the middle of the twentieth century. The plan of the city was concentric, with large quarters made of parallel streets surrounding the city center. The city was traversed by the channel Bega. On its banks large parks were created, making the walk to the center a pleasure. In Iosefin, houses were two-stories high: in many cases the ground floor was taken up by shops while the family lived on the first floor. We then reached the Catholic church that both Ricky's parents and his grandparents used to attend. The walk downtown triggered Ricky's memories of his childhood and youth in the city. As we drew nearer to the center he would get more and more excited: he vividly remembered the Romanian Revolution in 1989, how he joined the nascent protest against the communist dictatorship, how the secret police started shooting at people, and how they were running on the streets. He had even given an interview in Hungarian for the Hungarian radio station Kossuth Radio, which wanted to make the voice of the people heard in the turbulent times of December 1989.

After crossing the bridge over the Bega, we went through a park and reached the landmark of the center, *Piaţa Operei* (Opera Square), with its majestic *fin-de-siècle* buildings on both sides, the National Theater at one end and the Romanian Orthodox Cathedral at the other. Ricky took some snapshots. The center had changed over the past years. Italian restaurants, cafes, and pizzerias had mushroomed in the center, contrasting with the dark grey of the communist years when only a few pubs were open. In the fifteen years following the collapse of state socialism in 1989, many Italian investors had settled here, some of them introducing Italian cuisine into the local hospitality industry. After a long walk it was pretty difficult to make up our mind what place to choose for a chat over a coffee. There was a cheerful atmosphere everywhere: people rushed in all directions, youngsters lounged on benches, pensioners were feeding pigeons in the front of the National Theater. We then crossed Freedom Square, close to *Piaţa Operei*. The square got its name during the Hungarian Revolution of 1848, *Szabadság tér*, or *Freiheitsplatz* in German. It was given back its original name, Prince Eugen Square, once the Austrian army took over the city, but after 1920 the name was finally settled by the Romanian administration: *Piaţa Libertăţii*, Freedom Square. The people of Timişoara were proud of their historical legacy, that the city was a part of the Habsburg and later the Austro-Hungarian Empire. They considered it a cultural achievement and a symbol of the city's tolerant multiculturalism. We finally ended up on a terrace in *Piaţa Unirii*, the Great Union Square, a baroque landmark of Timişoara's architecture, with the city's

Art Museum, the Serbian Orthodox Church, the Catholic Cathedral, and the *Lenau Schule,* the German high school.

Ricky started to call up his friends and acquaintances, telling them he was in town. For an hour he was completely absorbed in endless conversations. When he finally put the phone on the table it was already late, so we decided to take a cab back to Freidorf. His friends started to arrive quite soon after. In a few hours the silent house in Freidorf was full with friends celebrating Ricky's visit. Oma's big old German house was full of life again. Layla, the dog, was the happiest. Ricky started to cook some meat, and Layla knew she would have a feast. Another German friend who had also originally left Timişoara dropped by. Luca was also living in Nuremberg, and for at least a week the two friends had been very excited at the thought of the partying and the trip to Timişoara. As the group of friends in Freidorf grew larger and larger so did the good mood. Ricky and Luca were getting updated about the most recent Romanian jokes and funny stories. They also made new acquaintances as new people dropped by, having heard by chance there was a good party in Freidorf. A mix of Serbian music from the 1980s, Gypsy rhythms, rock, heavy metal, and pop was played non-stop in the background.

Both Ricky and Luca had moved to Germany seventeen years before. But between 1990 and 2007, when this party took place, Ricky and his friends used to come regularly to Timişoara. Although they lived in Nuremberg, in Germany, they traveled to Timişoara whenever any free time was theirs. They were not transmigrants, migrants who have regular involvement in their country of origin. They did not remit money to Romania and did not make investments there. They left no relatives behind when they migrated to Germany. But they maintained relationships with Romania, and as time passed they created new ones. Their previous lives in Timişoara influenced their lives in Germany over the course of more than seventeen years.

* * *

Timişoara is the city where the Romanian Revolution burst out in the winter of 1989, when many people like Ricky went out on the streets to demonstrate against the dictatorship. Situated close to the border with Hungary and former Yugoslavia, it is a city with a multicultural tradition and with a sizable German minority.[2] Ethnic Germans had had a long presence in the city, as they arrived as colonists[3] in the eighteenth century.[4] After the retreat of the Turks following the Treaty of Passarowitz in 1718 the region of Timişoara, called Banat, came under Habsburg rule. It was underpopulated and Emperor Charles VI brought German colonists from Württemberg, Alsace, Lorraine, and Breisgau to colonize it. For almost three centuries, Germans[5] represented the second largest ethnic group in this region after Romanians. The planning and the development of Timişoara in the nineteenth century were credited to its German burghers and the Austrian administration. Due to its flourishing economy, for which the burghers were mostly to be thanked, and its large boulevards and squares and the architectural style of many of its buildings, Timişoara was named *Little Vienna*. In the nineteenth century it was a prosperous city: industry and manufacture developed and the city, along with the region, entered a process of modernization and industrial development. Public utilities improved: tramlines, public lighting, and telephone networks were introduced, among the first in the cities of the Austro-Hungarian Empire.

After 1918 the largest part of the Banat came under Romanian administration. The majority of the population were Romanian, but 275,000 Germans also lived there.[6] "Almost 80 percent . . . were peasants, whose standards of living were considerably higher than that of their Romanian and Serbian neighbors; 20 percent were town dwellers, mainly middle class" (Castellan 1971, 53). Timişoara, the largest city of the region, became a major Romanian city when the region was incorporated into Romania after 1918. In the interwar period ethnic minorities together still represented the majority, but in time they became less prominent in the city's population.[7]

During the interwar period Romanian Germans had a relatively favored position in Romanian society. Despite Romanianization policies

Figure 1.1.   Image from the Great Union Square. Source: Author's personal archive

Table 1.1.   Evolution of the population of Timişoara.

Year	Population	Romanians	Germans	Hungarians	Others
1920	86,850	16,047	32,097	27,189	11,517
1930	102,390	25,207	33,162	31,773	12,248
1941	125,052	46,466	37,611	24,891	16,084
1956	142,257	75,855	24,326	29,968	12,108
1966	174,243	109,100	25,058	31,016	9,069
1977	269,353	191,174	28,429	36,724	13,026
1992	334,115	274,511	13,206	31,785	14,613
2002	317,660	271,677	7,157	24,287	14,539

Source: Varga (2002).

undertaken after 1918 (Livezeanu 1995), there existed a well-established school system as well as strong religious organizations of both Swabian Catholics and Saxon Lutherans. In politics, *die Deutsche Partei* (the German Party) had representatives in the Parliament. In 1921 the Union of Germans in Romania (*Verband der Deutschen in Rumänien*) was established. In the 1930s they had twenty daily newspapers and about a hundred magazines and periodicals (Castellan 1971).

The Second World War and the post–War period brought about a major political and demographic change for the Germans in Romania (Castellan 1971; Dowling 1991; Totok 2003). The evacuation to Germany of substantial segments of the population, war losses, and postwar deportation caused a diminishing to about 65 percent[8] of the German population residing previously in the Romanian territories (Poledna 1998, 151-52). Blamed collectively as supporters of the Nazi ideology, ethnic Germans were excluded from the Communist Nationalities Statute and did not enjoy the same rights other nationalities had (Verdery 1985, 73). After 1945 in Romania, 75,000 Germans were deported on Soviet order:[9] all men between seventeen and forty-five, and all women between eighteen and thirty (Castellan 1971, 67). Out of these, approximately 10,000 did not return at all (idem). In 1951, the Romanian authorities also deported Germans from the Banat region to the southern part of the country, but they allowed them to return to their localities of origin soon after the start of the deportation (Andreescu 2005). The Germans' properties, including land and houses, were confiscated by the state (Poledna 1998; Verdery 1985; Weber et al. 1996). In many cases Romanian settlers were introduced into the ethnic Germans' former houses (Chelcea and Lăţea 2000; Poledna 1998). Germans were not allowed to vote and lost their civil rights. In the 1950s there were 385,708 Germans in Romania, of which 188,700 lived in Banat and 165,000 in southern Transylvania. Their situation gradually improved after 1950 when the deportees started to return from Russia. The Communist Basic Law of 1952, and the later Basic Law of 1965, stipulated equal rights for all Romanian citizens, irrespective of their ethnicity (Michalon 2003b). In 1954 ethnic Germans were granted again the right to vote, and they started to receive back their houses (Poledna 1998, 123). The anti-German measures were canceled by the decree 81/1956, but the properties lost by the Germans were only partially returned (Gräf and Grigoras 2003, 56). They received their houses back, but not their land. The confiscation of land holdings was not inherently an ethnic measure, as it targeted big landowners and the rich peasantry. But the German population consisted of just rich peasantry, and they came to be particularly affected. In 1948 the school system was nationalized but the possibility was maintained of receiving an education in the German language (Michalon 2003b). In 1952 there were 40,000 children enrolled in 356 German primary schools and more than 3,000 Germans in technical and secondary schools (Castellan 1971, 70).

The high social status that ethnic Germans enjoyed before the war was drastically curtailed in the 1950s.[10] The loss of land property forced ethnic Germans into a working-class status with the effect of forcing them to acquire technical skills and education (Poledna 1998; Verdery 1985). Many moved to cities or became commuting peasant-workers. This process was related to the development of the industrial sector in Romania under state socialism: the labor force employed in this economic sector grew from 20 percent in 1950 to 49 percent in 1975 (Verdery 2003, 41).

The German population of Timişoara slightly increased in numbers through urbanization while many individuals already lived in mixed families during the last decades of state socialism. Moreover, compared to the interwar period marked by nationalist tendencies (Chelcea 1999)[11] Timişoara was a more ethnically tolerant milieu. My interviewees insisted that there was a kind of ethnic peace between Romanians, Germans, Hungarians, and Serbs in Timişoara. There were no signs of ethnic segregation and there was no strong ethnic mobilization. As Verdery (1985, 63) also argues, during socialism "German ethnicity . . . ceased to mean belonging to a solidary and self-conscious ethnic group [entailing] group strategy or organization" (idem). However, most of the people I talked to contended that the prestige of the Germans in the region remained high in comparison to other ethnic groups (Chelcea and Lăţea 2000; Vultur 2000).

READINESS TO GO: GERMAN MIGRATION DURING STATE
SOCIALISM

The changes in the socioeconomic profile of Romania's ethnic Germans and the political repercussions following the Second World War increasingly encouraged trends to migration within the German communities. Migration to Germany during the war split families and communities between Romania and Germany.

The migration policy for the reception and support of ethnic Germans was motivated by Germany's responsibility for East European German refugees and expellees after the War. About fourteen million Germans from Eastern and Central-Eastern Europe[12] were expelled or had to flee, mostly to Germany. In the process of deportation and expulsion about two million people lost their lives (Tränhardt 1996). Yugoslavia, Hungary, Czechoslovakia, and Poland collectively expelled most ethnic Germans living there (Fassmann and Münz 1994, 532).

In recognition of the situation that ethnic Germans faced in the Central and Eastern Europe, article 116 of the German Basic Law[13] stipulated the right to repatriation for all Germans who lived in the former German territories.[14] Furthermore this right was extended in 1953[15] to other categories of Germans,[16] namely the forcibly displaced Germans[17] and the ethnic Germans from Eastern Europe (*Aussiedler*) (Groenendijk 1997; Weber et al. 2003). Thus between the 1950s and the 1990s West Germany received a high number[18] of Germans from the former German Democratic Republic (GDR) (*Übersiedler*) and about two million[19] ethnic Germans from Eastern and Central Europe outside of the GDR. The provisions adopted for the expelled and the refugees were maintained for these migrants until 1990. During the Cold War, *Aussiedler* received generous state support: German citizenship, housing facilities, reimbursement of travel expenses, language courses, and full access to the social security system. Their educational qualifications were recognized, and they received grants and tax facilities to start new businesses. In some cases these migrants were granted compensation for the years of political detention they had had to go through and for property losses in their countries of origin (Groenendijk 1997). To be accepted as *Aussiedler*, migrants had to be of German origin and to prove that they were persecuted because of their ethnic affiliation.[20] This policy of free entry did not change until 1989.

However, it was increasingly difficult for Germans to claim ethnic persecution in the last years of state socialism. "In Romania for example, Germans occupied a relatively favored niche in the ethnic landscape" (Brubaker 1998, 1051). Therefore, the main reason for granting such entitlements originated not only in the political responsibility Germany assumed, but also in the great influence of the ethnic German deportees and expellees in the FRG after 1949.[21] When the laws on ethnic Germans were ratified, provisions proved very generous (Groenendijk 1997).[22] Furthermore, there is also an ideological explanation which argues that by maintaining such provisions during the forty years of the Cold War, the FRG was proving the superiority of its democratic system vis-à-vis the East European states, especially the GDR (Dietz 1999). Finally, there is an ethno-national argument, stressed by Brubaker (1998), which claims that the pull effect of this migration was ethnic affinity but with no real link to the lived ethnicity of the East European Germans, or even to the alleged repression of their ethnicity.

Until the 1960s only a limited number of family reunions were realized, mainly through the intervention of the Red Cross (Diminescu 2003). After 1965, however, Romania was interested in establishing closer diplomatic and economic relations with Western European countries, Germany included (Weber et al. 2003, 444). From 1969 onwards the Romanian government allowed more Germans to migrate to Germany, at a rate of about 5,000 persons a year.[23]

In 1977, an agreement was reached between Nicolae Ceaușescu[24] and Helmut Schmidt[25] on this issue, which allowed a quota of ten thousand family reunions a year. Romania received important financial benefits[26] as Germany offered a compensation for every visa issued for Romanian Germans. For the next 12 years of state socialism, the migration of ethnic Germans was regulated by this agreement. This resulted in an increasing number of Germans from Timișoara deciding to leave the country permanently. In theory, this legal framework entitled ethnic Germans to apply for family reunion and to exit Romania legally. But in practice those wishing to migrate encountered innumerable obstacles[27] (Weber et al. 2003, 445).

Hungry for hard currency, the Romanian state allowed the ethnic Germans to migrate. But pressure was exerted on those willing to migrate, as waiting lists were quite long and in most cases the state's approval to leave Romania did not follow immediately after the application was made.[28] It would take months and even years of waiting. In the meantime, the financial and emotional state of applicants could often worsen. The administrative requirements were complicated: they consisted of two applications to state authorities, stressful interviews with the *Miliția*,[29] and an array of formalities involving different state institutions. Potential migrants had no choice but to sell their houses to the Romanian state at ludicrously low prices (Weber et al. 2003, 444-47). Finally, they had to give up their Romanian citizenship.

> In many cases people had to wait for a few years until they could receive the permission to leave. In most cases they had to bribe persons from the *Miliție* and from *Securitate*. They had to use intermediaries: in Timișoara there was a gardener, and everyone knew they had to go there, to give him 5,000 to 10,000 DM (2,500 to 5,000 Euros). After two weeks, they could receive the final application forms. Without bribery, it could take years before receiving approval (Otto).

There was a well-known joke in the 1980s Romania that "the last Romanian leaving the country should turn off the light." In a nutshell, it summed up the Romanians' struggle to cope with the hardship of life in the country that made migration a welcome option. Whenever I discussed the situation in Romania in the 1980s, migrants in Nuremberg recalled how bad it used to be. More than once people spoke not only of poverty and the lack of basic food, but of political pressure and the fear of secret police. In Romania, Timişoara was often referred to as an emancipated city, where people had more ties to Western Europe and were able to migrate more easily. Mathias and I discussed this issue a number of times. He left Romania in the 1980s by irregular means after his sister went legally to Germany. He considered life in Romania unbearable, and thought it was fortunate for them that Germans had a chance to migrate to the West. But for him migration wasn't easy. He was sure many people from *Securitate* [30] or the state authorities were watching over any attempt to go to the West. As he himself did, in such circumstances people would plan their emigration with the utmost care, not even disclosing their plans to their closest friends. The easiest way to get out, he decided, was to find state bureaucrats to facilitate the emigration procedures.

Migrants used their relationship with acquaintances and friends to get access to members of the state apparatus who were prepared to facilitate visa procedures: "In those times, even if you were [entitled to go], you had to pay a lot of money [to emigrate] and you had to make a deal with somebody from *Securitate*. There was a certain amount of money you had to pay" (Thomas). In the cases I analyzed, bribery involved financial and other types of benefits, and the payment could amount to some thousands of DMs[31] per person.

In other cases, they asked for favors, such as organized vacations in the West. Luca recalled how his uncle was desperate to emigrate to Germany. His wife and one child were there already, while he stayed behind in Romania with the second child. Life was hard indeed and deprivation was severe, yet he saw no chance to go to live with his wife and reunite the family. He was German, he had the right to emigrate, but he had to receive approval from the Romanian state first. Endless queues and trips to Bucharest led nowhere.

> In the 1980s my uncle went to Bucharest each month and asked: "I want to go, my wife and my child [are in Germany]." One day, one *Securitate* guy called him and said: "Hey, what's your problem? I can help you." That guy asked my uncle to be invited to Germany and to be hosted [several times]. When he [had the intention to go to Germany], he always said: "Look, I'll come to you and stay for this long a period of time" (Luca).

In the framework of the German-Romanian agreement, family reunions were the legal justification for migration, but migrants also needed the financial means to cover all the costs involved in relocation.[32] In many cases, relatives in Germany were the main provider. When I asked Ricky why he didn't come to Germany before 1989, he replied without hesitation: "I had no relatives here." Similar to Ricky, many Germans from Romania did not seek to migrate if they had no relatives to support them in this endeavor. Even going through official channels, migration still entailed risks and difficulties people were not always willing to face.

This critical situation generated dissatisfaction for many Germans. The long delays put people in difficulty; applicants could be harassed at the workplace or even lose their jobs. The atmosphere that characterized the German community in Timişoara at that time is depicted in the literary work of Richard Wagner (1991) as a tiresome oscillation between planning for departure and prolonging their stay, between ethnic solidarity and disillusionment. Wagner describes the political context in Timişoara in the late 1980s when pessimism, lack of prospects for the future, and political oppression made people determined to choose to go. Migration was the dream of many Romanian citizens in a period of stark deprivation of basic goods, endless queues for food, two hours of TV programs per day, and electricity breakdowns during winter (Verdery 1996). Romania in the 1980s was moving steadily towards deep economic crisis and state oppression. State control became ubiquitous in all spheres of the social life, intimacy included (Kligman 1988). Living conditions and the oppressive regime were the main driving forces that motivated international migration.

In that context, migrants in Germany used to send consumption goods, electrical equipments, clothes, and magazines like *Neckermann* or *Burda* back to their relatives in Romania. Some of these goods were sold for a profit to other Germans or to Romanian neighbors (Chelcea and Lăţea 2000). Ricky's room in Freidorf was a reminder of how Western goods were saved and valued during state socialism. It was not only the posters on the walls that brought back those years. There was an empty package of *Toblerone* chocolate "brought straight from Germany," music tapes, and an old tape recorder. The old recorder was often used to copy original tapes for friends and acquaintances. Ricky himself traded similar goods at the flea market in Timişoara before 1989. He also remembered how Oma exchanged *Burda* magazines with her friends. In those days the magazine had sewing patterns that Romanian women used to sew pants, dresses, skirts, and blouses for family members. New *Burda* magazines with new and fashionable patterns were therefore much sought after among friends.

In a country where sugar, oil, and bread had a limited distribution in the 1980s and where meat and milk were very scarce on the market, goods sent from Germany were highly appreciated. It consolidated the Romanians' widespread view of Germany as the *Wonderland*. In the Banat region migrants' visits back home motivated others to migrate. Vasile, an engineer from a small city close to Timişoara, remembered how migration was perceived at that time: "You heard all the time in town that somebody had left, and so had another one. A lot of people were [leaving] in 1980, 1981. There was a wave of departures. And afterwards my friends who were already in Nuremberg started to come back and visit us." He also remembered that migrants were admired not only for escaping dictatorship and state oppression, but most importantly for being able to attain a high level of economic prosperity in a very short time. He recalled how migrants' cars were appreciated by people in his town, comparing them with the Dacia cars available on the Romanian market. The homebodies always complained one needed to fix a Dacia constantly as they could break down at any time.

In Timişoara and in smaller nearby cities like Jimbolia or Reşiţa, migration was already significant by the middle of the 1980s and created a strong motivation for further migration. However, only a part of the population could actually migrate, and these were especially the ethnic Germans; the mobility of others was severely restricted by the Romanian state. In this context in the 1980s, many people, Germans included, started to migrate irregularly. Irregular migration refers to situations in which migrants do not comply with the requirements imposed by states for legal entry, stay, or work. It usually refers to foreign nationals seeking residence and employment in countries other than the country of their citizenship (Alt 2003; Ghosh 1998). But irregularity also refers to the noncompliance of citizens with exit requirements, as is the case of individuals who intend to move abroad from countries with oppressive political regimes or dictatorships. Often represented as large-scale geographical prisons (Diminescu 2003), the former socialist countries were classical examples of this latter category. In these countries, irregular out-migration was very dangerous and difficult, as it proved in the case of the Berlin Wall, when many people died attempting to cross it.

Today it is difficult to estimate the number of irregular migrants from Romania before 1989.[33] Steiner and Magheţi (2009) estimated that more than 16,000 persons tried to cross the Romanian borders irregularly between 1980 and 1989. More than 12,000 were caught. They further considered that in 1988 alone 400 people lost their lives in the attempt. Although the crossing of the border to neighboring countries was severely restricted by the state (Dietz 1999; Verdery 2003), in the Banat region many succeeded in leaving Romania irregularly. The migrants I talked to stated that irregular migration was resorted to frequently in the region in the late 1980s, especially in the border cities and villages. During socialism, while irregular attempts to cross the border were severely punished, the borders were by no means impenetrable.

The experience of migration varied considerably among the people I met in Nuremberg. Mathias, for instance, knew local inhabitants near the border and arranged his passage. Vasile, however, knew no one there. For him the process was longer. He planned his escape carefully: shift hours, patrol locations, ranges of visibility in the open. After long thought, he decided to cross the border together with his wife and child.

The border point was close to Jimbolia, a small city west from Timişoara, and the locals were often seen close to the border. As they were a family, border guards did not even think of them as escapees; they even greeted the border guard when they approached him. The night they left Romania the sky was cloudy, so visibility was very low. Close to the patrol booth, they entered the field and crawled along some ditches until they reached Yugoslav soil. They were eventually apprehended by the Yugoslavs but managed to continue on to Germany.

The land borders had been militarized and for those without local know-how, crossing the border could prove fatal. In order to deflect the intense surveillance, potential migrants had to make arrangements with the guards or to find out where the crossing could be made more easily. Crossing the Danube was another option. In such cases migrants had to swim or use boats or other improvised means.[34] In crossing the land border great attention had to be paid to the Romanian and Yugoslav guards. The border was on plain ground, and visibility was good, so there was a high chance to be caught by gunfire in the middle. Interviewees recall cases of migrants who died there, and how the Romanian army used to open fire "at whatever was moving in the border area" (Vlad).

Vlad, a Romanian, remembered he knew nobody at the border crossing point, so he and one of his friends decided to chance it crossing the border. They knew it was difficult and there were many risks. But they decided it was worth trying. When they approached the border there was a clear sky and a full moon. The border guards on both sides noticed movement in the field and opened fire. It lasted for more than an hour until the shooting stopped and they could move again. Finally, they reached Serbia and were caught by the Yugoslav authorities.

In other cases, people caught by the Romanian guards were taken to the *Securitate*. They then risked imprisonment, maltreatment, and later surveillance. Daniel was an ethnic German who tried to cross the Romanian border in 1986 but was caught by the Romanian guards. For this first attempt he paid the penalty at his workplace, being constantly under surveillance. The second time he tried to cross the border and was caught again, he was sent to prison. "This time I was caught at Orşova. I was imprisoned for one year and six months. For four months I was isolated, all by myself in one room. I thought I was going to die, that my end was at hand. But the Romanian Revolution came and I was released" (Daniel).

Migrants escaping from Romania were usually apprehended by the Yugoslav authorities and imprisoned for a while until their situation was clarified. Mathias remembered that many ethnic Romanians were sent back, but ethnic Germans were usually released and could go freely to Germany. They had to have a certificate of their ethnicity. Usually it was the *RU-Nummer*, a certificate obtained from the German churches in Romania. For them, the move to Germany was easy after crossing the Romanian border: "Serbs always caught you, very rarely could someone pass without being caught in Serbia. But only Romanians were sent back to Romania, about 50 percent of them. If you were German, you were sure that you would not be sent back" (Mathias).

A second route for irregular migration was through Hungary, but this was less used than the route through Yugoslavia. The passage was easy but it was more difficult to get to Western Europe from there. Tiberiu's parents went first to Hungary as tourists and from there they moved to Germany. "They went in 1988 and only with great efforts were they able to go to Germany. They didn't let anybody know about their intention to leave [that they wanted to go to Germany]. They simply left their jobs and that was all" (Tiberiu).

Studies of migration during the communist period reveal the importance of the political element in the emerging migration from Timişoara. As the political regime in Romania became increasingly oppressive, people decided to leave the country at an accelerating pace. The Germans' migration had the support of the German state, which paid a ransom for their migration. The migration of ethnic Germans was thus conducted mostly within the framework of the bilateral agreement between Romania and Germany. Irregular migration entailed difficulties, risks, and a good deal of uncertainty, but the situation of German irregular migrants was easier in comparison to that of Romanians. They needed "just" to pass the Romanian borders without being caught. Thereafter, migration was less hazardous and dangerous, as the Yugoslav authorities let them go. The irregular migration of Germans remained, however, less common. It involved a limited number of individuals in comparison to the yearly legal allotment. Legal migration, though difficult and costly for families, was preferred. Moreover, informal negotiation with members of the communist state apparatus was essential in order to obtain quicker exit and avoid useless harassment.

THE BIG WAVE: MASS MIGRATION OF THE ROMANIAN GERMANS

Migration took off after the enthusiastic moment of the Romanian Revolution. During the first two years after December 1989, most of the Romanian Germans emigrated. Between 1977 and 1989, 180,000 Germans had emigrated from Romania. Another 160,000 followed[35] in the first three years after 1989. Under state socialism, the migration of ethnic Germans took place in a context of political oppression, with people using their ties abroad to facilitate migration. It was a migration driven by the struggle to escape domination and fulfill the basic economic needs of migrants' households. The change of political regime led to a change of motivations. After 1989 it was mostly the harsh economic reality of post-socialist Romania that drove migration. As a consequence of decades of erratic economic policies and mammoth inefficient investments, Romania had one of the weakest economies in Eastern Europe (Neef and Stănculescu 2002), whose pillars were its big industrial plants (Chirot 1978; Turnock 1970). At no time was there any sign of large-scale privatization or any other effective economic measures to rein in the accelerating inflation, the unregulated processes of accumulation and de-accumulation, and the increasing economic uncertainty (Burawoy and Verdery 1999; Ronnas 1995). In a few years poverty was blatantly obvious[36] and living standards dropped further towards the middle of the 1990s.[37] Moreover, the period was marked by much political turmoil. The miners' march to Bucharest leading to the resignation of the government in 1991 and the violent interethnic conflicts in Târgu Mureş in 1990 were conspicuous elements of an unsettled political life.

For ethnic Germans, the decades of migration brought about a shared feeling of "losing their ethnic community."[38] The Second World War, significant population displacements, and later on migration during the years of communism had shattered the German communities in Romania. On the eve of post-socialism, ethnic Germans numbered less than one-third of what they were before the Second World War. In the 1980s, Germans' migration was built upon Germany's supportive policy towards ethnic Germans, which acted as a strong pull factor. Apart from this, migration was caused by the huge difference in the living standards between Romania and Germany. During the 1980s Germans' motivation for migration grew because of political factors. But after 1989, the political push factors were less important, and in most cases economic and individual motivations prevailed.

Such motivations unfolded during my research in Nuremberg. Interviews and personal life stories provided a more complex image on the causes of migration. Christian, for example, complained about the deteriorating quality of life in Romania and the "worsening" of social relations after 1989. He remembered the mix of feelings at the time. He stated his family lived well in Romania in comparison to other people and had a lot of hope that the end of the communist regime would bring prosperity and greater freedom. But soon after 1989 they realized the changes in the Romanian society would go in a different direction than they expected. Instead of more economic development, prosperity, and professionalism, he saw more corruption and nepotism: "We took the decision to come to Germany relatively late. I was more affected by corruption, injustice, and social aspects. I had [come to Germany several times] before [I made up my mind] to migrate, [so that I could see how it was]."

In some other cases, migration to Germany offered better life opportunities. Ionuţ's parents decided to migrate because they saw more opportunities in Germany than in Romania for Ionuţ's career and intellectual development. He came from a mixed family: his father was German and his mother Romanian. Ionuţ didn't intend to migrate. Neither did his father, who was stubbornly hoping for a better life in Romania. But his

Romanian mother insisted on going in order to improve the chances of life for Ionuţ and his brother. In 1995 they finally arrived in Germany after long family talks and making formal application.

> When Ceausescu fell, my father said, "Now, there is really no point to migrate any longer; it will get better." And in 1994 life was still not better than before; for us it was no better at all. And my mother had insisted we go, to improve our life chances. We were teenagers, me and my brother; we didn't want to migrate. We were in love for the first time. We did not want to come to Germany and we swore we would go back to Romania after coming of age. Finally my father gave in, we filled in the application and we came to Germany (Ionuţ).

Today, Ionuţ recognizes his parents made the right decision when they came to Germany. He was an independent individual who wanted to find his own path in life. In Nuremberg he went on to a postgraduate education and ended up in the liberal arts. "In Romania I could have easily become a hooligan," he said. "I had many restless friends and in the 1990s there were not many options for people like me who were looking to do something in life." Many of his friends, he admits, finally ended up in low-paying jobs. Some even became petty traders or petty thieves.

The case of Eugen further exemplifies the diversification of push factors. He migrated when he was eighteen years old, shortly after his sister left Romania. His decision was caused by family constraints. Eugen had the intention to continue studying and to live an independent life. Eugen's mother passed away and his father was a pensioner, so he was left with little financial support. Instead of continuing education, he knew he would have to go to work and earn his own money. When he compared that prospect with migrating to Germany to study, he realized he could fulfill his ambitions better in Germany than in Romania.

Whereas in most cases young migrants relied on the support of their families after they came to Germany, in this case Eugen's father was a pensioner and had stayed in Romania, while Eugen and his sister came to Germany by themselves: "[I came here] alone. My mother died in 1990, when I was 14. She was ethnic German and my father Hungarian. My father was already retired and he didn't come. When you are young you also want to be on your own, not to depend on someone else" (Eugen).

In the 1990s, migration involved most ethnic Germans who had remained in Romania. Germany was seen not just as a rich country. Migration also offered the solution to various problems and aspirations. The political regime of East–West migration changed. Migration of ethnic Germans was realized in the context of the politicization of migration policies, whereby "governments in the immigration states admit certain categories of migrants and exclude others" (Faist 2000a, 36). During communism, migrants from the Eastern block could remain in Germany as asylum seekers even if they were of a rather vague German descent, or were not German ethnics at all. Until 1989 also, the number of ethnic Germans arriving was relatively limited. But after 1988 there were more than 200,000 migrants arriving yearly in comparison to the yearly average of 50,000 to 60,000 during the 1980s. Between 1988 and 1991 the migration of 1.2 million ethnic Germans (according to the figures of the Bundesverwaltungsamt) created increasing housing problems and put extra pressure on Germany's budget (Tränhardt 1995, 29).

Perceptions towards migration also changed. Initially, the migration of East European Germans had had a positive reception during communism, but after 1989 resentments began growing (Groenendijk 1997). Besides, in contrast to the ethnic Germans arriving during the communist years, the newcomers of the 1990s had less knowledge of German and were increasingly part of ethnically mixed families.[39] Nevertheless, despite the burden on the German budget, the arrival of so many migrants produced economic benefits: "immigration generated positive short-run benefits in selected sectors of the welfare state. People who immigrated between 1988 and 1991 made significant contributions. Immigrant employees generated 30 billion DM (15 billion Euros) for social insurance, against the costs of only 14 billion DM (seven billion Euros)—thus a huge surplus of 16 billion DM remained" (Faist 2007, 8). But the *Aussiedler* program was very costly because so many migrants arrived at once.[40] The reception procedures for the ethnic Germans soon changed together with the legislation and admission procedures. The support schemes and fiscal privileges[41] were also reduced. For Germany, it was a political decision to continue to accept a large number of individuals whose ethnicity and the alleged prejudices they had suffered entitled them to be accepted as German citizens. Inasmuch as prejudices were hard to prove, ethnicity remained the decisive criterion according to which these migrants became eligible to remain "in the fabled 'new world' of Western Europe" (Brubaker 1998, 1052).

Those migrating to Germany up to August 1990 were allowed to enter without possessing an *RU Nummer* and were able to initiate the relevant procedures once in Germany. After August 1990 the procedures for the admission of new *Aussiedler* were modified.[42] Later on, the process of recognition of the status of *Aussiedler* had to be conducted in migrants' country of origin. In what follows I illustrate how people from Timişoara, both Germans and people of German descent, migrated to Germany after 1989. In the cases I will discuss, Christian migrated from Romania already possessing an *RU Nummer*; Ricky obtained one in Germany, while Emil had to go to court several times until he obtained the status of *Aussiedler*.

Christian had his German ethnicity recognized already in the 1980s. He came from a family of German intellectuals in Timişoara and had visited his relatives in Germany well before 1989. In 1990, his family debated whether to migrate to Germany or to wait and see how the political and economic situation in Romania would evolve. Their decision to migrate was hastened by the sudden announcement that Austria was about to change its visa requirements and entry procedures. In order to get to Germany, they had to pass through Austria. In March 1990 some relatives in Austria told them the news. They decided to migrate overnight. He and his mother reached the Austrian border on March 14, 1990, but the new visa procedure was already in force. At the border, an Austrian border guard was separating the Western and the Eastern cars into two columns. Christian asked in German about the situation. The border guard answered they should show a visa or a certain amount of money. Christian replied they had only the *RU Nummer*, but their relatives could come at the border with the required amount of money. "The guard was staring at us, surprised that we spoke German so well. We replied: 'We are Germans from Romania, as there are very many still living there.' He took us from the column of Romanians and sent us to the column of Westerners. He said: 'You should go there and cross'" (Christian).

Christian went to Germany. His *Aussiedler* status was automatically recognized and he received German citizenship soon after. Ricky's migration differed in some respects. He did intend to go to Germany since his girlfriend had migrated earlier. But he did not possess an *RU Nummer*, and he migrated spontaneously taking advantage of the first opportunity. This was in 1990 when the release of tourist passports was liberalized in Romania. He applied and got one. He decided to migrate alone to join his girlfriend, while his parents remained in Timişoara. He went to the tourist agency in Timişoara, where he obtained a ticket just to Budapest. He had no plans how to go further. Meanwhile, his cousin, now a German citizen, was coming to Romania. Ricky hoped he would bring him to Germany. They both went to the German and Austrian consulates in Budapest, where his cousin issued an invitation for him. His cousin took him on to Germany and left him alone in a parking lot in Munich. Ricky went to a reception camp for ethnic Germans: "I was hosted there and the following Monday some employees came and asked me: 'OK, what passports do we have here?' Almost all people had some [sort of] visas. The selection process started, and those without any chance were sent back" (Ricky).

Ricky was able to remain in Germany and was hosted for a few months in the camps for the reception of ethnic Germans, where he was interviewed several times. He obtained *Aussiedler* status without difficulty. For both Christian and Ricky, migration occurred more or less spontaneously in 1990. Up to 1990, migration to Germany was restricted by the burdensome procedures in Romania; it required clearly defined and well-organized migration projects. Migration was very costly, and strong social ties in Germany were often needed. Migrants had a clear knowledge of their rights in Germany, and migration was seen as a decisive act of moving to Germany permanently. After 1989, migration was still seen as a permanent act, but the resources and risks involved were now minimal. Networks in Germany were no longer needed.

After 1989 many migrants with mixed ethnic background used their *Aussiedler* status to gain access to Germany. Ethnic boundaries were often fuzzy in Timişoara, where many mixed families lived during socialism. Emil was such a case. His parents arrived in Germany in 1988 and were granted *Aussiedler* status. After 1989, they brought Emil's brother, Tiberiu, to Germany. Tiberiu was underage and was easily accepted as an *Aussiedler*. But the same did not apply for Emil, who was already eighteen years old. He had no *RU Nummer* when he came to Germany. His situation was in this sense similar to Ricky's, who also arrived in Germany without an *RU Nummer*. Yet Ricky entered Germany before August 1990 and was accepted without prior recognition. Emil arrived after this, but he was coming from an ethnically mixed family.

> In my case there was a problem because I did not have the *RU Nummer*. Since I did not have it, what else could I have done? My parents came to [pick me up] in August 1990. They didn't want to wait any longer, because Germany was changing its migration policy. In fact there was a change taking place already: without an *RU Nummer* you could be accepted only until the 30th of July. Afterwards, many were sent back. My parents told me: "Come over here!" I had my passport and they came with their car and brought me here. At the border crossing points nobody asked me anything. I just said that I was visiting my parents. When I arrived, I went to the *Aussiedler* camp [in Nuremberg, at the *Grundig* Center]. The janitor sent me to an office, where I was asked: "But sir, how did you get to Germany?" "I simply came with my parents, I came to visit them, but I want to remain here permanently," I said. He replied that that was no longer possible. Only those who were already registered could remain. All others had to leave. He sent me to another office and I was questioned [about my arrival]. They said I had to go back to Romania, to wait for my *RU Nummer*. Otherwise, I would not be allowed to return to Germany for another seven years (Emil).

In these three cases, migrants wanted to take advantage of the still unreformed *Aussiedler* policy. For Emil a strange situation emerged: while his brother was a recognized *Aussiedler*, he was not. In the following years he had to go through long procedures and finally even a trial in order to remain in Germany. To have his case heard in a court of law cost Emil much time and financial resources. He had no choice but to work informally in order to earn the money. Eventually he succeeded.

After 1993 the law for *Aussiedler* changed and the term *Spätaussiedler* replaced that of *Aussiedler*.[43] The new law had the aim of regulating migration to manageable levels. It signaled not only a change in terminology, but also decreasing benefits for ethnic Germans. Nevertheless, the quick acquisition of German citizenship remained in the provisions of the new law. A quota of a maximum 220,000 migrants per year was introduced (Dietz 1999; Faist 1994), and migrants had to prove persecution in their home countries. In addition, some objective criteria, such as knowledge of German, were also introduced for immigrants to be accepted as *Spätaussiedler*.[44] By the time the change of the law occurred, not many Germans were left in Romania. Their migration decreased dramatically, and those wishing to migrate had to wait until their *RU Nummer* was issued. Rolie, for instance, had a mixed ethnic background. His father was German, and most relatives on his father's side had migrated already. "Our application was rejected," Rolie recalled, "on grounds that my father had married a Romanian woman and therefore we were ethnically mixed. We went for help to a lawyer here in Germany and finally we obtained the approval in the autumn of 1994. In 1995 we came here, a few years after we had made the first application."

Gabriel's was a similar case. In contrast to Ricky and Christian who had no problems with the recognition of their Germanness, Gabriel's request was investigated and he had to prove his knowledge of German before arriving in Germany. Ricky and Christian were ethnic Germans and their mother tongue was German, so the process of recognition was unproblematic for them. But for Gabriel, like many others, ethnicity or ethnic background was insufficient, and their alleged affinity to German culture was inquired into, with knowledge of German being a decisive factor.

> We received the permission to come to Germany and I had not finished school. My mother had [applied previously] and [we received the acceptance after three years]. Many certificates were requested to come to Germany, to prove our German descent, to prove that we were German speakers, able to read German, and so on. We had to send such certificates constantly, and [the German authorities] were continuously requesting some other documents. We always had to prove something. So, my father is Romanian and my mother is German (Gabriel).

This alleged cultural affinity of the Romanian Germans became even more problematic for those arriving later. The number of mixed marriages was high in the 1980s in Romania (Poledna 1998), and social groups were often mixed. German high schools were attended by both German and Romanian children who socialized in the same milieu. Neighborhoods, like friendships, were not defined in strict ethnic terms in cities like Timişoara. In such cases, the cultural and ethnic boundaries were anything but clear, and Germanness was an expanded social category, which included mixed families and Romanians who were German speakers. This fuzziness became a challenge for the *Aussiedler* policy when people with ethnically mixed backgrounds had claims to be granted *Aussiedler* status. But in the end, Germany accepted the newcomers coming also from mixed marriages.

How inclusive this policy was can be seen when it applied to the relatives of ethnic Germans when they migrated to Germany. Adela and Horst, a mixed couple, arrived in Germany after 1990. Later on they decided to divorce. Because she was married to an ethnic German, Adela received *Aussiedler* status and German citizenship, which entitled her to remain in Germany. During the separation, she got to know Dan, a Romanian who later managed to come to Germany as Adela's husband after her divorce from Horst was finalized.

> [I met Dan, my new husband in Timişoara]. I became pregnant [with him] and as I already had a child with my ex husband, we thought it was better for us if he remained in Germany [with me]. [The authorities] wanted to send my new husband back to apply for family reunion from Romania. I went again to the authorities and told them straight out that [if he would go back to Romania], I would lose any hope for support. We were finally allowed to remain here (Adela).

In conclusion, migration from Timişoara to Nuremberg shows two distinct patterns, corresponding to the socialist and the post-socialist periods. In both cases, the German state was the main actor driving migration. In the former period, social ties were exploited, since relatives in Germany could issue family reunion applications and sent money to those in Romania planning to migrate. Irregular migration was risky, so people preferred to use the fussy but legal procedures. After 1989 we can see that by its inclusionary character the status of *Aussiedler* enabled the migration of most Germans from Romania as well as their non-German relatives. This post-socialist migration was not similar to many other migrations, in which migrant networks organize migration (Faist 2000a; Massey 1987). On the contrary, this was a quickly executed and massive migration, supported by the German state, who defined German ethnicity as the criterion according to which migrants were welcomed to stay.

If before 1989 ethnic Germans had to make applications and to undertake long formalities, after 1990 everything was speedy. In the cases I have presented, the migrants simply moved overnight to Germany, sometimes receiving a degree of support from their relatives or acquaintances. Furthermore, migration was boosted up by the changing of Germany's migration policy. In most cases migrants speeded up their arrivals, knowing that their rights could be diminished in Germany if they waited any longer.

The *Aussiedler* category (i.e., resettled Germans) was in many cases a questionable ethnic category, but it functioned in terms of policy and served to divide migrants into insiders and outsiders, some of whom could be granted citizenship overnight. Migrants' energies and funds were thus oriented towards obtaining *Aussiedler* status, which in reality determined their entry in Germany. A problematic aspect is that in many cases, such as the case of the Timişoara Germans, there were mixed marriages and many people who could plausibly claim German descent without necessarily knowing German, for example, or having a shared knowledge of German culture. And there were cases when migrants received apparently unfair treatment, such as the case with the two brothers, Emil and Tiberiu. Such cases were eventually settled in the courts.

The literature on migration often emphasizes the use of brokers and private companies as main actors in the migration industry. It tells of private companies, lawyers, or migration brokers (Cohen 1997; Garapich 2008) who establish and maintain links between the countries of origin and destination, thus facilitating the process of migration. These are "often seen as separate from—and complementary to—migrant networks" (Elrick and Lewandowska 2008, 724). In the case of Polish migration to Italy and the Netherlands, for instance, Elrick and Lewandowska (idem) demonstrate the role agents played in migration, and argue that an analytical separateness between migrant networks and the migration industry is difficult to sustain.

Nevertheless, as in the cases of Emil and Tiberiu, lawyers were very important actors for those with an unclear status. As Joppke (1998) has pointed out, the role of the courts is very important in Europe for migrants with unclear statuses. The changing migration policies of Germany left many migrants in an uncertain status and confused them about the concrete steps they had to take in order to complete the process—like, for example, where to apply for recognition and what test needed to be passed—so they had to use all avenues open to them to obtain permission to stay. Weak ties and family ties also provided migrants with information on migration, changing regulations, and possible opportunities for employment.

In the case of those coming during socialism, social networks with relatives were often exploited. But after 1989, networks came to be rarely used. However, we cannot generalize these findings, since in a different study about the ethnic Germans' migration from Romania, Michalon (2003a) shows that for some late migrants, networks did play a certain role in shaping migration decisions, yet not their migration strategies. Michalon has shown how Transylvanian Saxons from rural areas who migrated after 1993–1994 used their networks of relatives and friends in Germany when choosing their destinations and identifying future jobs.

Before migration, ethnic Germans had a high social status in Timișoara and they were able to keep their high status even during socialism.[45] In the 1980s, when shortages were acute in Romania, German products were sent by ethnic Germans who had started to migrate to Germany. Migration became a desired strategy. For the young ethnic Germans who were socialized in that context, migration was a legitimate and highly rewarding act. Migrants I interviewed did not see migration as compensation for something lost, or for maltreatment in Romania, but as something they were entitled to as ethnic Germans. Migrants expected that because they were ethnic Germans, or at least had some German descent, their presence in Germany would be well accepted.

NOTES

1. Names I used in this book are fictitious.
2. In 1989, the Germans in Timişoara were the third largest ethnic group in the city.
3. The region of Banat is located between the Danube and the rivers Mureş and Tisa. Towards the east it borders the Carpathian Mountains. Today, the Banat is shared between Romania, Serbia, and Hungary; the largest part of it, however, lies in Romania.
4. After the retreat of the Ottomans the Habsburgs tried to increase their revenues by colonizing the region of Timişoara with migrants from Alsace and Lorraine. In the following centuries, Romanians and Germans were the two most numerous ethnic groups. After 1778, when the Banat became part of Hungary, the number of Hungarians grew. In time some other ethnic groups arrived (Chelcea 1999).
5. In the Banat known as Swabians.
6. Out of about one million, the total population of the Romanian Banat region.
7. In 1930 there were 32 percent Germans and 25 percent Romanians, the largest group being the Germans. In 1977 Germans were still 10.5 percent of the population.
8. Accordingly, in 1950 there were 199,600 ethnic Germans from Romania already settled in Germany and Austria. These included former soldiers in the German army, ethnic Germans deported to Russia who were afterwards sent directly to Germany, and ethnic Germans evacuated during the war by the German army. Most German ethnics were evacuated in 1940 (Castellan 1971) from the territories ceded to the USSR (northern Bukovina and the eastern side of Moldova).
9. The deportation measures were carried out by the Romanian authorities.
10. See for instance Chelcea (1999) and Chelcea and Lăţea (2000). Moreover, Verdery (1985) points out that the situation of the Germans was reversed in Transylvania: from being large landowners who used to employ Romanians prior to the Second World War, Germans by the 1950s found themselves in the position of actually having to work for Romanians.
11. Accordingly, the interwar period saw strong nationalism in Transylvania and Banat, sustained by the centralizing and nationalizing actions of the Romanian state, including its attempts to "Romanianize" the administration (see Livezeanu 1995; Verdery 1991; 2003). During state socialism, ethnic competition in Banat was no longer important for various reasons, and attitudes were rather against "the center," Bucharest, or other Romanian regions. They would compete over resources allocated from "the center" (Chelcea 1999).
12. Thus, there were about 12 million Germans who migrated to Germany immediately after the war and another 2.6 million between 1950 and 1961, to the construction of the Berlin Wall (Dietz 1999).
13. In German, *das Grundgesetz*.
14. Such as *Übersiedler*, for instance, Germans from the former German Democratic Republic (GDR).
15. The law of expelled persons, *Bundesvertriebenengesetz*, BVFG.
16. I.e., *Deutsche Volkszugehörigen*.
17. I.e., *Heimatvertriebene*.
18. Thus it is estimated that about 3.8 million GDR Germans moved to West Germany during the Cold War (Hubert 1998).
19. About 500,000 of which in 1988 and 1989 (Bundesverwaltungsamt).
20. BVFG 1971, 58.

21. During the Cold War Germany was divided between the GDR, the communist German Democratic Republic, and the FRG, the Federal Republic of Germany.

22. Thus the number of the expellees and deportees was about one-sixth of the population of the German Federal Republic after the Second World War.

23. See Bundesverwaltungsamt, III Stabsstelle, Statistik—Dokumentation, 50728 Köln.

24. The Romanian communist leader.

25. The German chancellor between 1974 and 1982.

26. Thus in 1978 the sum was about 5,000 DM for any German allowed to leave Romania. This changed in 1983 to 7,800 DM and in 1988 to 11,000 DM.

27. Weber et al. mention there were two types of official applications to fill in, followed by interviews with the Romanian *Miliția*. Potential migrants had to obtain receipts to prove that they had no financial obligations towards the Romanian state. Some of these requirements were difficult to fulfill, especially for persons coming from rural areas (Weber et al. 2003, 445).

28. See Weber et al. 2003.

29. The socialist police.

30. The *Securitate* was the name of the Romanian secret police under state socialism.

31. 1 DM equals 0.5 Euros.

32. Many migrants considered that on the whole migration during the 1980s was possible only with help of relatives abroad who could send the necessary money. Romania's policy towards its German citizens was thus problematic in at least two respects: the state received money to allow the Romanian Germans to migrate, while the state apparatus received informal benefits.

33. The Romanian data show that between 1977 and 1989 the total number of legal migrants from Romania amounted to 342,427 persons altogether—Germans, Romanians, Hungarians, and Jews. The number of the ethnic Germans who migrated legally was about 152,000 persons. In Germany about 189,933 persons were registered as *Aussiedler* from Romania. The large difference might be made up by non-German spouses, by ethnic Germans visiting Germany and deciding not to return to Romania, or by irregular migrants. The *Saldo*—the difference between entry and exit from Germany—of Romanian citizens (non-German ethnics) was about 60,000 persons for the same period (BAMF). Yet it is extremely difficult to estimate accurately the number of migrants for each category. What we can observe is that 50 to 60 percent of legal migrants came from regions inhabited by Germans, which encompassed only 15 percent of the Romanian population, so we can conclude that migration in these regions was in fact much greater.

34. For instance, in the 1980s, instead of taking some fishing boats, which needed a long time to cross the Danube, migrants used oxygen tubes as a type of improvised motor boats.

35. See Bundesverwaltungsamt.

36. See also Neef and Stănculescu 2002. One should also take into account the social and economic effects of industrial involution and the weakness of the state when analyzing the informal economy after 1989 (Chelcea and Mateescu 2005).

37. See Neef and Stănculescu (2002).

38. See for instance Weber et al. (2003).

39. See Dietz (1999). This is mostly the case with the Russian Germans.

40. The *Aussiedler* program proved costly: about six billion U.S. dollars were spent by the German government yearly on migrants' accommodation alone (Kurthen 1995, 922).

41. *Gesetz zur Anpassung von Eingliederungsleistungen für Aussiedler und Übersiedler, Eingliederungsanpassungsgesetz,* 22 Dez. 1989.

42. *Gesetz zur Regelung des Aufnahmeverfahrens für Aussiedler,* 28 Juni, 1990 (BGBl I, 1247).

43. *Kriegsfolgenbereinigungsgesetz,* 21 Dez. 1992, BGBl I, 2094.

Spätaussiedler means "late resettlers."

44. Three cumulative criteria were considered: language, German origin and inherited German culture, and public recognition as a German (Groenendijk 1997).

45. For instance, even today when the German community accounts for less than 60,000 people, there are cities like Sibiu (in German called *Hermannstadt*) and Mediaş (*Mediasch*), where the current mayors are Saxons. Also, the German Democratic Forum won the elections in the Sibiu (*Hermannstadt*) county in 2004, although Germans accounted for less than 2 percent of the county population. In some of these cities, German names are still used. The education system, from kindergarten to schools, suffered no decline after migration, as Romanians attend them in high numbers. This is the remarkable case of a population that retains a very high prestige in spite of the fact that today there are so few members of the community left to represent it.

TWO

Living in Nuremberg

Accepted but Different

More than two centuries after their settlement in the Banat, Romanian Germans migrated *en masse* and resettled in Germany. One part of these migrants headed towards Nuremberg, where denser networks of migrants from Romania formed. As a large and rich city in southern Germany, Nuremberg offered a vast array of jobs and a rich multiethnic environment. The city of Nuremberg, accounting for about half a million inhabitants, became home for many migrants from all over the world, especially after 1989. In 2007, about 40 percent of the population claimed to have a migrant background.[1] As some of the migrants contended, Nuremberg was a much more tolerant place compared to other German cities in which they had lived previously. Ricky told me once that he felt at home in Nuremberg, and that people there were more communicative and tolerant than in the other parts of Germany where he lived before, where he had faced more conservative attitudes.

Migrants' incorporation in Nuremberg was realized in what has been called an "advantaged context of reception" (Portes and Böröcz 1989, 619), that is, they were supported by the state, were able to find good jobs, and enjoyed a favorable popular perception (Münz, Seifert, and Ulrich 1999). The German ethnicity of these migrants from Timișoara, and the support they received from the state, created high expectations of integration. In the present chapter I will look at the social and economic incorporation of these migrants, loosely coupled to ethnicity, and investigate how migrants' sociality was formed. I will show how, by providing privileged access and highly supportive measures, Germany encouraged these migrants to claim they were entitled to a privileged reception.

In my research I also asked if migrants' social status in their country of origin influenced their social and economic expectations. I analyzed how migrants positioned themselves vis-à-vis the local population and how they perceived their social status in the new context. I finally looked at migrants' identity claims and how they understood themselves, as German migrants in Germany.

* * *

On the Fürther Street, linking Nuremberg and the neighboring city of Fürth, Fabricius Butcher's Shop opened up in the middle of the 1990s. A profitable business thanks to the growing immigrant population of Romanian origin, the butcher's shop soon became a hub for Romanian associations and cultural activities in Nuremberg. They started to advertise tourist destinations in Romania and to organize and participate in the organization of different cultural activities in the region of Nuremberg. On one of the first days of my fieldwork, I spent a while in the shop. The butcher's shop was not full of customers, but their steady coming and going provided me an opportunity to learn more about them. The shop was a pleasant environment, as the owner was a very communicative person. There were all sorts of customers: some came only to do their shopping; others were interested as well in talking to the owners about upcoming events in the city. Some were labor migrants staying in Nuremberg temporarily; others were settled permanently. They were labor migrants, medical doctors, engineers, nurses, restaurant owners, technicians, and administrators. Some of them had just arrived in the city; others were second-generation migrants with a limited knowledge of Romanian. The customers bought Romanian ham, sausages, borscht, conserves, beer, and Romanian wine. My visit to the butcher's shop was short so my acquaintance with these people was limited. But it provided a glimpse into the diversity of professional patterns, careers, and backgrounds of the growing Romanian immigrant population. It became clear that it was essential to locate the social and economic incorporation of migrants from Timișoara into this broader social context.

I understand migrants' incorporation as a pathway, or a longer-term process of social, cultural, and economic interaction and change (Glick-Schiller et al. 2005) between migrants and the social context of arrival. Isajiw (1997, 82) defines it as "a process through which a social unit is included in a larger social unit as an integral part of it. Social units can be individuals or collectivities acting in a patterned manner" (idem). I also see these processes realized in the institutional contexts of specific integration policies that aim at ascribing migrants certain integration pathways. It includes reception policies and policies designed to provide access to education, labor markets, and the welfare system. Migrants' incorporation refers also to when migrants adapt to the social contexts of reception, interact with the local population, and construct patterns of sociality among themselves. It can thus be understood in terms of the number of social ties and the mechanisms underlying the formation of social ties (Eve 2010).

Migrants' incorporation is a salient political and social issue in immigration nations. In the 1960s, migrants' incorporation (called integration at that time) was seen functionally as a path leading directly towards immigrants' assimilation (Gordon 1964), but later evidence contradicted the assimilationists' claims (Glazer and Moynihan 1963). From the initial functional approach of the 1960s, assimilation (including cultural assimilation) was later conceived of as negative when the discourses on multiculturalism and diversity came to be celebrated in the 1980s and 1990s (Brubaker 2001). But over the years, one of the normative claims of initial assimilationists' accounts—migrants' better socioeconomic incorporation, leading to structural assimilation in the longer run—remained as one of the tenets of integration policies (Alba and Nee 1997; Brubaker 2001). This principle of structural assimilation guided policy makers who formulated and later applied the *Aussiedler* policy.

The ethnic Germans from Timişoara who appear in this study arrived in Nuremberg after 1989 having different socio-professional backgrounds and formed ethnically mixed social networks. I concentrate on a particular group. It is not my aim to generalize the findings to the whole of the migration of ethnic Germans from Romania. What I am attempting to do is to provide an account of how migrants seek to construct status during the processes of social and economic incorporation.

GETTING TO NUREMBERG

Migrants from Romania started to arrive in Nuremberg immediately after the Second World War, but more significant flows came during the last thirty years due to the steep increase of the migration of ethnic Germans. Consequently, a concentration of migrants from Romania emerged in the region, numbering between 10,000 and 15,000 families.[2]

Between 1990 and 1993 there was a steady migration of East Europeans to Germany. It was a period of policy change, of the tightening of the rules regarding the migration of asylum seekers and a limiting of the reception of ethnic German immigrants to a yearly quota. These were measures taken to regularize and control their mass migration (Finotelli 2006) after fifty years of successful control during which Germany received mostly migrants from other parts of Europe (Schönwälder 2004).

Migrants who arrived in West Germany, Romanians included, had to live initially in reception camps (Bauer and Zimmermann 1997), which were set up in all regions of the country. In Nuremberg there were two reception camps, one for German resettlers and another one for asylum seekers.[3] In such camps, migrants were hosted upon arrival and their legal status was investigated, including their ethnic affiliations and their reasons for coming to Germany. Their stay in such camps was generally short, and afterwards the migrants could settle and work anywhere in their state (*Bundesland*) of reception. After registration at one reception camp, migrants could move to independent housing. The arrival of migrants in the region of Nuremberg was encouraged by the previous arrivals of friends and relatives: "Because many had acquaintances here, many settled here. Let's say, at least 10 percent of those who used to come to these centers settled in Nuremberg" (Valeriu).

Romanian Germans settled overwhelmingly in the economically attractive regions of Bavaria and Baden Württemberg (Münz and Ohlinger 1997, 250). Their distribution depended on the infrastructure of arrival (such as the reception camps), the distribution of social networks, labor market demands, and available residential opportunities. Many migrants living today in Nuremberg had to reside initially in a different region of Germany, to wait there for a while, and to relocate later. Thanks to the high number of acquaintances, relatives, and friends they had in Nuremberg, these migrants remained only for a while in other places, and came to Nuremberg after receiving German citizenship. This was common practice among these ethnic Germans who, despite some settlement limitations, "moved in with friends and relatives who had already settled in Germany" (Zimmermann 1999, 8). Gabriel, for instance, arrived first in Nuremberg but was sent elsewhere in Germany. He considered it natural to decide to come back because some of his relatives were living in Nuremberg. Upon receiving German citizenship, the move back to Nuremberg was very easy.

> You were first asked where you would prefer to go. My uncle was here in Bavaria, and my grandmother had some brothers and sisters around. From the office, they told me that no places were available in Bavaria. They sent us to the *Grundig* Center [in Nuremberg]. We remained about two to three weeks to fill in some papers. But there were no available places in Nuremberg, and we were sent somewhere else. After four to five months, we came back (Gabriel).

Germans who arrived during the first months of 1990 received without difficulty permission to remain in the country. The situation was especially unproblematic for those who had obtained recognition of German ethnicity in Romania, as their stay in such a camp (*Lager*) was then quite short. In general, "the time an individual [spent] in a reception camp depend[ed] on the availability of accommodation and [could] be shortened if relatives and friends help[ed] to find housing space" (Bauer and Zimmermann 1997, 145). Migrants I interviewed preferred to live with relatives. But migrants without the *RU Nummer* had to apply for it at the reception camps. They had to prove their ancestry, their affiliation to

German culture, and their knowledge of German: "At the *Lager* they questioned me about my ethnicity, when I was enrolled in the army, what school I attended in Romania, and so on. I soon received temporary papers and a work permit" (Luca).

The settlement of migrants in Nuremberg was influenced by the easy economic incorporation of adults who encountered a very attractive labor market. The elderly too had an easy settlement, as they received pensions and could stay anywhere in Germany. Until 1991, the contributions to the pension system paid by migrants in their origin countries were generously compensated by the German state, so they received fairly decent German pensions. Later, pensions were reduced by 30 percent. After 1996 this compensation was even further watered down (Münz and Ohlinger 1997, 241). As I have shown in the previous chapter, the open-door policy that Germany had maintained over the past 50 years did not come to a halt, but the open door did start to slowly close. This becomes apparent if we consider the shrinking benefits that migrants received and the tightening of the admission procedures. Nevertheless, when the new law for ethnic Germans' migration was enforced in 1993, many of the Timişoara Germans were already living in Germany.

LABOR MARKET INCORPORATION

The migration of ethnic Germans was a politically legitimated migration, where networks of migration played only a marginal role. This migration differed from most cases of labor migration: migrants had not taken on jobs in the secondary labor market (Piore 1979). Their migration to Germany was not driven by the labor demand in Western Europe as it was for other East-European migrants (Cohen 1995; Favell and Hansen 2002), but by political reasons. Moreover, they did not have to attend universities or pass through examinations in order to obtain access to the labor market. They had their diplomas and degrees automatically recognized and full access to the labor market. "Germans had their diplomas recognized. No matter if they were medical doctors or engineers. [They had] a good chance to do something in life" (Marius).

Between 1988 and 1993, the economic opportunities in Germany were favorable to the comfortable incorporation of German resettlers: unemployment decreased by 500,000, and 1.5 million vacancies opened (Gieseck, Heilemann, and Loeffelholz 1995, 695–96). Ethnic German immigrants had a favorable qualification level: prior to their migration, a high proportion of them had worked as skilled workers or white-collar workers (idem). The employment potential of the German migrants was actually higher than that of the general German population: they had a younger age structure and better female labor market participation in their countries of origin (Münz and Ohlinger 1997). Prior to migration, 40 percent to 50 percent were employed in industry and 40 percent to 50 percent in services. However, their qualifications were not always compatible with those required by the German labor market, and for those who had worked in services in their origin countries language qualifications and nationally specific skills in some cases represented barriers for successful economic incorporation in Germany (idem, 243).

The situation emerged where ethnic Germans as well as foreign workers "[were] overrepresented among the long-term unemployed, namely those who [had] been searching for a job for more than a year" (Zimmermann 1999, 10). This paradoxical situation was mainly due to the relationship between unemployment, professional qualifications, and language knowledge (Koller 1997, 776–78): access to skilled jobs required specialization and a good command of German. Germans from Romania had a good knowledge of German (Münz and Ohlinger 1997): upon their arrival, and about 90 percent were able to speak and write good or very good German.[4] Bauer and Zimmermann (1997, 148) also mention that they performed well in the labor market, while Koller (1997) reaches the same conclusion when comparing them to Russian and Polish Germans.

Timişoara is a large Romanian city, with two of the largest universities in the country, German schools and higher education institutes, and quite a wide range of educational opportunities. When migrants arrived in Germany at the beginning of the 1990s, they found an economically advantageous context of reception. Most people I interviewed were satisfied with the opportunities in the labor market and their rapid access to German citizenship and welfare benefits. They were unemployed only just after arrival or when looking for better jobs. Ricky and Luca were euphoric. They were very young when they arrived in Germany and were enchanted with the opportunities they found. There was no problem with job seeking. Labor offices had many jobs to offer. Some were not rewarding by German standards, but for them it was a big deal. Another migrant from Romania, Horst, became a professional driver after coming from Romania. He had no specialized skills when he left the country and no idea what job he would get. But as a driver in Germany he was able to earn enough money to support his whole family and even to save a quarter of his income. For him and many like him, one year's work in Germany earned him more than what he would have gotten in 10 to 15 years in Romania.

Migrants could use formal means in order to find jobs: labor offices (*Arbeitsamt*) where they could register and receive job offers, or manpower companies (*Zeit Arbeitfirma*). Because of the many vacancies existing in the 1990s and through easily accessible institutions, they rarely used their networks for accessing jobs. Only in some rare occasions did they use weak ties when they learned about jobs from acquaintances.

Migrants with technical qualifications had the chance to find well-paying jobs appropriate to their qualifications, but others who arrived at an older age often had to accept underpaid employment. This was the case for professional migrants whose skills were unsuited to the German labor market, or those unable to adapt. Luca's parents obtained good jobs compared to their previous situation in Romania, but were underpaid in comparison with the local Germans.

> My mother got a job very quickly, but for my father it was a bit more difficult. He got a job after one year. They had to pass some tests and afterwards my father went to a job interview. He got it. It was a large construction company which hired *Aussiedler* and employees from the former GDR, whom they could pay less. My father worked about three or four years there. My mother earned about 4,000 DM (2,000 Euros) a month. A German engineer would gain about 6,000–7,000 DM (3,000–3,500 Euros) for the same job (Luca).

Those without qualifications could access jobs in the secondary labor market. Despite lower wages, they still thought that the economic gain of coming to Germany was huge when they compared their earnings to their previous earnings in Romania. This was apparent in the case of Martin. His mother was a technician in Romania and his father was a seller at a petrol station in Timişoara. In Germany, his mother worked as a cleaning woman and his father worked as an unskilled worker. In spite of obtaining jobs that required lower qualifications, they were pleased with the working conditions they encountered: their earnings allowed them to live well, save enough, and offer their children an education and a better future. Martin considered there were so many available jobs in the first years after their migration that even for unskilled migrants, economic participation was unproblematic. In order to illustrate migrants' opportunities for incorporation in the labor market, as well as the diversity of job openings that migrants encountered in Nuremberg, I provide here some case studies of Romanian migrants.

Sandu is a Romanian who came from a smaller city close to Timişoara. During the Romanian Revolution in 1989 he was completing his studies at the Technical University in Timişoara. He had no plan to migrate; he wanted to start working or open up a small business in Romania. But his girlfriend's migration changed his life plan. She was German and left Romania for good in the first months of 1990. He wanted to join her, but they had to marry first. After that he came to Nuremberg as the family member of a German citizen. Sandu had high aspirations upon arrival. As he had graduated from a good technical university, he thought he would be able to obtain a good job soon. The prospects were good: degrees from the Technical University in Timişoara were recognized in Germany without problems and there were many well-paying jobs in technical professions. But he spoke no German. At first his career did not run as he expected. He had to start from the bottom, washing floors and doing all sorts of unskilled jobs. After learning German and adapting to the new environment he finally obtained a job as an engineer. During the 1990s he was mostly involved in construction work in the Nuremberg area and in the former East Germany. In 1998 he opened an architecture office and a construction company. All went well until 2002. He closed the company down, as it wasn't profitable anymore. He finally obtained another job at Siemens, where he worked as an engineer in 2006 when I carried out the interview. In his career he had no complaints of discrimination, and was happy that he had achieved many things despite being a migrant.

The case of Sandu is revealing, as it displays the kind of adaptation to the market that was required in Nuremberg, and how professional success was attainable by legal migrants. Ethnic Romanians who arrived as legal migrants, mostly through marriage, and who did not receive the status of ethnic Germans, found a less propitious context, at least in the beginning. Their knowledge of German was not so proficient, and with some notable exceptions their qualifications were not recognized. Romanians had to attend professional schools in Germany and to pass exams in order to succeed in having their qualifications acknowledged.

Romanian legal migrants working in the secondary labor markets had multiple employment opportunities thanks to the availability of jobs. Ioan had just married Adela and decided to come to Nuremberg, where Adela was living with her daughter. His application for residence had not yet been processed and he had no rights to work there. But his case was positively evaluated by the immigration office, and it was clear he would be allowed to remain in Germany. Upon passing through a series of administrative procedures, he was concerned he would not get a job and went to an employment agency.

> I had a Romanian passport and they said: "From tomorrow you can come and work." I said I didn't have the right to work yet, but they answered: "It is all right, you will get it eventually." They sent me to a construction site where I had to install cables in walls and ditches. When I went to work I said to myself I would accept any job they would offer me. Afterwards [I got jobs] through acquaintances and I went to an electrical company. I thought I [had a great chance], I was to receive 16.5 DM (8.25 Euros) an hour. But they expected me to pack and carry the cables too, free of charge. And this took me about one hour a day. It was not convenient for me, so I went back to the *Zeit Firma*. They said they would offer me 18 DM (9 Euros) [for another job]. Finally, I got a job at the airport with some transport services. There I could get about 22 DM (11 Euros) an hour. I've stayed at the airport until today. In 1993 and 1994, I took an extra job as a taxi driver. I had the ambition to do it [and I did it] (Ioan).

In conclusion, migrants' economic incorporation was realized through formal market mechanisms rather than through networks. As the previous examples show, finding labor was relatively easy for legal migrants, whether Romanian Germans or Romanians. Education and a good command of German were important for finding good jobs. In comparison to ethnic Romanians, ethnic Germans received full recognition of their diplomas, while non-Germans had to attend specialization courses and pass examinations. For many this was an obstacle to vertical mobility, as it required time and effort. But in comparison to Romania, where salaries were about 100 U.S. dollars a month in the 1990s, and job insecurity was extreme,[5] Germany offered both job security and high salaries. Migrants declared they received decent treatment in the labor market and their life opportunities were enhanced by having a legal status. In the following section I look at migrants' education prospects, an issue linked to their career plans and access to specialized jobs and upward mobility. Middle-aged people were unable to pursue further specialization, but for the one-and-a-half- or the second-generation migrants, access to education was vital.

These ethnic migrants to Germany represent a very distinct segment of the Romanian migration, as migrants were overnight entitled to access the wealthy German labor market and enjoy welfare benefits. Their situation differed from other migrants from Romania, who usually found work in the secondary labor markets in Italy, France, Hungary, or Spain. By comparison, Hungarians from Transylvania migrating to Hungary encountered economic exclusion in the Hungarian labor market (Fox 2007). They developed labor migrant networks and came to occupy niches in the secondary labor markets, especially in construction. They hadn't the same access to jobs as migrants from Timişoara in Nuremberg, despite the political discourses in Hungary which incorporated them into a greater cultural nation of Hungarians. Furthermore, in a different study on ethnic Germans' migration, Michalon (2003a) describes how Transylvanian Saxons established networks of temporary migration between Romania and Germany, bringing Romanians and some Saxons to work as temporary workers. But these migrants from Timişoara only and rarely used weak ties for finding jobs. They had full access to the rich labor market in Germany through the use of recruitment agencies and firms, so networks of friends and relatives around Nuremberg did not play a major role in their labor market incorporation. It is a clear case of what we shall call a successful migration and labor market incorporation.

GETTING EDUCATION . . . AND BETTER JOBS

Education was very important for migrants' upward mobility. The migrants I interviewed were young when they arrived in Germany and some continued their education there, at universities, technical schools, or vocational schools. Altogether, I interviewed eighty persons—Germans, Romanians, and some Hungarians—of whom forty came from Timişoara or were spouses of migrants from Timişoara. Among the people from Timişoara, the level of education was generally high: fifteen had university degrees, while thirteen were attending courses and specializations in Germany. They were skilled workers, designers, engineers, or small entrepreneurs. Most of them completed their education in Germany and changed their line of business. Some pursued careers in the liberal professions and the arts. Ethnic Germans were entitled to free access to education through ordinary schools, universities, and language and special schools. Vocational schools were also an option for many. The schools for German resettlers aimed at promoting migrants' integration and language learning. In addition to language classes and the regular school curricula, social and cultural events were organized. In such contexts, young ethnic Germans could come into contact with other migrants, mainly from Poland, Romania, and Russia. The whole educational program was subsidized by the state.[6] As one migrant, Rudi, mentioned, the school he attended had about 80 percent Russians, 10 to 15 percent Romanians, and some Poles. There were some financial subsidies, such as for cinema tickets and excursions, as well as a program for integration, including football matches. This school provided help for young resettlers to adapt to Nuremberg. Migrants at first had no knowledge of the city and only a few acquaintances. In a few cases they had only a weak command of German. Most of them had attended high schools in Romania but, in order to continue their education, they had to adapt to the German educational system and have their previous studies recognized.

The schools for German resettlers were very helpful for the migrants' incorporation, as learning German was an intermediary step towards entering the German educational system. As some migrants confessed, ordinary high schools were more difficult, and in some cases migrants abandoned high schools and completed training courses for skilled workers or sales or administrative personnel. In attending schools, young resettlers, such as Rolie, had their first contact with the local population. In some cases migrants complained about discrimination.

> I was in the best class [at the *Aussiedler* school], among those with the best knowledge of German. We were five "Romanians," a "Polish" girl, and about fifteen "Russians." German Russian students didn't speak German at all. For me it was easy. I went to the *Realschule* (high school) afterwards. In the first two months I got poor results. For the first time I had contact with German society, this cold society. Teachers said that if I didn't master German perfectly, I could simply leave the school. In other words, "let others come, this is not your place." I quit. I went to a vocational school, to a specialization course. I left this school too and I started to work. It was not [an issue of capability, but of attitudes]. What I learned in Romania in seven years, I learned there in nine years, at least in mathematics and physics. I didn't get the feeling that they really appreciated me. In the tenth form, I had only German colleagues; it was all right, but, they would always say: "You know so many

things, but in fact you don't speak German properly." And even when you speak it well, you have an accent, and you will keep this accent [for the rest of your life] (Rolie).

In other cases, migrants from Timişoara were successful at school and later they were able to compete more equally in the labor market. Luca was one such migrant who adapted quickly to the educational and professional requirements. Different from Rolie, who ended up as a salesman, Luca attended good technical schools and later took up well-rewarded positions. He went first to a school for ethnic Germans, though he recognized he didn't need German classes because he was native in German.

He started to work and in the meantime he applied for different technical schools. His previous studies in Romania in mathematics were useful. He was flexible in the labor market and gifted intellectually. His attendance of good schools in Romania was of a great advantage for him. While he was attending a school in mechanical engineering, he went to Cadolzburg to visit a car company and looked for a job. He got it. In the following two years he attended the technical school and worked in Cadolzburg. He later started to work in car rallies, going to races all over Europe. After a while he decided it was too physically demanding, as he had to work the whole day during rallies: he had to install hot clutches, jumping into mud with oil all over him. Later, during holidays, he worked for a window cleaning company. Once there was an offer from the company Ina. Five scholarships were being granted to young students in engineering. The competition was high, as there were more than one hundred applications. Luca was awarded one of them. In the meantime, he took the entrance exam at Erlangen University. Once again, he was successful.

In the end Luca remained in Erlangen. After completing his studies, he took a job at Siemens, where he currently works. These two cases showed that migrants had different attitudes towards education. This will further influence their professional carreers. To most people I met, education was considered important, and migrants oriented their efforts to obtain some sort of qualifications in the market. In Romania these migrants had usually attended German schools, so that their command of German was good. Luca was a successful migrant. With Rolie it was a different story: he was not able to convert his qualifications to match the criteria in the labor market even though access to education was free. For ethnic Romanians, the situation was different: their education was recognized only to a limited extent and they had to pass further examinations. But the previous example of Sandu, who also became an engineer, showed that Romanians could be equally successful in the longer run.

On the other hand, there was not always a straightforward relationship between education and jobs. Gabriel, another German from

Timişoara, was educated in Germany and tried repeatedly to obtain a job. After several attempts to find employment, he gave up: "When I came here I found a job, but I [preferred to go] to school. I graduated, I worked for three months, and then the company closed down. I started to look for a job again, but I had to go into the army. [Now I am unemployed]." When I met Gabriel he was pretty skeptical about his future. He was the exception in the group, as he was one of the few longer-term unemployed.

Moreover, the labor market changed over the years. If initially migrants had multiple opportunities for employment, after 2003–2004 the situation worsened. Many of them recalled that in the 1990s there was demand for labor, whereas after 2000 it became difficult to obtain good jobs. Their living standards lowered, and for some of them the situation even became precarious. Horst had recorded his earnings from 1990 until 2005, when I interviewed him. He had kept the same job in this period of time. Initially, he and his family were able to live off his salary. But after 2000, the money was no longer enough, and his wife had to take a job too. Moreover, there was a growing feeling of insecurity, as the number of jobs on the market was significantly fewer. Another case was Ricky, who was left unemployed in 2006. For one year he looked for jobs and went to different professional training courses offered by the labor office in Nuremberg. After many applications he finally found a new job in 2007. His situation in 2006–2007 was very different from 1990, when he was unemployed for only a short period. He remembered that in the 1990s he had a choice of many job offers, but he waited for better ones. In 2007 he had to accept anything that was available.

At the time I spoke to them, some of my interviewees did not have jobs and lived on unemployment benefits. The most successful of them worked in management and engineering; some opened up small businesses, and some others were skilled workers. There was also initially a difference between ethnic Germans and their Romanian friends and relatives; but in time, Romanians acquired qualifications and reduced the gap.[7]

These migrants worked in a well-paying labor market and adapted well, securing employment in many sectors of the economy. They received substantial welfare benefits, as in Germany "not only the labor market, but all spheres of life [we]re highly regulated and coordinated with an extensive provision of social services" (Çağlar 2001, 603). In comparison to the majority of Romanian migrants cited in the literature, who worked overwhelmingly in the secondary sectors in different European countries (Anghel 2008; Cingolani 2009; Potot 2003; Şerban 2008; Vlase 2008), ethnic Germans and their family members enjoyed a privileged access to the labor market.

SOCIALITY NETWORKS, CLAIMS FOR IDENTITY, AND PRESTIGE LOSS

The intensive migration from Romania created a multifaceted social reality in Nuremberg. There emerged networks of migrants from Romania, cultural organizations, and small ethnic businesses, such as Romanian shops, restaurants, and discos. Romanian cultural events were periodically organized. There were doctors, lawyers, and insurance agents providing their services to migrants from Romania. Certain places, such as butchers' shops and the Romanian disco *Centro*, provided information for migrants concerning transport and tourist offers for Romania. Moreover, there are an array of ethnic Germans associations, especially for the Transylvanian Saxons and Banat Swabians, and Internet pages and publishing activities concerning the Germans from Romania. The Romanian associations issue their publications in Romanian and German. Ethnic Germans' associations have websites and publications in German along with some sections in the Swabian, Saxon, or Zipser dialects.

Migration was positively perceived by the Romanian Germans when they lived in Romania. And their expectations were indeed not disappointed upon arriving in Germany: institutions were very supportive, and these migrants could hope for a positive reception from the local population. As noted elsewhere, the conditions of reception in the host country "tend[ed] to form more or less coherent patterns organizing the life chances of the newcomers. . . . [They faced] these realities as a *fait accompli* which alter[ed] their aspirations and plans" (Portes and Böröcz 1989, 618). Arriving in new social contexts, migrants created a sense of their locality, appropriated a space, maintained social ties, and constructed new social ties at their destination (Smith 2001). Some elements were particularly discernible here in the creation of migrants' locality: social ties were established or maintained in migration, and networks of migrants formed (Smith 2001).

Ethnic Germans had diversified incorporation pathways and identity claims. Migrants arriving before 1989 usually severed their ties to Romania, and many considered themselves pure Germans. Others kept their group identity alive, attending Saxon and Swabian events. The ethnic Germans' associations are diverse. There are hometown associations for almost every city and village from Transylvania, and nation-wide German associations for Saxons and Swabians. There are also independent groups of Germans from Romania that meet regularly. Finally, many ethnically mixed groups emerged, usually arriving in Germany after 1990. I carried out my research with networks of migrants from Timişoara, a mix of ethnic Germans, Romanians, and Hungarians. Their networks formed in Nuremberg after migration. These networks perpetuated over time and enlarged in size. Although it is difficult to estimate the size of these groups in the overall population of migrants from Romania, interviewees in Nuremberg were under the impression that migrants arriving after 1990 often lived in such ethnically mixed groups. In one of the fieldwork encounters, I happened to meet Karina, who came from a Transylvanian village and grew up in Germany. She and her sisters met regularly with a group of migrants from Romania. The group was created on the initiative of a few migrants who enjoyed spending time together. It later expanded and started to announce events on the Internet. These meetings are now organized three to four times a year and attract mostly first- and second-generation migrants from Romania. Besides parties they sometimes organize trips to Austria or elsewhere. The event I participated in was in a village about twenty kilometers from Nuremberg. It was held in a ballroom at the outskirts of the village. The atmosphere was relaxed. Many people I met spoke German among themselves, but were prepared to speak in Romanian. The group was mixed, made up of Germans and Romanians. Outside the room some of them prepared the Romanian dish *mici*, a type of Balkan meat rolls. When they learned I was Romanian, they welcomed me warmly, asking where I came from. With some I spoke Romanian and with others German. This type of ethnically mixed atmosphere I encountered whenever I attended events with migrants from Romania. In some cases people spoke mostly German, while other events attracted more ethnic Romanians and the language spoken was Romanian.

Given the diversity of these migrant groups, I did not focus only on ethnicity, approaching this research from a migrant network and social capital perspective. Migrant networks, as sets of interpersonal ties "that connect migrants, former migrants, and non-migrants to one another" (Palloni et al. 2001, 1263–64), will be examined by looking at the social capital mobilized in migration. The concept of social capital was coined by Bourdieu and later developed by Putnam and Coleman (Portes 1998). From a functionalist point of view, social capital enables social actors to achieve their goals by relating individuals to social structures like networks, groups, and organizations, and thus facilitating cooperation (Faist 2000a, 103; Lin 1999, 471; 2001). In the work of Putnam, Leonardi, and Nanetti (1994) and Coleman (1988), social capital is given a normative value, as a public good meant to enhance democracy, human capital, and trust in public institutions. Yet Portes is more equivocal, identifying not only its positive but also its negative attributes, the so-called "downside of social capital." For him social capital can promote "public bads" (Karner 2000, 2640) just as easily as "public goods:" it may restrict the entry of migrants to labor markets and may create "downward leveling norms" (Portes and Sensenbrenner 1993; Portes and Landolt 1996). Social capital appears in both strong and weak social ties (Granovetter 1973).

Migrants use different types of social capital during the processes of social and economic incorporation (Portes and Böröcz 1989; Portes and Sensenbrenner 1993): value introjection, reciprocity transactions, bounded solidarity, and enforceable trust. In real-life situations, though, we often see combinations of these used in transactions that take place within social ties. Value introjection is based on values and moral obligations among the members of a given community. "Individuals behave in certain ways because they must—either because they have been socialized in the appropriate values or because they enact emergent sentiments of loyalty" (idem, 1332). Reciprocity transactions are obligations and expectations based on norms of reciprocity (Karner 2000, 2640). Such transactions are not about money, but about social intangibles (Portes and Sensenbrenner 1993, 1324). The kinship obligations of migrants, for instance, could be based on value introjection and on reciprocity exchanges. Reciprocity exchanges appear when kinship ties are used instrumentally, for instance, in situations where migration is based on kinship networks and where kinship networks provide jobs and business opportunities to migrants. But value introjection comes into play when migrants socialize. Solidarity is based on a "willingness to transcend immediate self-interest, grounded in emotional identification with the others" (Faist 2000a, 109). Bounded solidarity is limited to the members of a specific group or class, and it is based on moral imperatives. It may emerge as a reaction towards the majority population and can be based on a common cultural repertoire (Portes and Sensenbrenner 1993). Using this conceptual framework, I will analyze how these forms of social capital were used during migrants' incorporation in Nuremberg.

In what follows I show how two migrant networks came into being and how migrants perceived their own ethnic identity and social prestige. In the first network certain migrants accidentally met in Nuremberg in 1990 and recognized each other on the street. Then they decided to see each other again.

> It was a coincidence. I was walking down the street. Suddenly I saw Marius. We were sitting [in a restaurant] and looked at each other. I was wondering if he was from Timişoara. I was reluctant to ask him anything and I did not go to his table. I left the restaurant. But we met again at the metro station. I asked him: "Bist du Marius?" (Are you Marius?) "Oh, Ja," he replied. We then started to talk Romanian (Emil).

It was not surprising that migrants from Timişoara were likely to meet up in Nuremberg. The city center is not big. Given the size of migration from Timişoara it was actually quite easy to meet acquaintances and friends. I happened to be present on one such occasion. I was with Ricky and Luca. We were in a Turkish restaurant waiting for the meal. A tall guy was standing next to the cashier waiting to pay. Luca thought he was from Timişoara. He suddenly asked: "Excuse me, aren't you from Timişoara?" This happened in 2006, sixteen years after their arrival from Romania. Luca and Ricky had their circles of friends and had no interest in getting to know lots of new people. But they were simply curious to see if that tall man was from Timişoara or not. "Yes, I am," the other replied. He said where he lived in Timişoara, and when he came to Germany. He told Luca where he was living, not very far from the Turkish restaurant. During the talk we finished our meal. It was already evening and it was growing darker outside. We headed towards Ricky's place. On the left side was the area of the city that the person we met had mentioned. Luca and Ricky went there to have a look. "We were just curious to see where he lives," giggled Luca happily.

Other migrants in this group were friends in Timişoara, while some others were relatives. Shortly after arriving in Nuremberg, these migrants started to meet regularly, and the group grew in size. Emil recalled his first years in Nuremberg, when he had no friends: "I had no German friends, [and no friends from Romania]. I was [practically] not integrated here. [But] one time I met Sergiu, a tall guy; afterwards he introduced me to Tiberiu, his brother, and so on. Afterwards I met Alexander, Gabi, Georg, Ricky, all of them."

Relatives and acquaintances were added to the network at a later stage. It expanded and finally reached twenty-eight persons. Migrants had diverging personal and professional interests and were involved in different jobs, but were happy to maintain close ties to each other. These migrants had opportunities to socialize and meet many Germans, *Aussiedler* or *Ausländer* (foreigners), but they still forged stronger social relations among themselves. Luca invited me once to his place. "There is a gathering of the group," he said, "some other friends from Würzburg and Frankfurt are coming too." I reached Luca's house in the evening. Some cars were parked outside his two-story house. Luca's brother had painted "Timişoara" on his jeep; others had TM, the Romanian abbreviation for Timişoara, on their German registration plates. About twenty people had met on the top floor of Luca's house. There was a lively, happy atmosphere, people recalling good times and swapping jokes. The whole group had arrived, including the ones from Frankfurt and Würzburg. Two of Luca's colleagues, a German and a Serbian, were also there. With Luca's friends everybody spoke German, but mostly they spoke Romanian. "I've known these Romanians for many years," said one of Luca's colleagues. He thought Luca was well regarded, knowing everybody at the job. He could not explain why the Timişoreni did not invite other Germans to their parties, and why so many years after their arrival they continued meeting only among themselves. The answers to these questions came later while I was analyzing how migrants spent their time together and related to one another.

However, membership into the migrant network was not exclusive, since *de facto* they had social ties with other migrants, as well as with Germans, even if to a lesser extent. The network provided migrants with sociality based on value introjection and the solidarity they needed: "I don't have real friends here; this is the truth. I maintain a sort of distance from [other people from Nuremberg]. I've kept among those who came from Romania. I stay in the same neighborhood in which I've lived since I came here. I go to work and spend time with my wife. The rest of the time I spend with my friends from Timişoara" (Luca).

In the diagram below, I present a schematic representation of the network, which will serve as a basis for further discussion. Women are represented as circles, men as triangles. Grey represents Romanian ethnicity; stripes stand for Hungarian, and black for Turkish. The unfilled ones are *Aussiedler*. Two women are German. All men but two are ethnic Germans; half of the women are Romanian, four are Hungarian. All the men came from Timişoara, while the women arrived from different regions of Romania, though predominantly from Timişoara. The two surrounding circles signify that migrants lived in the same neighborhoods: four couples lived in *Nürnberg Südstadt*, and two couples lived in *Fürth Klinikum*.

Numbers 11 and 13 were already couples prior to their migration to Germany. In all other cases, marriage occurred after the migration of the men. The men in couples 3 and 4 were brothers, as were those in couples 5 and 6. The women in couples 4 and 5, and also in 6 and 7, were sisters. Number 3 represents the marriage between an ethnic German and a Turkish woman who had been living in Germany before they met. In all cases excepting couples 11, 13 and 3, the women arrived in Germany through marriage. The women in couples 5 and 6 were already married when their sisters, the women from couples 4 and 7, came to visit them in Germany. On that occasion they met their future husbands. In the rest of the cases, the men traveled to Romania as German citizens and there met their future wives. Couple 14 returned to Romania in 2007. Couple 9 was

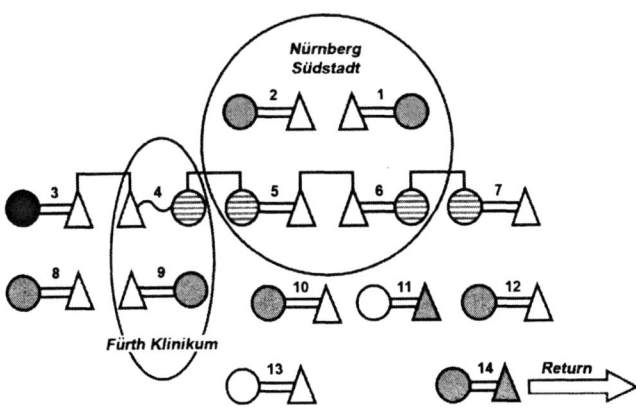

Figure 2.1. Network of migrants from Romania. Source: Author's personal archive

in the process of separating, the woman moving to Munich, while couple 4 was not yet married.

Some of these migrant men got to know each other prior to their migration, and after arriving in Germany they tried to re-form previous friendships and acquaintanceships. At the same time they also developed relations with other migrants from Romania coming from different cities, such as Sibiu (*Hermannstadt*), Braşov (*Kronstadt*), and Bucharest. Furthermore, as the Romanian women arrived, some of these migrants became connected through kinship (couples 3, 4, 5, 6, and 7), so that kinship reciprocity also appeared. Some of them indeed had multiple simultaneous social relations with members of the group, and with other foreigners and other German migrants. Alexander was a young lawyer who joined the group after marrying Aniko, one of the Hungarian women in the group. He came to Germany in the 1980s when he was a teenager. From the time he arrived he had lots of German friends. He was pretty successful in his business and had no complaints of discrimination. He received a graduate education in Germany and had a relatively good job. Unlike other members of the network he had no preference about socializing with people from Romania. But he started to come regularly to the group's gatherings after marrying Aniko, who was the sister of one of the oldest group members. "I moved to many German cities and I had friends everywhere," He said. "First, in the *Lager* I had friends from Romania, Poland, and Russia. Afterwards, when I came here to Nuremberg I started to make friends here." In contrast, though, the other members of the network had the tendency to socialize mostly among themselves.

The second network was formed by migrants who got to know each other in Nuremberg while attending the school for German migrants. They became friends over the course of many years. In the beginning, the group consisted of a small number of persons, migrants who met regularly at school. Differently from the first case, when the migrants had a very good knowledge of German, in this case the first step for some of these migrants was to learn German. They considered their friendship with other migrants from Timişoara very important for their incorporation.

Ionuţ came from an ethnically mixed family and spoke German poorly. He graduated from high school in Romania. Upon arriving in Germany, he had to attend a school for ethnic Germans and learn the language. He never went on to graduate education; however, he ended up in the liberal professions after a few years in Germany. As he always stressed, his friends from Timişoara were a great help to him: "I was lucky to find these Romanians here. In the beginning I didn't know a word of German. It was very lucky that we could integrate into a circle of friends who were here already and had relations with other Romanians. It was indeed a sort of first friendship, arriving here and knowing nobody. It could have been more difficult without them."

The migrants started to meet weekly at the school for German migrants, which was attended by migrants from Romania and the former USSR. There they organized sports activities, parties, and excursions together. Over the years, these "Romanians" were able to maintain their relations among themselves, whereas the relations with their Russian German colleagues faded out. Like the first network, this one too was based on value introjection and bounded solidarity. The members of the network had different professions, and some were just graduating from university. In time these migrants expanded their relations and a number of other Romanians joined: "We met there [at the *Aussiedler* school], and through these relations we got in contact with others and so on" (Lucian). They also established contact with migrants from other countries, and with local Germans. As was the case with the first group, they maintained multiple relations outside the group too. At the time my fieldwork was carried out, only two migrants from this group were married, as they were younger than migrants from the first group.

Both networks were established by men from Timişoara. Surprisingly, only two German women were part of the first network. The migrants did not concentrate in certain neighborhoods. They lived in different parts of the city or in the surrounding areas. Social ties were rarely used for instrumental purposes, usually only when the migrants turned to each other for various household tasks, such as painting or renovating: "Dan from Braşov, for instance, knows how to put in parquet; I can help with something else. So, it is also a friendship based on need" (Ioan). Their incorporation was therefore mainly through socialization networks and those institutions supporting the migrants' labor market incorporation.

I have pointed out before that the use of social capital did not bring migrants a better status attainment, and they displayed a rather high degree of individualization. Migrants' status attainment was realized in Nuremberg mainly through education and specialization. At the same time, even if they were successful in the labor market, as was the case with Luca and Alexander, they perceived a prestige loss. In the following, I will analyze this paradoxical process and reveal its mechanisms.

In Germany, the issue of migrants' social incorporation was linked "to the question of acquisition of cultural and social competencies, solidarities and loyalties" (Çağlar 2001, 603). In a similar vein, Glick-Schiller et al. (2005, 1) considered that the "dominant discourses about migration stress[ed] that it [was] only through a form of cultural change that foreigners [could] become a part of Germany." The case study I discuss here is intriguing precisely because of the cultural similarity which authors like Çağlar and Glick-Schiller invoke, and which legitimized the ethnic Germans' migration. And yet they constructed an idiom of their separateness from Germans based on two arguments. First, they referred to an alleged anti-*Aussiedler* attitude among the German population. Second, they emphasized the commonalities they shared because of the experience of migration and the difficulties of their prior life in Romania. They felt the insights they gained from similar personal histories set them aside from the rest of the German population.

Regarding the first argument, migrants underlined the Germans' reservations towards them and complained about a perceived feeling of exclusion. Tiberiu was a teenager when he arrived in Germany. He attended a technical school to study architecture and was between jobs when I first met him. The jobs he had obtained in Germany were nothing special, but he was able to secure a good standard of living for him and his family. Throughout his youth and adult life, however, he thought of finding something better and never stopped sending off applications for better jobs.

> [In the beginning] everything was rosy and nice. In time I realized that I could not make that many friends here. I went to a school where I had German classmates. They were alright, we had no problems, but it was difficult to relate to Germans and become friends. I think we understand each other much better: Saxons with Saxons, Swabians with Swabians, and those of us who are a bit more mixed [among ourselves] (Tiberiu).

Tiberiu put a great value on his friendships with migrants from Timișoara and was not very enthusiastic about non-"Romanians." Migrants like him did not attempt to enlarge their networks of acquaintances. They thought it unnecessary to develop stronger ties with Germans even though they attended schools in Germany and worked with German colleagues. They justified their reluctance by Germans' perceived negative attitudes. Ioan was a technical worker in Germany, but had received university training in Romania prior to his migration. He was well regarded by his colleagues, but his social interactions with his German colleagues were limited to the time they spent at the job. "When [Germans] speak about foreigners, they say: 'That guy is a very good guy for a Romanian.' They never speak about a foreigner the way they speak about themselves" (Ioan). In some other cases, they resentfully accept a situation of non-integration. "How to explain it? You are not one of them, they simply say: 'You are not a German.' They say you are an *Ausländer* (foreigner). But I tried very hard to show that I deserve the place I have in [this] society" (Berni).

The lack of recognition of these Germans' ethnicity came as a total contradiction of their own clear sense of their Germanness, which was highly prized in Romania. But once in Nuremberg, they were considered Romanians by the majority population. Their ethnicity was denied. Migrants often complained that Germans don't make the distinction between foreigners and East European Germans. Christian was not happy with this situation. He received graduate training in Germany. He came from an old intellectual family from Timișoara, with a clear sense of their position in the Romanian society. Migration to Germany posed new challenges to him, making him reflect on his ethnic belonging.

> I observed that Germans [do not make] this difference, [that I am a Romanian German and not a Romanian]. Then, I stopped denying that I am Romanian. Anyway, I was born [in Romania], I married a Romanian woman, I lived twenty years there, and my ancestors lived there for many generations. So, Romania left a trace on me, a sort of blueprint in my behavior, mentality, and so on. And I don't want to give it up (Christian).

When they discussed their status in German society, the jobs they had obtained and how they were regarded as foreigners, migrants often compared their current situation with that of their families in Romania, the regard they enjoyed "back there" and the quality of their friendships. Besides, most of them were considered to be Germans in Romania, but they were considered "Romanians" in Germany. Comparatively, similar identity shifts have been identified in other cases of ethnic migration: Hungarians from Transylvania in Hungary, other groups of East European Germans in Germany, as well as Russian Jews in Israel (Münz and Ohlinger 2003). The issue of Transylvanian Hungarians was salient in Hungary's political debates inasmuch as Transylvania, a region heatedly contested by Hungarians and Romanians alike in past centuries, was very present in political debates in Hungary. Transylvanian Hungarians were integrated politically into a greater cultural Hungarian nation. But when they started to migrate to Hungary for work as labor migrants, they were pejoratively called "Romanians" (Fox 2007). These migrants started to reconsider their identity, claiming a purer Hungarianness for themselves in opposition to Hungarians in Hungary, whom they considered somehow mixed with Jews and Swabians. In Nuremberg, Timișoara Germans did not compete for jobs with the autochthonous population, as was the case with the Transylvanian Hungarians in Hungary. But similar to Hungarians, they were considered Romanians abroad. In Germany, ethnic Germans from Timișoara felt they lost the high prestige they once held in Romania. When they arrived in Germany, they became migrants. They had to climb up the social ladder.

> Ethnic Germans came here with the idea that this was their home, and were not accepted "by their own." So they said: "I won't accept them either." They are not accepted. And they played everything on a single card, because they left Romania, where Germans were always respected. In a way they have a big problem [in accepting their current position], and now they are nowhere at home, [neither here, nor there] (Christian).

Most migrants expressed dissatisfaction with this state of affairs. Yet there was no apparent relationship between these complaints and the success migrants had enjoyed in Germany. It was rather a feeling they shared in common, irrespective of the jobs they held. It was like this for Luca and his brother, who were both engineers, and also for Rolie and Tiberiu, who were still struggling to find jobs.

The second argument shaping their separateness is the common migration experience and the perceived common identity based on country of origin. The similarity of difficulties was seen as a factor that both united and separated. On the one hand it was regarded as grounds for bounded solidarity (Faist 2000a; Portes and Sensenbrenner 1993) that generated social support among migrants. On the other hand, it was evoked as the experience that constructed a different set of attitudes and behaviors than those of the local Germans. Cultural differences were embedded within different patterns of communication, in the view of Christian, another member of the group. As he saw it, it was culture, and not language barriers, that was important in forging sociality among migrants. The fact that migrants lived in a culturally different environment like the one in Nuremberg influenced their choices in making friendships. He also thought that there was an easiness of communication between people who had grown up in the same social context.

> After finishing high school I thought it was high time to get to know some Germans, and if I happened to run into anybody from Romania I would simply avoid contact with him. I thought that was the only chance I had to integrate here. In the same class with me there was a Transylvanian Saxon. I did my best to refrain from talking to him for about six months. But once we sat down near each other. Afterwards, during my studies, [I remained friends with him and his group], another twenty persons from Romania. During my studies we studied together, went on excursions and parties together. Afterwards, as an undergrad student, I would always go out with Transylvanian Saxons and with people from Bucharest. We had a very good time together. And again I could not integrate here. When you have a party, you tell jokes, and Romanian jokes are much funnier than German jokes. [Afterwards I got to] know Luca, and in this way I entered into a different group, with Toni, Georg, and in time they brought some others, and so on. Each of us knew someone and introduced them to the group. I think what united us so much was the fact that we are all from Timişoara. As a matter of fact, this is a sort of magic, the fact that we are so close to one another just because we came from Timişoara, or from Romania (Christian).

In a similar vein, Berni, a Transylvanian Saxon, complained about the Germans' reluctance to accept migrants and stressed the positive effect of migrants' sociality: "I remained together with groups of Romanians, Transylvanian Saxons, and Banat Swabians. It's been like that ever since I came here. We meet and take care of each other."

Romanian Germans did encounter in Germany a different society than the one they were accustomed to. And many depicted it as "cold" and "estranging," lacking a certain type of communication they knew from Romania. At the same time, in many cases, such declarations disguised migrants' own lack of interest and ability to communicate with the majority population. This would become apparent when listening to other migrants, who held a more nuanced opinion about Germans. Lucian, for instance, thought that many Germans were in fact interested in foreigners, keen to learn about their culture and their experiences of migration, and that they were pretty tolerant. In his view, migrants often have false ideas about Germans: he considered Germans are very often tolerant and cultivated people. For him, it was the migrants' failure and the fault of their reluctance to communicate to Germans, not the other way around.

So far, I have discussed the emergence of migrant networks and the migrants' preference to not socialize with the local Germans. I have shown that this was not a complete group closure, since they maintained multiple relations outside the group. Second, the construction of migrants' locality was accompanied by a complex process of identity repositioning as migrants' self-perception altered. The migrants also developed a sense of identity difference from the majority population and reconsidered their Romanian origin. As I will further show, gender relations and the preference of migrant men to marry Romanian women were other elements which influenced the changing of migrants' attitudes. Marriages with Romanians ultimately completed the process of migrants' ethnicization as "Romanians" in Germany.

MARRIAGE TO ROMANIAN WOMEN AND "ROMANIANIZATION"

> Let's say the following: [you take a Romanian woman] because you have more in common with her; it is not just about aesthetics. [. . .] The ideal choice is to take someone with similar [interests]. You went to the same places [so you have something in common]. Also, it is preferable for her to be from Timişoara. At least, to be from Banat, or from Romania (Ricky).

In the previous sections I argued that a perception of losing prestige was not directly related to the jobs migrants had. It was rather related to the fact that migrants felt they were not considered Germans but Romanians, and that they were separated from the local Germans. A more puzzling issue was the absence of German women from the first network of migrants from Timişoara[8] and that the latter married Romanian women. The causes could be quite diverse: the men's lower socioeconomic position in comparison to the local Germans made migrants unattractive as partners; or the men's inability to adapt to gender relations in Germany.

It is also possible that *Aussiedler* women had different life trajectories, preferring to remain single or marry German or migrant men outside the circles of Romanian Germans.[9] In this section I further seek to unfold the men's discourses and perceptions towards their lives in Germany and how their social repositioning made them reconsider their ties to Romania and their identity claims.

After 1989 these male migrants started to go back to Romania and marry Romanian women. Such marriages prevailed in the groups of migrants I analyzed, most of the women arriving a few years after the men's migration. Networks of migrants already existed in Nuremberg, like the first network I analyzed above. In Germany migrants attended schools and went to work. Nevertheless, they often traveled to Romania as "tourists," like Ricky who went to Freidorf from time to time. They partied there, met people, and made friends with women. In time, they started to marry and their wives were assimilated into their networks. Emil used to go to Timișoara regularly and spend time with friends and acquaintances. He said he had no interest in meeting German women. On one occasion in Timișoara he published an advertisement that he was looking to meet and marry a woman from there. He met Réka, who found him funny and attractive. He was enchanted by her. After meeting many times and spending time together, Réka eventually came to Nurnberg. Christian, on the other hand, had a different experience. He had known Anca ever since he migrated to Germany, but they were only friends in those days. It was only several years later that Christian got to date Anca, as both were involved in other relationships. But eventually they got together. There were cases, too, when couples formed in Nuremberg when the women came around to visit, as happened with Réka's sister, Aniko, who met Alexander once when she came to visit Réka. In Nuremberg, men met their future wives through common friends or relatives, in Romanian discos, or through attending Romanian cultural events.

As I argued in the analysis of the first network, the migration of non-Germans to Nuremberg happened mostly through marriage, and the largest part of this migration consisted of women. For the migrant men, marriages to Romanian women reconnected them to Romania, where they acquired new relatives and friends.

One can build different typologies by following men's personal histories: migrants had relations with German women but preferred to marry women from Romania, or they had no German girlfriends at all. What I am interested in, though, is how the migrant men I interviewed articulated a coherent understanding of their selves as "Romanians" in Germany, and how marriages with women from Romania helped in sustaining their views. Luca, for instance, never had a German partner, and his girlfriends were mostly from Romania.

> After my arrival here, I met one girl in 1990. She was a Transylvanian Saxon, and I was with her until February 1992. Then I had no girlfriend for about two years. [Afterwards I had a] Czech girl. Afterwards there was someone from Timişoara, who came here to be with one of my friends. I was with her for a while and then I met a Saxon girl from Transylvania. I later met another girl from Timişoara [and we stayed together a very short period of time]. Finally, I met Anna, my wife. I never had a German girlfriend (Luca).

Luca remained within the networks of people from Romania, mostly from Timişoara. All his girlfriends came from Romania with only one exception, the Czech. His wife was from Romania, but they divorced in 2008. In the meantime, he started a new relationship with someone from Timişoara. In other cases, migrants had both German and Romanian girlfriends, but preferred to marry those from Romania. They shared an idealized image of Romanian women, justifying their choices as the right ones and putting forward a series of arguments in favor of Romanian women. They first invoked aesthetics and the femininity women from Romania displayed in contrast to German women.

> I can say that 90 percent of people coming from Romania marry women from Romania. It is an emotional issue here, and it is hard to define it, but femininity is different in the countries of the South, or the Balkans. It is simply a different femininity. I always said that you go to Romania and see so many beautiful girls. German women are tough. There are beautiful women here too, but they don't have the same warmth. And if you lived many years in a country with Romanian women, and if you have seen them, you would like that [type of woman] (Christian).

Migrant men also referred to the importance of communication and cultural intimacy between partners. They considered their previous life in Romania decisive, as they had different attitudes and interests from local Germans. Marriage implied for many, such as Emil, Ricky, and Tiberiu, the sharing of similar views, so they preferred rather to marry someone from the same country of origin with likely similar interests.

> I can observe the difference between the [German] girlfriends I had here and those ones born in Romania. The ones from Romania could understand me much better. She knew where I came from. She understands a part of my history, even though we did not meet in Romania. And we had a similar mentality, we have things in common. A German woman is not interested in knowing [anything] about Romania. She would not understand what it is all about, mentality, and one's own history (Alexander).

A third argument, related to the second one, was about differences in family organization and lifestyle. Migrants set importance on the fact that non-migrants were, in their eyes, born in a wealthy state, whereas they themselves grew up amidst scarcity. They claimed a different understanding of money is always at issue, of what was financially affordable, and what was not, and of how a family should be managed. As Udo considers, "[people here] are brought up in wealth. [A German woman] doesn't do housework, because one can buy everything. And they don't clean too much. They are good for holidays, to go out in the city, but they are not good as housewives." His opinion was similar to that of Emil: "I had [German] women. They say: 'Why should I go to Croatia or Bulgaria? Let's go to the Caribbean Islands.' They don't pay attention to money. They say: 'Money is to be spent, that's all.' And this is why I didn't want a woman like that."

Finally, most of my interviewees praised Romanian women as good housewives. They held them in higher regard in comparison to German women and considered them to have a different understanding of motherhood. In their view, German women did not take care of the household properly: they did not cook, did not iron the clothes, and did not clean the house properly. They claimed they did not have the same attitudes towards men and children: "The understanding of being a mother is different [here]. There is a different spirit of sacrifice, and Romanian women [dedicate themselves more] to their men and children" (Christian). In all these cases, migrants stated that they were "accustomed to [a family] model from Romania, with women used to cooking, cleaning, and being good housewives" (Daniel), while in Germany gender relations were more equal between partners. In coming to Germany, some men felt they had left behind a different notion of family, and this put a lot of pressure to adapt to Germany: "At the beginning we said that it was not possible to live in the circumstances [that we found here]" (Daniel). In this sense, the networks of migrants from Timişoara shared some similarities with other migrants, in that "preferring partners of the same ethnic background may result from everyday pragmatics of adaptation rather than from a conscious strategy of ethnic closure" (Wimmer 2004, 18).

When socialism collapsed in Eastern Europe, West European citizens could enter and exit Romania easily, and marriage and family reunions could be arranged without difficulty. During their process of social incorporation in Germany, migrant men commonly chose to marry women from Romania. On this point, I have analyzed some of the alleged reasons for this migration of women by looking at men's attitudes and perceptions towards marriage, family, and gender relations. According to the men's own claims, it was their migrant status that accounted for their fewer marriage opportunities to Germans, or different gender relations that the men were not keen to comply with.

After 1989, Germans migrated *en masse* without any intentions to return. In most cases they left no relatives behind, and many of their friends were also migrating to Germany. But with the migration of the Romanian women, a re-linking to Romania was established. This was a process tied up to migrants' changing self-perceptions in Germany and to the production and change of migrants' locality in Nuremberg (through networks and organizations), and was followed by a process of Romanianization.

This process of redefining belonging and Romanianization was realized within a milieu of "de facto multiculturalism" in German society (Joppke 2010). Individuals socializing in such groups continued to speak Romanian and listened to Romanian music, and new Romanian acquaintances were attracted into their networks. "They've started to speak more and more Romanian because of the women. They had no other choice. Until their arrival, they wouldn't listen to Romanian music, it was only afterwards they started to listen to it" (Udo).

I describe as Romanianization the gradual and subtle process of cultural and social change in which some of the Germans from Romania started to reevaluate their ethnicity and their relationships to Romania and took steps towards improving their command of Romanian. Ricky's case offers some more concrete insights into the process.

> I had a limited vocabulary [in Romania], [I talked a poor Romanian language]. My colleagues, friends, family, everyone, including even the neighbors, were 80–90 percent *Deutschstemmig* (of German origin). I had no other friends to talk Romanian with. Even with my girlfriend I used to speak German. The [most important] contact with the Romanian language I had was when I started to attend the Romanian high school. Here [in Germany] I Romanianized myself. I had to learn the language again (Ricky).

Some migrants had left Romania when they were too young to have a good command of Romanian and solid social ties to Romanians. In Germany, when they married Romanian women they started to speak the language again.[10] Initially many migrants were not interested in maintaining strong relations to Romania, and constructed their entire life projects in the context of Germany—friends and relatives included. After marriage, this orientation towards Germany changed, and they started to issue invitation letters to their Romanian relatives and friends. As a consequence, the number of Romanians visiting Nuremberg increased over time. In Nuremberg, the presence of Romanians in the city became more visible than before: "Until 1990, 1991, 1992, there were not many Romanians here, only the half Romanian–half Germans would come. Afterwards more Romanians started to arrive" (Alexander).

Romanian music was listened to in mixed families, and satellite TV broadcasted news and movies from Romania. This process is indeed surprising, since in Romania many Germans had a clear sense of their Germanness. Such a situation is not unique, though. In a study of Bosnian refugees, for instance, Jansen (2008) analyzed migrants' downward mobility and showed how hierarchies bounded to certain places (or states) were not transferable abroad, even though "migrant men often [relied] on cross-border networks in order to create and maintain hierarchies of status and recognition" (Jansen 2008, 194). In my research, migrants from Timișoara felt a prestige loss due to the misrecognition of their ethnicity and the loss of the high symbolic status they once had in Romania. Besides, these migrants were not able to gain social recognition "back home," as there was no community in the eyes of which such prestige could be gained. Meetings with friends were important for them, but these migrants' stakes were in Germany and not in Romania, where they had no intention to return.

To sum up, migrants' arrival in Nuremberg was realized in the context of a very supportive German migration and integration policy towards the East European Germans. Migrants considered they were entitled to come and live "as Germans among Germans" and had high expectations of incorporation. They fitted very easily into the mainstream economy. They had diversified educational backgrounds and professions, and ended up well integrated into the German labor market. But migrants claimed their ethnicity was not recognized socially. The migration of Romanian women set in motion a paradoxical process. Although in Romania the men were Germans, some of these migrants "Romanianized," not

Figure 2.2. Romanian open air events are organized every year. Source: Author's personal archive

in Romania but in Germany, and eventually reconnected to Romania through a Romanianness constructed in Germany. Today, these migrants live in ethnically mixed groups with Romanians or persons coming from ethnically mixed families.

NOTES

1. Source: interview with BAMF, the German Office for Refugees and Migration.

2. There are no clear data in support of these estimates, and the information is gathered from different sources. However, because migrants from Romania concentrated mostly in southern Germany (Bavaria and Baden-Württemberg), we may consider that these data approximate the real situation.

3. This was located in Zirndorf, a small village in the vicinity of Nuremberg.

4. This figure is, however, relative, since these ratios are based on self-representation. But the same research shows lower rates among Polish and Russian *Aussiedler*.

5. In the course of the 1990s Romania lost about 3,533,000 jobs, about 40 percent of those that had existed in 1990, the majority of them in industry (Horváth and Anghel 2009).

6. The per capita expenditures of the German government for the whole support package, including pensions and welfare benefits, were 4,308 DM (Bauer and Zimmermann 1997).

7. I have included the cases of the Romanian migrants here in order to underline that ethnicity was not a decisive criterion to enter the labor market and be succesful, but rather legal status, command of German, and qualifications.

8. I was not able to investigate fully the incorporation of *Aussiedler* women due to the limited period of my fieldwork. So I have no details on their sociality in Nuremberg and why they are not part of men's networks.

9. In my fieldwork it was not my intention to look more deeply into gender relations. I therefore keep a distance from offering explanations on the issue of marriage migration and the factors conducive to the current marriage preferences. My aim is rather to analyze what men have to say concerning women from Romania.

10. I met several cases of migrants who had had no previous knowledge of Romanian but who learned the language in Nuremberg.

THREE

A Weak Transnationality

Memory, Leisure, and Plans to Return

Ricky recalled his trip to Freidorf a while after he returned to Nuremberg. He was asked by the others how the trip was, and if there was anything new there worth reporting. Like Ricky, all members of the network used to go from time to time to have short vacations there. In the meetings I attended, people often brought up stories from Timişoara and swapped news about common acquaintances and friends. Despite the fact that they lived in Germany, Timişoara still played an important part in these people's lives.

The proponents of migrants' transnationalism argue that nowadays migrants forge social, economic, and political relations transcending the borders of nation states, and that migrants maintain simultaneous multiple relations in home and host societies (Basch, Glick-Schiller, and Szanton Blanc 1994; Glick-Schiller, Basch, and Szanton Blanc 1995). In the last fifteen years, this research agenda produced substantial evidence showing that even when migrants' transnational practices are not recurrent, they nevertheless link migrants and non-migrants in origin and reception societies in an enduring manner. Migrants are very often carriers of long-distance nationalism (Levitt and Glick-Schiller 2006), being part of what is called transnational social fields, or transnational social spaces (idem; Faist 2000a; b).

The ethnic Germans' migration diverges from this understanding in several ways. First, upon migration ethnic Germans left no relatives and only a handful of friends behind. Different from cases of labor migration documented elsewhere (Massey, Goldring, and Durand 1994; Portes 2003), they had no community left behind to remit to. Instead, they re-made their communities in Germany by making new contacts there or

81

maintaining prior friendship and kinship relations. Second, ethnic Germans from Timişoara migrated with a clear idea that they were going back to their Fatherland, and that they belonged there. They had no or a very weak idea of developing a long-distance nationalism towards Romania. This expectation was built upon the prior experiences of migration to Germany of their relatives and friends who had settled permanently in Germany. When ethnic Germans migrated after 1990, one of the main issues was whether to remain in Romania, where only a residual German ethnic community remained, or to go to Germany.[1] Life in Romania no longer offered people a sense of belonging to the ethnic community as it had before when German communities were larger. Even when the education system provided education in German, there were too few co-ethnics to maintain community life and ethnic customs. For many, migration was the sole solution left. Furthermore, in the case of the ethnic Germans, there was no sign of their sending back remittances after their migration to Germany, and until now no studies on the Romanian migration mention it. However, a weak form of transnationalism did develop. This came about because of difficult social incorporation accompanied by perceived cultural differences and gender imbalances between them and the local German population, their failed expectations, and their re-linking to Romania through marriages with Romanians.

To recall the facts, migration from Timişoara to Nuremberg occurred at the beginning of the 1990s and it led to the emergence of an increasing number of migrant networks within Nuremberg. Ethnic Germans achieved an advantageous economic status and had diversified professional careers. In the previous chapter I explored the ethnic Germans' social incorporation, noting as well their tendency to marry Romanian women and claim a Romanian identity. On the other hand, many other ethnic Germans from Romania opted for assimilation, setting aside or even denying their Romanian origins. As interviewees admitted, many of them were too young at the time of migration to identify in any way with a Romanian background. Such tendencies towards assimilation were especially frequent among migrants who arrived in Germany before 1989. As I further stressed, migrants from Romania opted for diverse identity claims and group membership. In addition to the two main tendencies, assimilation and ethnicization, there were migrants who established groups based on a common place of origin, as well as associations organized to represent ethnic German sub-groups of Transylvanian Saxons, Banat Swabians, and Zipsers. Migration to Germany put entire communities on the move, and in most cases migrants left behind only a few acquaintances and relatives. There was hardly any practical reason for traveling back and investing in Romania given the lack of communities and social ties there, the post-socialist political uncertainty, and the adverse economic reality.

Some other migrants, though, such as the migrants from Timişoara I interviewed, migrated after 1989 and made a living in-between Timişoara and Nuremberg, where Timişoara was a place of leisure and recalling memories. As early as the 1990s the literature on transnationalism has emphasized migrants' in-betweenness, their living between the social contexts of reception and origin (Basch, Glick-Schiller, and Szanton Blanc 1994). This refers to migrants' multiple belonging, that they are simultaneously involved in social relations in the countries of origin and destination. In the present case, migrant transnationalism was made possible because of the changing political context in Europe after 1989. Before 1989, migrants had difficulties in sustaining transnational relations because the communist authorities in Romania made problems for them to travel back there. Migrants coming back were followed around by state agents, and their relatives in Romania could be victimized if they hosted their visits. After 1990, migrants' transnational practices suffered no such hinderance. In that context, over the years the ethnic Germans I analyzed developed a weak form of transnationalism between Nuremberg and Timişoara. They did not send remittances nor did they become involved in political activities in Romania. For the most part, their connectedness to their country of origin remained limited to visiting friends and relatives and to tourism and leisure activities in Romania.

Furthermore, it became apparent that within the last ten years, their transnational practices intensified, strengthened by the migration of women and by the economic changes in Germany and Romania. Germany started to experience labor precariousness for certain categories of people, whereas for the first time in many years Romania had a degree of economic growth generated by the country's accession to the EU. This development changed again with the current economic crisis. Whereas Germany experienced growth, Romania went into crisis. Migrants' perceptions changed again. They still expect to see growth in Romania, but later. In the following I will describe migrants' transnational practices in order to show how migrant transnationalism evolved over the years.

REMEMBERING PLACES: TRANSNATIONALISM AS MEMORY

Migrants who were the subjects of this study visited Romania to recall memories and to find friends left behind in Timişoara. Such visits were very much influenced by personal feelings, and related to positive or negative experiences in Romania. Many migrants who moved to Germany before 1990 were not very enthusiastic about visiting Romania again, and they traveled back only up to the time when the rest of their families managed to move to Germany. Memories and unpleasant incidents during communism made them quite uninterested in going back to see their places of origin or to visit their acquaintances. Even though the agreement from 1977 between the Romanian and the German governments created a framework for legal migration for ethnic Germans, in practice applicants encountered numerous difficulties in trying to migrate. It is perhaps unsurprising that they were reluctant to return after the change of the political regime in 1989:

> In my family there is this situation that those who came to Germany before 1990 wouldn't go [back to Romania] any longer. They migrated in a period when it was very difficult for everyone, and they had serious problems. They got burned, so to say. The [Romanian] state took their properties, did bad things to them. Therefore they said: "Once we escape this shit, we'll never go back." There are many people like them. They had to queue at the *Miliție* to get their passports, put up with months or even years of waiting. The *Securitate* interrogated them and they had to hang in there and not to withdraw their applications (Luca).

In such cases migration to Germany became permanent migration; migrants' families no longer lived in Romania, and there was no transnationalism. "People say that they don't want to hear anything about Romania. They say: 'I'm proud to be Swabian, Saxon, or Hungarian. But there is nothing left for me in the country I came from'" (Otto).

Those who migrated after 1989 had a different attitude towards Romania. Their migration was free, and not restricted in any way by the Romanian state's discretionary policy. In contrast to those who migrated during communism, migrants from the 1990s commonly maintained some transnational practices and forms of in-betweenness. Migrant transnationalism was first expressed as memory, the migrants' practice to pay visits to Romania in order to remember previous events and see their acquaintances, those very few that were left behind. For such migrants also, there was very little left to return to.

> I had many classmates in Romania, but they all came here. Between my departure and my first visit back, some came here [to Germany]. When I was there for the second time, already half of them were here. [Then] there was nobody left behind. Only the church and the places I know still stood. In the end there was just one friend of mine who remained. When I met him I had a strange feeling, since neither of us knew what to say to the other (Alexander).

In other cases, the trips to Romania in the early 1990s turned out to be a complete disillusionment for those returning to visit their friends. Ricky kept in contact with his friends, wrote them letters after his migration, and sent them photos. But the encounter with the grim life in the 1990s during his visit back to Romania killed any desire to visit Timişoara again.

> I left [Romania] in 1990, and I went back in December 1991 for one week. When I saw how they looked . . . after 24 hours I wanted to come

back. For me, the language was the only familiar thing because otherwise they were completely different people [from those] I left in 1990. They looked differently, thought differently. In Romania, or to the people over there, they seemed all right, since things changed in a certain direction after 1990. But I hadn't taken part in that change; I had a different life [in Germany] and I was disappointed in everybody . . . I wanted to get out of there and to come "home." [At that time] I could identify myself better with Germany than with Romania (Ricky).

Because of such personal reasons and keenly felt differences in lifestyles between Romania and Germany, many migrants no longer showed any wish to visit Romania. These persons underwent a process of self-redefinition, and Germany became their home. Sometimes migrants can forget about their societies of origin (Carsten 1995), and this is what happened to some extent to part of the group of Romanian Germans who had moved to Germany. This process of "forgetting Romania" gained in momentum in the 1990s. In such instances migrants considered that "my house is where I feel best, and where I live. I don't have such feelings towards Romania now" (Ionuţ). Furthermore, migrants' relatives and acquaintances migrated *en masse* to Germany and migrants were able to refashion their social ties there. They felt there were not sufficient reasons to establish new social relations in Romania, which would have required the extra effort of transnational mobility.

However, other migrants, generally young men, continued to visit Romania, either for sentimental or for more practical reasons, such as taking care of real estate property, meeting friends, partying, or looking for partners.

I'm sure that it is about affection and it is also about practical reasons. [Some have properties] in Timişoara; they go to see what tenants are doing or to collect the rent. Third, it is about memory, people visiting family graves. These are the reasons for going back. All families I know go there regularly. But others don't go there any longer. They say they don't want to have anything to do with Romania any more. They feel at home here (Otto).

The German migrants displayed various attitudes in relation to the country of origin. Some thought of Germany as their "home"; others maintained steady communications with Romania. The migrants I interviewed were of the second kind. They redefined their identity and maintained transnational relations to their context of origin. With the arrival of Romanian women, the tendency to develop transnational practices intensified. In the following section I describe the types of transnational practices these migrants developed between Nuremberg and Romania, paying particular attention to their changing perceptions about economic life in Germany and in Romania.

"ROMANIA TOURISTS": TRANSNATIONALISM AS LEISURE

Some of the ethnic Germans now living in Germany, mostly young men, visited Romania regularly. They went back to have fun and spend their holidays there. In the 1990s, when Romania was in deep economic crisis, they could travel there and flaunt their wealthier position. They called themselves "Romania tourists," traveling there two or three times a year. The migrants I interviewed had very vivid recollections of the utter poverty in Romania during those years. They also recalled how they could have great holidays there with very little money or how showing up with cheap cars from Germany would gain anybody a high social recognition. As Tiberiu said, "I left when I was young, but every year I would go back to Romania. Until 1991–1992, there was nothing there [but sheer poverty]. You would go with a 5,000 DM (2,500 Euros) car and you were the best in town. You were somebody, and you could feel great. You could have a lot of fun, and you could speak to [so] many people."

In these cases, migrants' friends visited them regularly in Germany and new friendships were established with Romanians from Timișoara. Over the years migrants would start their own families and a pattern emerged: the "Romania tourists" proved to be among the first to marry Romanian women, just as was the case with the migrants in the first network I discussed.

> I think that, to some, Romania is a sort of paradise. With the money from here they could go to Romania and have great holidays. There are many who go there whenever they have a holiday. Especially those from mixed marriages, they have this idea that they go back to Romania, see beautiful girls, go to great parties, and for that they are much looked up to (Marius).

The casual lifestyle and the possibilities of entertainment available to migrants visiting Timișoara caused these people to return from time to time. The feeling of "being home" could be strong, migrants retaining memories of their life in Romania prior to migration: "When I am in Timișoara, I don't want to come back to Germany, and I'm happy with every day I stay there. I like it there, I stay in my flat, just as I used to before, so there is something familiar. I'm never in the mood to leave the place soon" (Luca).

Tourism to Romania was much practiced at the beginning of the 1990s. In time however, it became less popular. As Romania turned into a more expensive destination, it was no longer such a good deal or affordable for those without a reasonable income. Moreover, after marriage, partying was no longer possible like before. Also, these migrants started to diversify their holiday locations with other destinations in Europe or overseas instead of spending them in Romania only.

These people did not travel to many places, to ski [in Europe for example], but always went to Romania. Now, they don't see as much reason to go there as before because it has become expensive. To go for tourism in Romania is no longer affordable. Besides, I want to go to other places and see something else. And once you found a wife, why should you go there? You would go to Romania to meet girls and have fun. That is why you went there (Tiberiu).

Migrants continued going to Romania after marrying Romanian women, but not as much as before, and for different reasons: partying and going out was replaced by family visits to their new relatives. Migrants would organize their trips back together with their friends in Nuremberg, as Ricky and Luca did when they went to Freidorf. This form of transnational tourism was often undertaken by people who were visiting friends of friends and who thus enlarged their networks of weak ties. Social ties and networks were rarely used in migration after 1989. But social ties were used for creating networks of incorporation, for sociality and solidarity purposes. Social ties were also used in migrants' transnational practices. Incorporation and transnational practices evolved together for a while. Having their ethnicity not fully recognized in everyday life in Germany, these migrants tried to compensate for this by frequently visiting Romania. There, their Germanness and related historically constructed high prestige went unquestioned. Certain other cases, too, demonstrate how migrants aim at acquiring prestige in their origin countries (Nieswand 2011; Salih 2003) when they experience lack of prestige in the destination countries, and this happened with the ethnic Germans from Timişoara to some extent. However, as compared to many other cases, such a strategy remained rather marginal for these persons, and the migrants' acquiring of prestige in Timişoara did not trigger intense transnational practices, such as investments or remittances.

TRANSNATIONAL PENSIONERS

A second type of transnational practice was that of retired persons who moved back to Romania for a part of the year, generally during summers, while staying in Germany during the winter. I did not notice this pattern among the migrants I interviewed, who were generally young people. But it was mentioned several times as a growing trend among senior citizens and as having the potential to further develop into a settled pattern. This transnational practice has developed over the last few years and has multiple causes. Because they were already somewhat advanced in age when they left Romania (i.e., in their late forties or fifties), many ethnic Germans continued to be engaged in employment only for a few years after their arrival. Their pensions were thus smaller than those received by other German senior citizens and insufficient for their needs.

In order to eke out their budgets, these migrants choose to spend part of their time in Romania. They remained registered as residents in Germany, where their children and nephews lived, but also lived in Romania.

> It started a few years ago, I mean many pensioners going back. They speak Romanian so they move there. These people told me: "We get only 700 Euros a month, me and my wife, and we cannot survive here on that money." It pays the rent, the phone bills, and that's it. In Romania they can take care of their gardens, plant potatoes, breed animals; they can live cheaper. They can go out to have a beer and talk to people. In the end, they may even manage to save something (Thomas).

Pensioners' migration is a more general phenomenon in Europe, for example, the rich North Europeans residing in Spain (Janoschka 2008). These senior citizens, often successful professionals, chose to settle and enjoy the climate and lifestyle of southern Europe. Nonetheless, the Romanian case is different. Such migrants are not rich pensioners going to live in the south but poorer pensioners seeking to employ coping strategies to make their incomes go further. German pensioners' residence abroad is allowed within the EU. Romania's accession to the EU, therefore, provided a legal basis for these pensioners to return and receive their retirement money without restrictions.

Moreover, these people were adults when they migrated to Germany, so they do not necessarily see their previous life in Romania in negative terms. Some even complain they missed in Germany a particular type of communication, friendship, and social relatedness that they had been used to in Romania before. In such cases, a return may be interpreted as regaining some cherished habits. Lucian's parents arrived in Germany in 1994 when they were in their forties. In Romania they were blue-collar workers. Even after coming to Germany they earned less than the average German: his mother worked as a cleaning lady and his father did non-specialized work. So their pensions were going to be significantly lower than average and they were worried about their future.

> My parents are retiring so they plan to go back, buy a flat and stay half a year there and half a year here, or something like that. When they came here my mother did not get a full pension, so that the money from her pension is small. She might be getting about 400–500 Euros, not more than that. If my parents were getting 800 Euros, this would be all right for Romania; one can live there on that money. And social relations are different. You can visit neighbors, have coffee together, chat with them, and so on. I think [my mother] misses that society very much (Lucian).

Nevertheless, despite the trend to spend more time in Romania, migrants also complained about the disadvantages of return. The quality of the health services is much lower in comparison to what they have access to in Germany. The social benefits people receive in Germany offer them more security, and state care is seen as very comprehensive.

> When they are 60–63 years old, they weigh the question: "To go there or not to go?" There is a problem with the quality of the services "down there"[2] [in Romania]. It is not like here, especially when it comes to medical assistance. Here in Germany, if I need something I give a call and in five minutes a medical doctor comes to my door. This never happens in Romania. And no matter what you want to do with your life here, the state doesn't allow you to starve. In Romania nobody cares about you. The Romanian state doesn't care if you sleep in a shack or in a cow stable (Mathias).

Furthermore, inasmuch as the pensioners' children are living in Germany, they feel they would be deprived of family support and affection, and their families, too, would miss them. Thus, even if such a pattern of mobility might leave these pensioners better off financially, they do not tend to stay full time in Romania in great numbers.

PLANS TO MOVE BACK

Finally, there is another category of migrants who consider moving back to Romania. Their plans of returning are surprising in the context of this migration. Migrants received full citizenship rights and social benefits upon migration to Germany and initially had no intention to return whatsoever. But given the uncertainties concerning their economic perspectives in Germany, some of them would prefer to go back in the hope of benefiting from the growing Romanian economy. Indeed, the contexts of origin and destination have changed dramatically over the years. In the 1990s, Romania was passing through a very deep economic crisis, with a rapid falling of living standards. Almost half of the people lost their jobs. At that time, Germany offered many job opportunities for the Romanian Germans and any thought about return would have seemed unreasonable. After 2001, Romania's economy started a process of rapid growth, with income increasing more than three times in about seven years. The accession of the country to the EU stimulated hopes of economic prosperity. This tendency to return was visible until 2009, when the crisis hit the Romanian economy and when post-EU accession enthusiasm in the Romanian economy stalled. During the crisis, migrants stopped thinking about returning to Romania or postponed their plans.

Conversely, after 2000, migrants started complaining about the deteriorating economic situation in Germany. The ones with lower specializations in particular have felt growing uncertainties around work and the fall in living standards. Although labor opportunities are still available, as well as state support for the unemployed, child allowance, and other social benefits, some migrants have begun to lament their present-day

situation and compare it to their economic well-being at the beginning of
the 1990s: "The job market looks pretty bad in Germany nowadays. Entire factories are moving to the East and thousands of workers have lost
their jobs. Stabilo is going to the Czech Republic, Ina is going from Her-
zogenaurach to Romania. In two years they will all be gone from here.
Bosch is going to Russia. They are going because everything is cheaper
there" (Mathias). Or, as Ioan considered, "[Entrepreneurs are trying to
bring down] living standards in the West to the level in the East and not
the other way around. In my view, in twenty years it will be better in
Romania than here: there will be more work available and people will be
able to earn good money."

In this context, some migrants predict a leveling of earnings between
Germany and Romania when the crisis is over, a crucial factor for their
future choices. Many complain that the money they earn is no longer
enough, and that the change from the German Mark to the Euro brought
about a decline in living standards. They feel strongly the effects of these
changes. In their view, "those who came earlier, in the 1980s, are better
off. [The same goes] for Germans who don't have real problems" (Tiberiu). These migrants compare their current situation to the one when they
migrated and are nostalgic for the 1990s: "It is no longer working out in
Germany. And how good life was here from 1980 until 1995! Those were
Germany's glorious years. Since 1998, everything started to decline dramatically" (Daniel).

Despite this perceived change, a clear decision to go back is not without problems, as re-adapting to Romania entails its own risks. Compared
to what they are used to in Germany, they see prices going up in Romania, yet without much social protection. "I consider that in Germany you
have social protection. You are not kicked out into the streets, even
though you may have difficulties. It is no longer as it used to be, but it is
still something" (Tiberiu).

However, return is still seen as a viable alternative for migrants who
plan to open small businesses in Romania. Some in fact did return with
such aims. By these means their living standards do not sink and they can
even plan to develop their businesses. "There are some people moving
back to Romania. They launch businesses there. I know someone who is
constructing a hotel at the Black Sea. Every year there are some who
invest money there, in a house or something like that" (Marius).

In other cases, migrants look for positions in German companies with
businesses in Romania. For German speakers there are openings like this
in Romania, and migrants may even obtain better jobs than their current
ones in Germany. For architects or civil engineers, for example, there is
room for opportunities in the future when the market resumes its growth
and the German and Austrian companies start to invest there again. Before 2010 I had an interview with Christian, who at that time was trying
to find work as an architect in Germany. The situation looked gloomy. At

that time, the real estate market in Romania was booming, attracting large investment from Western Europe. Christian thought seriously of going back.

> When you write in an application [that you are an] architect, [you have few chances, as] companies receive hundreds of applications. I have no chance to get a job. In nine months I had no success. When I wrote that [I spoke Romanian and I came from Romania and was willing to work there], I was invited to three interviews out of five letters. This was already a success. I plan to return eventually to Romania, from a professional point of view, but I don't know how easy this will be for my family. It is difficult, but I am going to try to go back (Christian).

The crisis altered his plans of return. Inasmuch as it hit the real estate market particularly hard, prices and wages in his field fell dramatically. So Christian had to postpone his plans for the future.

In summary, I have argued that migration from Timişoara to Nuremberg resulted initially in a redefinition of the notion of home, as migrants were often disappointed with what they saw during their visits back in Romania. Due to their legal status in Germany and the economic and social opportunities on offer there, some of these migrants re-evaluated their connection to Romania and finally ceased to maintain relations with their country of origin.

At the same time, others continued to maintain ties. Some of them became "Romania tourists": they went there to meet their friends, find girlfriends and future wives, or simply to have cheap holidays. As a consequence of these relations and especially of marriage migration, migrants from Nuremberg strengthened their transnational ties. People interacted with their new relatives in Romania and multiplied their social ties between Romania and Nuremberg. Furthermore, over the last few years a shift has occurred in the case of some migrants, as they seek to return either as pensioners, traveling regularly between Germany and Romania, as small-scale entrepreneurs, or as professionals employed by German companies in Romania.

In the first part of this book I described how ethnic Germans from Timişoara migrated to Nuremberg. This was a politically legitimized migration process in which migrants received strong institutional support from the German state in order to live "as Germans among Germans" (Oltmer 2006). I analyzed the situation of the German community in Romania and their historically constructed position of high prestige. Germans started to migrate during communism, especially after 1977 when a legal framework was established for this migration. However, the emigration process was costly and full of harassment, and very often people had to resort to informal payments to obtain a quicker exit. Once the communism system collapsed in Eastern Europe, migration boomed. Migrants arrived in Germany, where they had to prove they were ethnic

Germans. Afterwards, state institutions in Germany assisted them in obtaining a proper education and finding work. These migrants obtained citizenship overnight and ended up in financially comfortable circumstances. But during their social incorporation, migrants I interviewed claimed they were not recognized as Germans equal to other Germans but as "Romanians," despite their previous expectations to be regarded socially as equal. A context emerged in which the migrants' German ethnicity came to be questioned. And they were conscious of a loss of the prestige they had previously held in Romania.

Simultaneously, they started meeting among themselves and developed an attitude of being different from the Germans around them. Indeed, their identity claims were redefined in the direction of asserting their Romanian identity. They strengthened their transnational ties to Romania, where they traveled often as tourists. This tendency was further strengthened by their marrying women from Romania, which completed their reconnection to their country of origin. They ended up as "Romanians" in Germany, involving themselves in a process of ethnicization in which they started using the Romanian language, reevaluated their Romanian identity, and strengthened their connections to Romania.

NOTES

1. Weber et al. (2003); see also Wagner (1991).
2. To the south.

II

Romanians in Italy

FOUR

"We Need to Get Out of Here"

From Borşa to Milan

The road through the mountains had almost reached Dealu Stefăniţei, a peak 800 meters high, when the view unfolded before me of the great valley of the Maramureș below, in the northernmost side of Romania. From Cluj, the largest city in Transylvania and the second in Romania after Bucharest, it took three hours to reach. It was a hilly region with hamlets and small villages located on the slopes of the Carpathians, sparsely populated and visibly poor. The largest cities in the region had no more than 30,000 to 40,000 inhabitants. The road was the only one linking Transylvania and Maramureș, the historical alpine valley bordering Ukraine. After I crossed the peak the road crawled downwards. Maramureș, one of the most isolated regions of Romania, was by then known for its wooden architecture and the traditionalism of its people. Twenty years ago, just after the collapse of communism, the region was advertised as a tourist attraction, a living village museum with wooden houses and centuries-old wooden churches, now part of the Unesco world heritage. This marketing strategy did nothing to alleviate the poverty of the region, however. The houses looked like they did a hundred years ago, and there was barely any sign of modern facilities in many of the villages. But people of the region were proud of their identity as "Moroşans," of their traditional music, and of the local traditions which they never missed the chance to exhibit.

The road continued northwards. The beautiful mountain landscape towards the east had significantly altered after the collapse of the state socialism, as illegal logging has been practiced on a large scale and many of its forests were cut down. Fifteen kilometers after entering Maramureș, I came to a crossroad with a petrol station. Towards the West, the road

went to Vișeu, a small city of 25,000 people, thirty kilometers away, and
further to Sighetul Marmației, a larger city a further seventy kilometers
on. Towards the east, the road went to Borșa and further to Vatra Dornei
on the other side of the mountains. I turned eastwards. After a while,
some remnants of former socialist industry, now in ruins, appeared on
the left-hand side. And after crossing some train lines, the name of the
city appeared on the right side: Borșa. It was an old, decrepit sign nobody
had thought of changing for a new one in more than fifteen years.

The landscape was hilly and everywhere houses were scattered on the
slopes. There were also many big new villas, a contrast to the rudimen-
tary infrastructure of the place. Only the main streets had asphalt; the rest
were earth roads. Public lighting was rare. Despite the local investment
in houses, the local administration hadn't kept up with the speed of
development and the urban infrastructure remained poor. Because of
this, over the past fifteen years people had started to construct houses
close to the main road, to benefit from the existing infrastructure. Towards the center, houses were jammed on both sides of the main street.
There was a strange mix of kitschy architecture and strident colors,
where new two-and-three-story houses randomly alternated with old,
small, run-down buildings. The older houses, many of them once inhabited by Jewish traders who had lived here prior to the Second World War,
were in poor condition. The new houses had been erected in the past
fifteen years by labor migrants who after the collapse of state socialism
had started to migrate towards Western Europe to work.

The city center was dominated by grey four-story blocks of flats constructed when the city was developing during the communist period
from the 1960s until the 1980s. There was a large regional hospital, some
administrative buildings, and an array of shops. In the center, pizzerias
and cafes had opened up. The small center, made up of a few streets with
four-story blocks, houses, and new buildings, concentrated a significant
part of the population of the town. The rest lived scattered on the valleys
nearby and five kilometers to the north in Baia Borșa, a mining colony
that developed in the 1960s, on the site of an older mining settlement
from the nineteenth century.

I first went to Borșa in November 2004, after I met Dragoș in Milan. It
was his city. In Milan he gave me his father's address. "My father will put
you up," he said. Upon arrival in Borșa, I took a walk in the center,
looking at the shops selling cheap products and having a coffee in a
newly opened cafe. I then went in search of Dragoș's house. When I
finally got there, it was four kilometers away from the center, on a slope
close to the main road. A dog started barking outside the house as I got
closer. The family's living conditions were primitive. The house was
small, and three of Dragoș's siblings were crowded into one small room.
His older sister taught the younger ones to read and write. On the win-

dow I could see Pietrosul Rodnei, the highest peak in the eastern Carpathians, 2,300 meters high.

The father turned up shortly after I arrived. He lived on casual employment, usually in construction, but had not had much work that day. He was happy I had come with news from Dragoş, as he had heard nothing about him for a while. As he showed me around his run-down house, Dragoş' father proudly described how they were going to build a fine big one up there on the hill with the remittances that Dragoş and his mother were going to be sending back home. Like Dragoş, many people from Borşa had left their hometown dreaming about a better life. Dragoş left behind his father and three siblings, and in Milan he lived together with his mother and a younger sister. As has happened to many people in the region, migration to Milan has greatly changed the life of Dragoş and his family.

People from Borşa like Dragoş and his family departed from a remote valley in Romania and arrived in one of the most enticing and glamorous cities in Europe, Milan, center of Italy's business and fashion industry. In the present chapter I analyze the principal migration strategies pursued by these people and highlight the main periods of their migration. Included are data about the push factors and the use of social networks by migrants. My approach will be based on network analysis and the theory of cumulative causation. In keeping with this, the analysis will be comparatively based, with reference to the theoretical model of Mexico–U.S. migration, where this approach originated. I look at the development of migrant networks and at the resources in social ties mobilized by migrants. Finally, I provide comparative insights from other research on Romanian migration.

* * *

Borşa is a former industrial town of approximately 30,000 inhabitants in the northern part of Romania. Under socialism, mining and forestry employed the majority of the local labor force. Urban planning and industrialization were implemented here, as in many other Romanian cities (Chirot 1978; Turnock 1970; 1991), through extensive development of heavy industry. In the 1960s and 1970s, when socialist industrialization arrived in Borşa, the town developed from a quasi-rural settlement with a small mining industry into a mining town. The town itself maintained its rural outlook, and with the exception of a regional hospital and some hotels in a tourist resort a few kilometers away, there was a marked absence of urban services.

This pattern of development was quite common for many small Romanian towns which were industrialized during socialism. Industry was distributed throughout the country, so the absence of a massive concentration of industry in specific regions favored a balanced regional devel-

opment. This led to the development of short-distance commuting, trans-
forming much of the peasantry into a class of commuters. Very often,
these peasant-workers had double employment, in industry and in their
household farming activities (Turnock 1970). At the beginning of the
1960s the mining industry developed intensively and Borşa became the
core industrial site of a larger area. The population increased through
inner migration. In the 1960s there were less than 20,000 inhabitants,
while in 1977 there were almost 25,000. The town was further urbanized
through the construction of new blocks of flats, although these were not
supported by adequate infrastructure. "The Colony," a new quarter for
new inhabitants arriving in Borşa, was constructed five kilometers away
from the center.

Most of the people worked in mining industry or forestry, but also in
transportation, small-scale manufacturing, and commerce. As a consequence of industrial development Borşa became an industrial center, providing jobs in the region. As Radu, one of my interviewees, noted, "Borşa
developed through the arrival of labor migrants from other regions: from
central Transylvania or from the Moldavian region."[1] Some of these la-
borers settled there. Besides them, until the 1990s commuters used to
come from about sixty to seventy kilometers away. Migrants and commuters represented about 40 percent of all employees. Because of this
internal migration, about 2,000 flats were planned and constructed.

As one of the Ceauşescu regime's goals was to achieve energy inde-
pendence and to generate raw materials for industry, many mines were
operating in Romania, often despite their economic inefficiency (Chirot
1978; Turnock 1970). This was also the case in Borşa, where, even if not
profitable, mining was subsidized by the state. As was commonly the
case in Romania at that time, miners lived relatively well. "People here
lived well during the Ceauşescu era. The food shortage was not as great
as in the rest of the country. Salaries were higher, 30 percent more than in
the rest of Romania. It was similar to other mining regions, where work-

Table 4.1. Population of Borşa, displaying the demographical evolution of the city.

Year	Romanians	Hungarians	Jews	Germans	Total
1930	8,183	374	2,486	106	11,230
1956	12,483	871	166	50	13,600
1966	17,659	1,097	13	57	18,926
1977	23,096	1,108	4	47	24,406
1992	26,476	753		77	27,450
2002	26,263	522		49	26,984

Source: OSB (1993; 1978; 1967). See also Anghel (2010).

ers had good salaries. As long as the mining continued, people could get good money" (Dumitru).

In addition to mining and forestry, households benefited from land owning and the secondary economy, which helped to fill consumption demands, especially food, which was scarce in the 1980s. The socialist economy was not oriented towards consumption and market demands, but was organized around planning and top-down resource allocations (Verdery 1996). Collectivized agriculture was quite inefficient. Authors like Sampson (1984; 1995) and Turnock (1991) note that although most of the agricultural land was included in the state-owned collectives, a considerable percentage of Romania's agricultural production used for internal consumption was actually harvested from small individual plots. In the 1980s, Ceauşescu started a policy of paying off foreign debts through controlling and severely restricting food and energy consumption (Turnock 1991; Verdery 1996). Even though people had enough money, there were no goods to spend it on (Chelcea 2002a, b). Basic products such as milk, bread, and meat were in painfully short supply, and the secondary sector went part of the way to fill these shortages (Anghel 2005; Chelcea and Mateescu 2005). In many areas where land was not collectivized by the state, people could still satisfy their living requirements and even make a profit by informally selling such goods. Such was the case in Borşa, a town where landed property remained in people's hands and access to basic agricultural products was secure. "People could save from salaries and food was often produced at home. Household consumption was covered, as everyone could get potatoes, onions, and meat" (Radu).

Commuting and seasonal work were the Borşeni's main forms of mobility during socialism. Sometimes the production of basic food was sustained through temporary migration for agricultural work, as some Borşeni used to work during the summer in Banat, Western Romania. In exchange for their work, they received grain with which they were able to raise cattle and poultry. They also witnessed the process of migration and settling in Borşa of those people who came from other regions and were employed in mining. By and large, international migration was a rare phenomenon, with only a few cases of migration mostly to the United States and Western Europe. Although the international migration of ethnic Germans did take place after 1977 from some surrounding places like the cities of Vişeu and Vatra Dornei, this had little impact on migration from Borşa during the years of state socialism.

After the collapse of state socialism, several major changes occurred at the local level. There was a growing impoverishment of the population, and the restructuring of industry brought about a sharp economic decline. Mining was not profitable and the Romanian government began a program for closing down the mining industry. A process of industrial involution emerged which greatly affected the economy.[2] This was not a peculiarity for the town of Borşa. If we look at the general figures for

Romania, we can see that between 1989 and 2000 the number of employees in industry declined from 3,846,000 to just 1,991,000 (Horváth and Anghel 2009). The situation was now exactly the reverse from during socialism. In those days, there was money in their pockets but no goods on the market; now Romanians saw merchandise flooding the market but could hardly afford basic foodstuffs (Chelcea 2002a). In many cases people left the cities and moved back to the villages in order to live on their pensions and to cultivate their plots in an attempt to secure enough food to live on. If the 1990s were characterized by extremely high inflation, in 1997 a radical restructuring of industry was carried out which resulted in large-scale unemployment. Most studies on the migration of Romanians mention this year as a turning point (Baldwin-Edwards 2007; Sandu 2006). After this major change in the economy, international migration started in most Romanian regions. It became the main strategy to combat impoverishment and to reduce households' risks in the face of such dramatic changes.

The process of mine closure started in Borşa in 1990, and for the first years it proceeded at a gradual pace. But in 1997 there was a radical restructuring: about 2,000 people were fired, though they received relatively generous financial compensation.[3] As presented in the following table, less than half of the people employed in industry in 1989 in Borşa were still employed in 1997, and in 2002 only 20 percent still held a job.

The restructuring was conducted by the Romanian government under the guidance of the World Bank and IMF, as part of a general policy to rapidly restructure and reduce the heavy losses in the mining industry.[4] Uncertainty grew during that year, and the Romanian currency lost much of its value. People saw their savings destroyed and businesses ruined. Private initiatives in Borşa often failed in a context of a decaying economy, generalized corruption,[5] and accelerated inflation. For Romania's mono-industrial areas, the results of this policy were in many cases catastrophic, and the compensation money was mostly spent on consumption (Crăciun, Stan, and Grecu 2002). In Borşa, though, it was invested in migration. "I know that they were smart, I remember, one visa was about 1,500 DM (750 Euros). When they received compensation, [miners already had information] on how to migrate to Italy. They didn't spend their money on drinking, as happened in other regions. They changed the money into DM [and migrated]" (Constantin).

Borşa is located in a mountainous area, and there were several attempts to invest in forestry and tourism. When the political regime changed in 1989, people were able to cut timber and sell it informally, at least for a period of time. Soon thereafter, labor migration developed, fed by the information on migration and resources generated by some prior migration. In a short time, migration became a stable and profitable economic strategy. Thus, compensation money that was initially regarded by the Romanian government as a means to ease workers' lives and to gen-

Table 4.2. Employment in Borşa.

	1989	1997	1998	1999	2000	2001	2002
Employed persons (total)	14,492	6,351	5,537	5,178	4,759	4,366	3,903
Industry (mining and forestry)	9,300	3,770	3,008	2,568	2,149	2,099	1,940
Energy				67	54	50	55
Commerce	1,000	132	121	411	367	365	165
Constructions		471	197	251	225	163	146
Transport	7 – 800	389	349	351	258	189	213
Administration		62	65	71	68	60	63
Education		484	526	473	455	472	456
Health		725	800	714	769	679	708
Total Population	30,055	27,493	27,262	27,275	27,267	27,166	27,677

Source: Combined data OSB (1993; 1978; 1967) and information gathered in Borşa. See also Anghel (2010).
Note: For 1989, the data are estimations. In 2005 there were also 180 family associations and 320 registered companies.

erate small business initiatives was used instead for migrating to Western Europe. "About 30 percent of miners who lost jobs migrated with this money in the first or second month after the restructuring. Another 30 percent followed in the next year. With the second wave of restructuring, in 1998–1999, about 70 percent requested voluntary leave in order to migrate. [Migration] was [already] the main motivation [to leave mining]" (Nicolae).

At the time when these waves of migrants left, a large number of pioneering migrants were already in Western Europe, providing a source of information and funds for would-be migrants at home. In the following years a complex system of migration developed, directed particularly to Italy.

MIGRATION FROM BORŞA: CAUSES, PERIODS, AND MECHANISMS OF MIGRATION

This case study of migration presents a contrast to the one previously discussed. It is based on a study of migrants who went "illegally" to Europe and managed to find work and settle in Italy. While migrants in the first case benefited from a great deal of state and institutional support, the second case was precisely the opposite: migrants in Italy did not receive any form of institutional support. Additionally, if in the first case the pull factors were essentially political, migration to Milan was pulled by market demands in Italy. In the first case study I showed how Germans from Romania "Romanianized" in Germany. This process of ethnicization was generated by migrants' perceived loss of prestige and lack of recognition of their ethnicity. The second case, as we shall see, evinces a different process of changing social status and prestige. In order to explain how people migrated and obtained a particular socioeconomic status, I apply theories of labor migration, showing both their usefulness and their limits in the case of the Romanian irregular migration. The following two chapters will deal with migration and migrants' incorporation in Milan. I will show how, despite their marginalization and the precariousness of migration, migrants eventually succeeded in gaining a satisfactory socioeconomic status. This process occurred in the context of a laissez-faire migration policy on the part of the state and a lack of institutional support for migrants. It stands in contrast with the first case study, where migrants benefited from a great deal of support.

Migration from Borşa to Milan evolved in the broader context of the substantial development of migration from Romania to Italy. In the last few years, the Romanian community has become the largest migrant community in Italy, with almost one million migrants in 2011. Already in the autumn of 2002 the regularization of migrants in Italy recorded 180,000 Romanian migrants. In 2008 the number of Romanian migrants was estimated at somewhere between 630,000 (ISTAT 2013) and 1,016,000 (Pittau, Ricci and Silj 2008).[6] The last official data record 970,000 Romanian citizens in January 2011 (ISTAT 2013). In the largest Italian cities the number of Romanian legal migrants increased steadily. In 2007, there were 62,000[7] registered Romanians in Rome, 44,000[8] in Turin, and 20,000[9] in Milan.

Romanian migration to southern Europe (Italy, Spain, but also Greece and Portugal) occurred in the context of a rapid general increase in the migrant population in these countries: after 2007 migrants became a considerable percentage of the population, as much as 6 percent in Italy and up to 10 percent in Spain. In the case of Italy, the migration developed rapidly and in substantial numbers. A high proportion of these migrants were undocumented (Zincone 2006a; 2006b, 3). As recruitment programs were modest and did not attract sufficient workers for the needs of the Italian economy, the demand for labor came to be filled by the hiring of irregular migrants who were already there. Although it is often claimed that Italy is a new country as a goal of migration, in reality migration to Italy had already started in the 1970s, after the oil shock. More consistent flows developed between 1984 and 1989, when 700,000 to 800,000 migrants entered Italy, out of which 350,000 were irregular (Allasino et al. 2004, 1; Zincone 2006b). Thereafter, the expansion of migration to Italy was tied to the changes in Eastern Europe and the Balkans: the fall of the communist regimes, and the availability of a pool of cheap labor that existed there. Besides these parts of Europe, migration chains to Italy developed from Africa and Asia (Colombo and Sciortino 2003, 196).

For many years the only migration law in Italy was an act from the old fascist regime of the 1930s concerning the presence of suspect aliens. Only in the middle of the 1980s did a series of laws and amnesties, triggered by the growing number of migrants, begin to regulate the process of international migration. In 1986, the first law of migration was passed, altering the discretionary way of managing migration (Colombo and Sciortino 2003, 197). On the face of it, the 1986 legislation looked generous and liberal, but it lacked force. "In theory, immigrants were not only given equal welfare but also special opportunities to study in their own language and to learn the Italian language. In practice no national public funds were devoted to sustain immigrants' rights . . . the burden of implementing these rights mainly fell on the already over-stretched regional and city councils" (Zincone 2006a, 19).

The 1986[10] law and that of 1990[11] looked to the example of other European migration policies after the Second World War, which aimed at regulating migration according to the labor demands of Fordist industry. At the same time, and under European influence, Italy adopted stricter policies of entry for tourists and for legal migrants (Colombo and Sciortino 2003, 198). But the small-scale of planned legal recruitments, "the higher costs and, to an even greater degree, the complexity of the procedures, were real deterrents for employers [who wished] to officially hire non-EU workers" (Zincone 2006a, 19).

These two main factors led to an increasingly unfilled labor demand arising especially in small and medium-size companies and from Italian families who needed informal domestic workers. It caused endemic irregular migration and brought about discretionary administrative practices (Colombo and Sciortino 2003, 198). Migration expanded through a developing migration industry (Castles 2004), and nowadays most of the legal migrants are former irregular migrants legalized through large-scale amnesties.[12] Some authors consider that at a certain point in this development, control over migration was lost (Colombo and Sciortino 2003, 198). And, as Zincone (2006a, 20) argues, "the process of legalization of illegal behaviors characterizes more generally the Italian policy style, not only in the field of immigration, but also in other fields. . . . Italian policies are characterized by a long succession of amnesties. . . . Unauthorized building, tax evasion, and unregistered labor are frequent objects of [such] amnesties."

Nonetheless, between 1992 and 2008 a series of laws and measures were introduced that signaled an increased structuring of Italy's migration policy. Today, there are three acts regulating migration and migrants' rights: the 1992 Nationality Law,[13] the 1998 Turco-Napolitano

Act,[14] and the 2002 Bossi-Fini Law[15] (Zincone 2006a; b). Of these, the 1998 law was the first to acknowledge migration as a permanent phenomenon (Zincone 2006a, 23). In time, efficiency in controlling irregular migration increased, and repatriation agreements were signed with the transit and origin countries (Colombo and Sciortino 2003, 200). The number of expulsions increased, but there were more opportunities for those arriving in Italy as regular migrants. Nevertheless, there was still "no reform in the administrative apparatus and much arbitrariness [was] allowed" (idem).

Compared to Germany, where potential irregular migrants were labeled *a priori* as asylum seekers (Finotelli 2006, 203), Italy managed the irregular flows of migrants differently, through *post factum* regularizations[16] and a reactive policy based on emergency measures. Migration was strongly linked to legality and security in developing a "model of reasonable integration" based on four principles: interaction based on security, respect for human rights, integrity for legal immigrants, and interaction based on pluralism and communication (Zincone 2000).

In this context of endemic irregular migration to Italy, the migration of Romanians developed very quickly based on networks from particular regions and locales from Romania. Italy soon became the Romanians' preferred destination in Europe. The movement of people between the two countries has increased dramatically over the last few years, migration affecting entire Romanian communities, such as Borşa.

Migration started in Borşa during communism, with small numbers of inhabitants migrating to Western Europe and North America. Migration was essentially a post-1989 phenomenon, however, categorized by three distinct periods, roughly corresponding to the main stages of Romanian migration (Horváth and Anghel 2009): (a) the early stage of migration and the emergence of migration networks, when migration strategies were unsettled and dynamic, involving individuals and small groups of migrants; (b) the development of networks and a migration industry (through informal brokers), when migration reached a certain development. The critical point was 1997, when migration was strengthened by the restructuring of mining. In the period between 1997 and 2002, migration was irregular, but entry controls to Western Europe made migration difficult and costly; (c) after 2002, the last phase, during which Romanians traveling to the EU were exempted from visa requirements. During this stage, migration spread to the majority of the population in Borşa. It became a mass phenomenon.

Studies on the Romanian brain drain (Csedö 2008; Ferro 2004a; Nedelcu 2000) do not mention networks, but rather institutions (companies, universities, and state agencies) as the major players in the migration of highly qualified Romanian citizens. By contrast, aggregate data at the national level (Sandu 2006), and also qualitative research on Romanian migration (Bleahu 2004b; Cingolani 2009; Elrick and Ciobanu 2009; Horváth 2008; Potot 2000; 2003; Radu 2001; Vlase 2004; 2008), show that networks played the main role in irregular migration. Even when migration was institutionally determined, as was the case with Romania's ethnic and religious minorities (see Şerban and Grigoraş 2000; Stan 2005a; b), migration propagated through networks outside these groups and involved large numbers of Romanians. Given the wide variety of migrant networks, I will examine here the particularities of such networks and identify what resources of social capital were exploited in the process of migration.

THE INITIAL PHASE: INVENTING MIGRATION STRATEGIES

As in the case of migration to Nuremberg, motivations for migration to Western Europe were very powerful after the collapse of state socialism. Romanians' mobility was no longer controlled by the Romanian state and people could now travel abroad. But Romanians had no easy access to Western Europe. In comparison to the socialist period, after 1990 motivations for migration modified. During socialism there were both economic and political concerns which persuaded people to migrate, but after 1989 economic motivations prevailed. At the beginning, there was much haziness on the part of migrants concerning patterns and even motivation for migration. For some, migration was initially a touristic decision, as people were eager to see other countries after forty years of travel restrictions. For others, migration was economically motivated, a perspective that started to gain much importance over the years due to better earnings and working conditions available abroad. "I don't think that [only] money was the most important push factor [of migration, but also better working conditions]. [At the beginning, there were] young people [who migrated], in the twenty-to-twenty-five age range. They moved because [mining work] is difficult. They took vacations [from their jobs] and left" (Radu).

Although they were the exception, some early migrants managed to take advantage of asylum regulations and the (still) unchanged asylum policy in different West European states. Tudor was eighteen when he first left Romania, soon after the regime change in 1989. He went in 1991 first to Hungary, then to Czechoslovakia, and from there he had to walk all the way to Austria.

He put in an application for political asylum and received it. They offered him financial assistance. From there he went to Switzerland, where he stayed another three months. He returned to Borşa because he was in love. But after six months he went to Italy again, this time on a tourist trip. In Italy there was no possibility to apply for political asylum, but he received some social benefits. Although there were no major political problems in Romania at that time, the Italian authorities allowed him to stay.

After 1989, irregular migration from Borşa expanded to all parts of Europe, with migrants trying to access labor markets and find states where irregular migrants were allowed to stay. Among the countries targeted by migrants, France, Belgium, and Greece were the first in line. But Italy soon became the main destination of migrants from Borşa, driven by the developing irregular migration and laissez-faire policies. In comparison with Germany after 1989, where millions of migrants arrived in a short period of time, there were only 600,000 migrants (ISTAT) in Italy in 1992.[17] Migration was not a "public problem," and there was also a tolerant attitude on the part of the authorities towards the first Romanian migrants. Some benefited from this state of affairs. "The first migrations were to France and Belgium. At a certain point, some went to Italy and got jobs in agriculture; they found the conditions there attractive" (Marian).

At the beginning, migration involved the irregular strategies of individuals and small groups crossing the border. These strategies were usually improvised. However, some were prearranged, such as those used mainly by first movers going to the West with the help of their German friends. A pioneer of migration, Călin arrived in Italy with an invitation he received from a friend in Germany. He had worked in Vişeu[18] and had acquaintances among the German *Zipser*.[19] With the invitation he went to Sibiu to the German consulate, where he was able to apply for a thirty-day visa. He stated he would go to Germany, but in fact he went straight to Italy.

For the majority, however, strategies of migration were unclear and migrants could not rely on networks or institutional support. In order to exemplify these migratory practices, I introduce three cases of migrants who succeeded in entering Italy irregularly. In two of these cases, the migrants managed to get to Italy on several occasions and they traveled back and forth irregularly. Although these may be exceptional cases, they vividly show the permeability of European borders and the difficulty in stopping irregular migration when migrants were able to mobilize social ties, financial resources, and the necessary information.

THE STORY OF DUMITRU

Dumitru was a technician in Borşa before migrating to the West. When I conducted the interview with him in 2005, he was already fifty-five. He was a very cheerful person and a good storyteller. He proudly remembered his migration experience, the difficulties he went through, and how he was finally able to succeed in what he set out to do. He first migrated in 1990 to the former Yugoslavia with five other persons from Borşa. They found work in the forestry industry for about three months. He was teaching at the high school at home, but in Serbia he did other work. He did not think he was likely to earn much money, but anyway it was better than in Borşa. A Serbian who was a resident in France made them an offer. He asked them to work for him for one month, and as a reward he would take them to France. Dumitru accepted the offer, together with another person from Borşa.

Dumitru, some of his fellow Borşeni, and the Serbian middleman went on to France. The Romanians crossed the Slovenian border to Italy irregularly, near the border crossing point. The war in the former Yugoslavia had already started, and migrants heard gunfire along their way. After crossing the border to Italy, they met their Serbian guide. All of them reached Trieste; however, their guide decided not to continue the journey to Paris. The Romanians decided to go on by themselves. They took a train to the French border, then crossed it by night, passing through a long train tunnel. By the time they reached France, they had no money or food left.

> In the first city in France we took a train and we finally reached Paris. We had problems there. We did not know anyone. There was a moment when we had to share the last tin of meat. I said to my friend: "This is the last one; after that, we are finished. We do not have anything else to eat, just what we will find in the garbage dumpster." I just remember [the situation]. Once I tried to steal a peach but the seller, an African guy, noticed what I was up to and shouted at me loudly. I was not able to run, I was powerless. I had to give back the peach. [In Paris] I happened to sleep in garbage bins [at that time]. [I was fortunate enough to run into] my brother-in-law. He sent me to some places where [the poor could eat] for free (Dumitru).

Dumitru managed to survive. In time, he obtained residence papers allowing him to work temporarily, but he overstayed. He was helped by a Frenchman, who found him a job in the field of forestry. Dumitru was able to work for about three months irregularly. With the savings he bought a car, but unfortunately he had an accident, which was reported in the local newspapers. His employer fired him so as not to be caught with irregular employees. Without a job, Dumitru was forced to return to Borşa.

Dumitru stopped several times during our talk so as not to leave out any important information. He recalled difficult moments from his migrant life, but he often chuckled remembering how he was able to get through them. Looking back, he described his migration as a trial he had to pass to eventually achieve success and a better life.

He then resumed his migration story. He tried to start a business back home but it didn't work. He was heavily in debt, and in 1996 he tried once more to emigrate. One of his friends was a truck driver carrying goods between Bucharest and Venice. Ten people from Borşa gathered and went on his truck. They met him at the Romanian border, but had to wait until the border guard sealed the truck; then everyone entered through a small airway. Dumitru was lucky to remain outside as a second driver. Nobody inspected the truck the whole way. The truck arrived in Budapest. Afterwards it was transported on a train through the former Yugoslavia. Somewhere in Bosnia-Herzegovina the army checked the train, but they did not discover them. In Slovenia, near the border with Italy, everyone went outside the truck. They entered a restaurant. Just across from it was the border to Italy. They got through. Afterwards, each of them called on acquaintances and relatives in Italy for help. Dumitru moved to Bergamo, where he stayed with his brother and worked on a cattle farm for the next two years. In 2007, when I saw him for the last time, he was living in the region of Bergamo, working in construction.

This case reveals how migration routes were created. Dumitru first migrated to the former Yugoslavia. Afterwards he moved to France and finally remained in Italy. This example shows how migration to Italy, unlike to other countries in Europe, became possible because of the permissive conditions regarding irregular entry and stay. In comparison, Romanian migrants to other European countries encountered a less easygoing reception. In France (Potot 2000; 2003) migrants found a more regulated labor market, where trade unions were a strong lobby, restricting migrants' labor to that of newspaper sellers. In Germany, Romanian migrants had to apply for asylum, as irregular stay was very difficult. They either legalized their status, as political refugees, marriage migrants, or stateless persons,[20] or moved elsewhere. In Germany, to be sure, Romanian migrants had more social networks. But this alone did not create a strong irregular migration towards Germany, as happened in the case of Italy. In comparison to continental Europe, migration was more difficult to the UK, as it required crossing the Channel and both formal and irregular access in the UK were highly selective. Although migrants considered that the labor market in the UK had better jobs to offer than in Italy, they often indicated that they regarded this migration as more difficult. In Italy no similar difficulties were present and Romanians arrived in the context of a strong informal economy and growing irregular migration. In the following part, another two personal histories will illustrate how migrants continued to establish migration routes, as well as the difficulties encountered by the Romanians in the first years of migration.

THE STORY OF DAN

Dan had one of the most engrossing migration stories, as he managed to cross to Italy irregularly several times. His stubborn will to succeed, the difficulties he passed through, and his ability to find new and innovative ways to reach Italy made him one of the most interesting migrants I met in Borșa. Once we met, he started recalling the story of his migration:

I first went to France in the spring of 1994, on a tourist vacation. [I was together with a group of people from here.] We had to stay for three days in France and then to come back [to Romania]. We remained for two days in Paris. From there we went straight to Italy, to some other people from Borşa. There were [Borşeni] also in Greece and France at that time, but our friends in Italy [could help me]. [They were] a family of friends of my mother-in-law who was living close to Verona. I got off the bus in a parking lot in Verona. My acquaintances lived about sixty kilometers away. I was carrying a lot of luggage and gifts. I managed to hide these bags in some bushes close to the highway and I started to walk all the way towards that village. It was June and it was hot. When I arrived at the destination, I was exhausted. I immediately drank about four bottles of water. The following days I rested there, in order to recover after the long trip. Later on, I went to Milan, where I had some friends (Dan).

Dan remained in a tent camp organized by migrants from Borşa at the outskirts of the city. About sixty to seventy persons lived there, all of them from Borşa. He had no luggage with him, and he had to improvise a sleeping place in the open air, borrowing cover sheets from the others. The living conditions were miserable: "There were lots of mosquitos, there was no toilet, no washing facilities." Everything was improvised. Even the washing of laundry was done in a lake not far from Milan. Tents, marketplaces for informal labor, and a few acquaintances among migrants: these formed these newcomers' locality in the beginning. In the absence of institutions or networks to accommodate the newcomers, the pioneers had to rely on new acquaintances. Places like open markets or certain squares, such as the one in the front of the *Milano Centrale*,[21] had the function of mediating first contacts to the new environment.

During his stay among the tents, Dan looked for employment: he asked for jobs directly at the janitor's office of different plants, and went regularly to the informal marketplaces. He also asked other migrants about any labor opportunities. Nothing showed up for him. Among migrants there were some rumors that labor was available at the Venice harbor. He traveled there with his brother-in-law. They slept for three days in some boats. Nonetheless, the information proved false and they had to go back to Milan. After many attempts to find employment, Dan was ready to give up. One of his acquaintances from Como[22] asked if he would be available to take a car back home to Borşa. He could not stand the thought of the tent camp any longer and accepted the offer, returning to Romania together with his brother-in-law. He stayed home for another year, but by that time people in Borşa were starting to migrate and to find jobs abroad. The guy from Como whose car Dan brought back home promised to help him find a job. So Dan decided to go again. He sold some wood in order to get some money. He went with two youngsters and a guide who charged 700 DM (350 Euros) for each of them. One of them decided to remain in Romania after all.

They went through former Yugoslavia and got through some of the borders by bribing the border guards. The trip lasted one and a half weeks. There was war there and at home nobody had any news about them. They tried repeatedly to cross to Croatia, but every time border guards turned them back. At a border crossing point over a river they put the car on a boat and finally they were allowed to pass. At the border with Slovenia they left the car and crossed the border irregularly. They went through forests at night. It was difficult since there were rocks and bushes everywhere. Dan ruined his clothes and was bleeding. The person accompanying him lost one of his shoes. In all, the passage from Croatia to Slovenia took several hours. They tried to find one of their guide's cars in a parking lot, as they had previously agreed, but there was no sign of him.

Dan started to walk along the road and went into hiding from any car that approached. At a crossroad the police suddenly showed up and arrested him. He had to pay a fine of about 200 DM (100 Euros) and was returned to Romania. He remained in Borşa for two to three months, but finally decided to go to Italy again using his ties with migration brokers.

> I had a friend who was able to obtain one-week invitations to Austria. He asked me to pay about 500 DM (250 Euros) [for such a visa]. This time I had only a few things on me. I had no money left, I was bankrupt. I did not even have money for the train ticket. I hitchhiked to the Romanian border. At the border crossing point I found some ethnic Germans from Vişeu going to Germany and I went together with them. Thus I was able to reach my destination in Austria. I remained one and a half days and afterwards I went to Udine [with a guide]. I finally reached Milan at one o'clock in the night. Next day I went to Como, to the guy whose car I once brought to Romania (Dan).

He tried to find his acquaintance, but nobody was at that address. A neighbor said no Romanian had ever lived there. Dan had another acquaintance in Trento whose address he had received from one of his relatives. He went back to Milan and then to Trento. He checked out the address. Again, nothing came of it. His last resort was the contact of one of his cousins in Modena. He found him living in a caravan and working for an Italian family. When Dan arrived, his cousin Paul tried to get rid of him. However, Paul was questioned by his Italian employers whether he knew Dan at all. Paul confirmed he did and finally had no choice but to share his caravan with his cousin. Dan got work with that Italian family and had to pay Paul for accommodation. He worked for a while for these Italians. As the Italian employers did not fulfill the official criteria, they could not issue papers and legalize him. After a while, Dan decided to come back to Borşa, as he missed his family.

[Then, two to three months after coming back to Borşa], I decided to go again [to Italy]. [This time] I took more money with me. I had a good knowledge of all borders between Romania and Italy. I went with another three Borşeni. I was their guide now. We were planning on passing through Croatia but the police caught us. We stayed half a day at the office of a border crossing point and they sent us back. "No problem," [I said]. They let us go, but I knew another crossing point a bit further. Croatians let you go, but the Slovenian border guards could also stop you. When [we finally crossed the border illegally], the police chased us by car. We ran through bushes and managed to escape. It was eighty kilometers to Trieste and we decided to walk the whole distance. It took us about three days of walking in the mountains along the road to Trieste. We had no food and no water; it was terrible. Finally, we arrived in Italy, in a village near the harbor of Trieste. We had some money and entered a restaurant. We made a phone call to Treviso to some friends to come and pick us up. We hid the bags outside together with our passports in case the police caught us. The *Guardia di Finanza*[23] turned up and we could not run away. We stayed one night in detention. They issued expulsion letters for us [and let us go]. We didn't [go back] and remained in Italy. [From Trieste] I took the train to Modena [where I was able to find work]. I worked there for the following years (Dan).

Finally, Dan's employer issued papers for his legalization. After many irregular crossings, Dan was finally able to travel legally between Italy and Romania. He currently works in Modena, in charge of the operations of a construction company at one of its sites. Over the years he was able to bring his family over too, and planned to remain in Italy for a longer period of time.

My analysis of these two cases highlights the difficulties encountered by first migrants in their attempts to stay in Western Europe. In both cases, the migrants had to come back to Borşa on repeated occasions. For the first migrant, the accident in France changed his plans, while for the second, the living conditions in Milan and the desire to see his family made him return. Both cases also show the fragility of migration arrangements and the problem of scarcity of available information. In the first case, Dumitru was not at all prepared to migrate to France, and he had a great deal of luck finding assistance centers in Paris. On his second migration trip, Dan also repeatedly tried to find his acquaintances from Borşa, but he failed twice. Only the third attempt was successful. Migration was risky. Both migrants chose the passage through the former Yugoslavia. In other cases, migrants crossed irregularly through Austria, but the territory of former Yugoslavia was more often preferred during the first years of migration.

Although the migrants repeatedly returned to Borşa, they were pushed into migration again by the worsening economic situation back home. The sharp decline in the economy plus stories of other migrants' success, as well as the increasing number of acquaintances they had in Italy, motivated these people to migrate again. It is thus apparent that for these two migrants, migration, though difficult, was still seen as a means of financial salvation when they decided to try again to migrate. Moreover, even when a migration attempt failed, migrants gained knowledge and skills, thus increasing their chances for a successful migration later.

Gradually, too, migration tended to become easier and procedures standardized. This was the case when migrants made irregular crossings of states' borders near the border crossing points, instead of choosing random points. Again, when arrangements with their guides failed, they knew enough to walk along the main roads until reaching the nearest city. These migrants continued their migration projects despite difficulties and lack of information. During this period the success of migration was random, depending on the migrants' luck and the living conditions they had to put up with, especially situations of human degradation and with high social costs. Dumitru, who was a technician in Romania, had to starve in Paris, to eat from garbage bins, and to sleep in inadequate conditions. Dan was often in the situation of having to walk long distances to reach his destinations. He lived in tents in Milan, and on boats in Venice harbor. These people left their families behind in order to escape impoverishment in Borşa. Even though they had a marginal position abroad, they felt they had no other choice. As the situation grew progressively worse in Romania in the 1990s, these migrants considered they had to take risks and accept the situation as it was until they could obtain some sort of work. They had to accept the fact they were irregular migrants and had no possibilities for ascending the social ladder abroad, only to be able to feed their families back home.

The migration of another first-mover, Adrian, will show that incipient migration was not always so difficult, as migration control was often ineffective. Despite the risk of possible imprisonment, people continued to migrate and some made their way without being stopped. Over time multiple migration routes and strategies developed. At this stage migration was unorganized and supply-driven: people migrated in the absence of migration arrangements and social ties to Western Europe because of the degrading economic life in Romania.

THE STORY OF ADRIAN

I conducted the interview with Adrian in his newly opened pizzeria in the center of Borşa. He was not the first one to open a restaurant in the center, but he was confident it was going to make money. He was a successful migrant in 2005 when I carried out the interview. He had started a company in Italy, where he had employed some other people from Borşa, and now his investment plans in Romania were also looking bright. In Borşa he opened a pizzeria and was also involved in the construction sector together with two of his brothers, building houses for other migrants in Milan. Adrian had intended to return to Romania at the time of the interview. But he remained in Italy until one of his daughters received Italian citizenship. As he maintained, ever since he migrated from Romania at the beginning of the 1990s he was determined to succeed.

> I went in 1993 because I wanted to build a future for myself. In Romania I worked as a bookkeeper and administrator at a school, I even had three jobs at once. Despite this, my salary was meager. I decided to migrate illegally. I went with three other persons to Hungary. [In a town] we took a taxi to the border with Slovenia. We crossed the border [illegally] and used the same taxi in Slovenia until we reached the first town. We traveled further by bus until we reached the Italian border. We crossed at night at Opicina, but we were not able to catch the bus in Opicina on the following day. After ten minutes, the police arrived and took us to their office. The interrogation started, on how and through where we arrived in Italy. We were returned to Slovenia and imprisoned (Adrian).

In that prison, Adrian was locked up with some fifty other Romanians. They had no information about whether they would be released or sent back to Romania. Living conditions were poor: rooms were overcrowded and food was bad and insufficient. They initiated a strike, but nothing changed. Surveillance conditions were not strict, and he was able to escape one afternoon together with some other Romanians. They managed to find a taxi driver who brought them to the Italian border, and they all crossed the border irregularly. Afterwards, they moved to Milan. Adrian stayed with some acquaintances from Borşa. They finally reached the tent park on the outskirts of the city, where they were able to find shelter. They learned about seasonal jobs in Venice and moved there, but eventually they made it their practice to come to Milan whenever their work was over. Finally Adrian moved to Trento, where he managed to find longer-term employment.

From the analysis of these three cases one can see that the migration of these pioneers was originally directed towards different European countries, and they eventually moved to Italy, where they found better conditions. We can conclude that for these early migrants their social ties abroad were not always useful. They used "checking" strategies. When something failed, other strategies were used, as happened with Dan on several occasions. They employed a multitude of strategies to overcome control by state authorities. Especially the first two cases illustrate this. The police caught the migrants, but the penalties they applied did not make these people abandon migration. Furthermore, when no labor opportunities presented themselves, they could still use Milan as a place to rest and from where they could continue their search for work. Even though living conditions in the tent camp were poor, the emerging web of social ties and the sources of information it offered were crucial for the newcomers who were in desperate need of employment.

Despite the difficulties migrants encountered, structural conditions in Romania, namely the sheer impoverishment, pushed migration from Borşa in this initial stage. These structural causes had a different role in the following two migration phases, when other causes, such as the establishment of migration networks, the labor demand in Italy, and particular circumstances in the origin community, became the essential factors driving migration.

In the beginning, basic shelter was a main problem for Romanian migrants. At the tent camp in Milan migrants could find supportive relations by living among their own. Basic concerns included savings, sanitary conditions, and the minimizing of risks.[24] The inadequate living conditions were not unique; on the contrary, we can find similar situations in other cases of irregular migration (Bleahu 2006; 2007; Massey et al. 1993; Todesco 2008). In the Mexican case for instance, "during the first few trips and in the early history of migration from a community, migrants tended to live in rather Spartan conditions, sleeping in barracks or sharing apartments with other men and sleeping in shifts to save money" (Massey, Goldring, and Durand 1994, 1499).

In my case study, migrants did not come from the middle class and were not among the richest in their origin communities, as is documented in other cases (Durand and Massey 1992). Although there were economic differences within the origin community, the resources used for migration by the first movers were provided to a large extent by the Romanian state, which offered severance payments during the process of restructuring industry. The first migrants were among those with more initiative and more support from their families; indeed, some were even postsocialist entrepreneurs whose businesses had collapsed. The decaying economy did not mean that people had no financial resources, but that living standards were rapidly decreasing and savings were being lost.

Besides, whereas under socialism people had secure jobs, this situation had changed in post-socialism. When people lost jobs and migration came to be seen as a profitable investment, they mobilized money to migrate: especially after 1996–1997, they used savings, sold wood, took loans from relatives and friends, or even used wedding money to finance migration. The increase in insecurity and the compensation payouts when the mining industry was restructured pushed migration tremendously. Then people started to migrate on a large scale, being helped both by the development of the visa industry and by the networks of Borşeni residing abroad, who were able to arrange invitations for others.

In this period, some of the main strategies for migration included: (a) invitations received from Germany followed by an irregular move to Italy; (b) labor contracts in Western Europe (such as for temporary agricultural work) followed by irregular stay; (c) tourist trips to Western Europe; (d) visas bought from migration brokers;[25] (e) irregular group crossings of borders; and (f) individual or small group border crossings.[26] These strategies of migration towards diverse European destinations fueled the growth of migration. The infrastructure of migration developed through the visa industry, which provided visas for Western Europe, and through transport companies, which brought migrants to Italy. Networks also consolidated, driving migrants predominantly to certain specific places of destination. Information on migration spread within Borşa, encouraging the migration of others. Because of the multiplication of social ties abroad, the risks and uncertainties of migration decreased over time. In the initial stages, however, migrants faced miserable living conditions during their move to the West and encountered a number of risks and difficulties.

THE DEVELOPMENT OF MIGRATION: KINSHIP NETWORKS

The rapid development of migration to Milan had been brought about by a combination of factors, among which the most important were the demand for informal labor and the lax regulation of migration. Besides consideration of structural factors, my analysis was carried out using migrant network theory, because the development of migration from Borşa was triggered by the expansion of migrant networks. Migrant network theory attempts to bridge the gap between structures and individuals in explaining international migration (Goss and Lindquist 1995). Migration is not driven solely by individual migrants' decision-making processes, or by structural labor demands and the logic of capital expansion in the destination countries. The theory argues that migration develops over time its own social structure that perpetuates it.

The development of migration relies on social ties and on the spread of networks (Faist 2000a; Massey et al. 1993). Through the use of social capital, resources for migration such as financial means and information accumulate. The extent of network ties is related to the richness and diversity of social resources (Lin 1999, 483). Since migration implies costs and risks, the first migrants are those who are better able to take on these risks. Analyzing a number of migrant communities in Mexico, Massey argues that migration becomes less selective and more families become involved in the migration process (Massey 1987, 1374).

This theory is often used together with the theory of cumulative causation to explain how migration perpetuates itself in migrants' origin communities. It states that "once initiated, the process [of migration] builds upon a growing base of knowledge, experience, social contacts, and other forms of social and cultural capital in self-reinforcing fashion" (Massey, Goldring, and Durand 1994, 1503). Moreover, research on migration networks recognizes that networks develop in phases (Düvell 2005; Faist 2000a; Guilmoto and Sandron 2001; Massey et al. 1993). The first phase is that of the pioneers of migration (Cvajner and Sciortino 2009; Düvell 2005; Massey et al. 1993), when relatively little migration occurs. After pioneers report success in their migration and small migrant communities are established in the destination countries, migration chains develop (Düvell 2004; 2005). In Borşa, the transition from the first to the second phase of migration coincided with the compensation received by the Borşeni from the Romanian state. Suddenly, many were able to finance their migration. Because people lost their jobs, they felt their households were at risk. This increase of migration that developed after 1997 was mainly supply-driven. However, as time went by and networks developed, the demand side gained primacy.

During the first years of migration individuals or small groups had multiple migration strategies. In time, more organized strategies came about. In most cases, they appeared as specialized forms of guiding and managing irregular migration, conducted by migration brokers and migrants' weak ties. In either case, they provided visas or guided new migrants over the borders. Still, the crossing of borders often remained irregular and entailed risks, which were, however, lower compared to the risks that had existed in the early stages of migration, when migrants migrated autonomously.

> I left in 1997. We are a big family. We told one another that there was a person who could carry migrants to Italy for 2,000 DM (1,000 Euros). I talked to that person and I went. [From Romania] to Hungary we crossed the border with our passports. From Hungary we had to pass with a guide to Austria, [crossing the border] through forests. We were five persons, three women and two men, all from Borşa. In Austria the guide waited for us and brought us further, [to the border with Italy]. From Austria to Italy, we again had to cross the border [irregularly]. The guide waited for us [in Italy] and brought us to Milan (Marin).

The development of the visa industry played an important role in this migration, and migrants could simply buy West European visas on the informal market in Borşa. These were either tourist visas or invitations that entitled the carrier to apply for a visa for a West European country. Vlad, who was thirty years old in 2005, recalled how he moved to Italy in 1998. He had to pay about 2,200 DM (1,100 Euros) for a two-week Austrian visa. He gathered the money in Borşa while working at the school, and afterwards as a public guard. In addition, he made money by selling wood. His wife worked too. They managed to save money regularly, 100 DM (50 Euros) one month, 50 DM (25 Euros) the next. After one or two years he had the money to go to Italy.

In these cases, trajectories were clearer and migration simpler than before. Compared to the first period of migration, these trajectories had also changed. If initially many migrants used the territory of former Yugoslavia, which involved more risks, in the second phase the visa industry re-routed migrants through Hungary and Austria: "In 1999, I went to Hungary on a tourist visa. I stayed in Budapest together with two other boys from Borşa. [We had to wait about] two weeks in order to get Austrian visas. Then I went straight to Italy to my cousins" (Octavian).

Organized tourist vacations were also used. The advantage in such cases was that transportation costs were included. Ioana migrated using a trip to Switzerland. When I did the interview at her place in 2005, she was living close to the main road, four kilometers away from the center. Ioana was an engineer in Borşa and the decision to migrate was not easy. But in 1998 she got pregnant and hadn't enough money to raise her child. But she knew very well about the difficulty in migrating to Italy and how the first movers went there. She was unwilling to take the risks this involved. She preferred to borrow money from one of her uncles who had worked in Germany previously and went with a tourist trip to Switzerland and then to Italy. When she arrived in Italy, she called her cousin who came to pick her up from one of Milan's bus stations. She didn't feel that migration was risky. Indeed, the possibilities of being caught by the authorities were lower compared to other migration strategies. Although her migration entailed costs, these were preferred to the migration strategies, and to the risks they involved, that migrants had recourse to in the first years of migration.

In comparison to the first migrants, Ioana adopted a safe strategy. There were financial risks, and she could not allow herself to fail and to lose her investment in migration. But she took the loan in Romania judging that the risks were low and she was sure of success. In similar fashion, others migrated to Milan irregularly, but they had the support relations in Italy on which they could rely. Already at this stage potential migrants were aware of more successful strategies and their migration chances. Many of them had extended social ties in Italy, ready to provide support.

Access to Western Europe was thus gained either by paying for costly visas or through organized excursions, or by having relatives or acquaintances in Western Europe who could provide invitations. In Borşa there were still many people choosing to cross the borders irregularly, but many now tended to prefer the safe (and even legal) strategies where migration was organized by brokers and through social ties abroad. The example of Ileana shows how different migration strategies might be employed, how migration decisions were made, and how social ties (here kinship) functioned in facilitating access to Italy.

Ileana and her husband had jobs at home but decided to migrate to Italy after hearing the many success stories of acquaintances and relatives who went to Italy. Ileana's husband, Ion, was a miner and had taken voluntary retirement. He received a financial compensation which he used to migrate to Italy, buying a visa from a broker in Borşa for 2,500 DM (1,250 Euros). Once Ileana's husband made it to Italy, she also wanted to migrate. But she complained to her father-in-law, Vasile, about the high price she was expected to pay for a visa. Vasile was from Vatra Dornei, a town ninety kilometers away, that had once had a significant German population. He had German friends living in Germany. When he heard about the prices, he contacted his friends in Germany who issued an invitation to Ileana for free. With that invitation, Ileana was able to migrate to Western Europe, and she went straight to Italy.

Finally, in other cases migrants obtained temporary labor contracts in agriculture in Italy and then overstayed. Compared to other migration strategies, this was safer because it involved a labor contract, hence financial support and accommodation for the first period of migration. When their labor contracts ended, large numbers of migrants remained in Italy: "There were groups of fifty to sixty persons, in general organized by one person. They moved there and remained. Some worked on agricultural farms, and they gained contracts for the others" (Tudor).

At this stage, migrants tended to employ more costly but safer migration strategies and trajectories, but this did not mean that risks could be completely avoided. In all cases there was an element of risk. Even when official arrangements allowed legal entry to Western Europe, people were sometimes forced to undertake irregular crossings of borders in order to go from one country to another.

> I went to Italy with a contract for work in agriculture, with a friend from here, a neighbor. My wife went first [legally] to Germany in 2000. She worked there for two to three weeks and then went to Italy. She was caught in Austria together with five other women but they were released. [The Austrian authorities] said that if they caught them again, they would go to jail (Alex).

In this period individuals preferred to choose formal arrangements. As migration was already developed, the effectiveness of various different strategies had already been tested. Migration brokers were generally people from Borşa on whom others could rely. Trust was involved from the very beginning when pioneers moved to Western Europe, but it gained in significance in the second phase of migration, when the structuring of migration and of migrants' labor market incorporation was based on enforceable trust and kinship obligations. Trust is a form of social capital (Portes and Sensenbrenner 1993) that can serve to regulate free-floating social relations in unstable economic contexts (Hart 2000). Different from kinship or contracts in regulating a negotiated order among individuals, trust is based on the belief of social actors that a certain conduct on the part of others will be realized. In contrast to generalized trust as a category entailing an element of belief, enforceable trust retains a sanctioning capacity within a given community. Migration from Borşa was first based on enforceable trust emerging from membership in the community of origin. In time, however, it was increasingly kinship (and kinship obligations) that came to play a prominent role in migration and in migrants' incorporation.

Initially, kinship did influence migration in a limited manner, by providing resources for migration. This was the case when people borrowed money from their relatives, for example. Nevertheless, migration was then rather a matter of individual projects. As migration developed, kinship provided the main support, allowing not only other household members to migrate, but extending migration to the larger kin group. In Borşa, there were large networks of kin relations,[27] which became extensively exploited for the purposes of migration, especially when the state offered severance payments. Migrants used kinship obligations to finance migration, and enforceable trust to get access to Western Europe when they made use of migration brokers from Borşa.

In this respect, I consider the case of Sandu typical for this type of migration and for the ways in which migrants' kinship networks functioned. I met Sandu for the first time in August 2005, during his summer holiday. He had come back home with his wife and four children. The first interview I carried out with him was in the house of some relatives they were visiting. There were some other people there as well, as Sandu's brothers also dropped by. During our talk Sandu said more than once they were sort of migration brokers, in fact, and they had helped a large number of his relatives and friends to get to Milan.

Sandu arrived in Milan with a false visa that cost about 2,000 DM (1,000 Euros) in 1997, together with two other people from Borşa. After three months, he got his first job in construction work through the help of a friend of his. After one year, he started to send money back to Romania, to help others to migrate. After attaining legal status, which happened in the second year after his arrival, Sandu rented a flat in Milan. He lived there with his wife, who moved there from Borşa. Their house became a transit house. "We were a sort of migration office," Ruxandra, Sandu's wife, said cheerfully. They first paid back about 5,000 DM (2,500 Euros), representing loans taken in Borşa to finance their migration. Afterwards they started to facilitate the migration of their relatives.

The mechanism of migration was the following: Sandu sent money back home to one of his relatives, Vali, in order to help him migrate. With this money Vali bought a Schengen visa in Borşa and went to Italy. Sandu had already looked for a job for Vali and put him up when he arrived. After getting a job, Vali started to contribute to the household's expenditures. Finally, Vali paid back his loan and remained in Sandu's flat. The money of his loan was sent back to Borşa to finance the migration of others. Afterwards, migrants moved to other houses in Milan. A system of common housing emerged. This mechanism was part of a kin-based migration strategy that facilitated migration. It illustrates how migration developed from Borşa and how kinship networks functioned.

> Once you tell them to come, it becomes your responsibility. We lived together with my cousins, and they started to come one after another. In our case, we gave money to most of those that passed through our house. They bought visas; it was pretty expensive at that time, and then they came to live with us [in Milan]. My husband's brother-in-law, his sister, and others came and we had to host them for a while in our house and to find work for them. We sent word to the others to tell them when to come. Sometimes we were ten to fifteen people living in the same flat (Ruxandra).

Sandu's case shows the ways in which kinship was mobilized and helps explain the quick development of migration. In such cases, kinship primarily provided support in Milan, and channeled information and financial resources. Although this mechanism was typical for the migration of the Borşeni, there were cases when kinship had a more limited role. For instance, people could migrate using their kinship ties but were not helped by their relatives in finding jobs. In other cases, migrants were able to migrate without the help of their relatives, but were hosted in Milan by them. There were also cases when kinship did not provide much support at all for newcomers.

In this second phase, migration from Borşa was similar to other migrations, where networks became autonomous from the conditions that generated them (Massey et al. 1993). As we have seen in the case of Sandu, the loan was used to bring a second migrant to Milan. By doing this, his network expanded and the chance of bringing other migrants increased as well. However, as migration standardized and more and more Borşeni resided in Milan, migration became increasingly driven by demand. Finance became an important factor, and newcomers were brought over by their relatives only when labor was available on the informal market. At the maturation stage of the networks, kinship represented the main migration mechanism—mobilizing information and resources and helping the newcomers to find accommodation in Italy.

Different studies have shown that Romanian migrants coming from the same locales of origin had multiple destinations (Stan 2005a; b; but also Bleahu 2004b; Cingolani 2009). But migrants chose predominantly certain particular destinations in accordance with how their networks developed: for example, from Marginea to Turin (Cingolani 2009), Vulturu to Rome (Vlase 2008), Negreşti to Paris (Diminescu and Lagrave 1999; Alexandru 2006), Dobroteşti to Madrid (Şerban and Grigoraş 2000), and so on. Similar to the migration of the Borşeni, other Romanian migrants used multiple strategies to reach their destinations. Networks were formed based on kinship and friendship ties. In the case of Spain, for instance, Bleahu (2004b) shows that a pioneer brought to Barcelona his friends first and then his relatives. In some other cases (Şerban and Grigoraş 2000; Stan 2005a; b) members of religious minorities migrated first, and then migration expanded to the migrants' kin relations.

In all these cases, migration expanded due to labor demand overall in Western Europe, although the decaying Romanian economy was what pressured people to migrate in the beginning. Thereafter, local labor demands in Western Europe shaped how networks adapted and developed in the destination countries. This was the case of the migrant network from Vulturu to Rome (Vlase 2008) that subsequently feminized due to the increasing demand for female labor in Rome. In Milan, migrant networks were very large and included kin members, both men and women, who found jobs in construction and the caring industry. This extensive net of relatives and acquaintances would be crucial for people's economic participation and success in the next few years.

FREEDOM OF MOVEMENT IN EUROPE

A major status change occurred for Romanian migrants after January 1, 2002. At that date the visa requirements to enter EU countries[28] were removed for Romanians. Migration was no longer difficult, and most studies of Romanian migration speak of 2002 as a turning point. Migration increased dramatically after this date. Before 2002, the maximum rates of departures of Romanians[29] were estimated at about 7 per thousand. After 2002, it reached as high as 28 per thousand (Sandu 2006, 24) of the Romanian population between the ages of fifteen and sixty-four. In the following years, Romanians migrated *en masse*, mainly to Spain and Italy.

In other cases, for example the Mexico–U.S. migration, the costs of migration fell due to the development of networks. "After the first migrants [migrated] . . . the costs of migration [were] substantially lowered for friends and relatives living in the same community of origin" (Durand and Massey 1992). But the Romanian case differed. The costs of migration dropped substantially, from 1,500 to 2,000 Euros, the costs of visas and transportation, to just 150 Euros, the transportation costs, when Romanians were exempted from EU visa requirements. Risks of expulsion also decreased at this time. In the following period, the role of kinship in migration decreased.

In Borşa migration increased dramatically from this point, and mostly in just two years: "The big outflow was in 2002, when the border was no longer closed. Before, only those who had money could go, or those with acquaintances abroad. But after 2002 everyone could go" (Sanda). Today we can realistically estimate that between 30 and 50 percent of the population from Borşa has migrated[30] in the last fifteen years.

In the Mexican case (Massey, Goldring and Durand 1994) migration needed to acquire a certain level of momentum and then turned into mass migration through the development of networks. When freedom to travel in the EU was granted to Romanians in 2002, migration from Borşa was not yet at this level. Hereafter, the changing structures of opportunities available to Romanian citizens turned it into a mass migration. People migrated mainly to northern Italy, to Milan, Treviso, and Trento, where they could find many opportunities for informal work. Moreover, the numerous groups of friends and relatives from Borşa already residing there were able to provide support for the newcomers, which was essential under conditions of irregular migration. Around Milan and the nearby cities, the networks of Borşeni multiplied. There were also migrants without much support, but for most of the Borşeni, migration to Italy was no longer difficult. People had enough information concerning migration, and the risks they might encounter were easily overcome. In order to highlight the shift in migration strategies that happened after 2002, I present the case of Vlad, which displays the ease with which people with established networks in Italy could migrate and find jobs after 2002.

Vlad was thirty-five when I saw him in Borşa in the summer of 2005. He came from a well-off family. Prior to migration he attended the university in Cluj, the largest university center in Transylvania, and dreamed about moving there at a certain point. But he was not successful in finding a decent job, despite having a degree in technical engineering. He also tried to go to the UK, but had no clear opportunity to move there. So he gave up the idea. The alternative to migration to Milan would have been to stay at home and live off his parents' income, which he rejected altogether.

He then moved to Italy to his brother who lived near Milan. He went first to Italy during holidays and didn't have to pay anything for accommodation. Only when he obtained a job did he start sharing household expenses with his brother. In Milan he was able to meet other Borşeni, and by chance one of his former schoolmates offered him a job.

> I got used to life in Italy. I first worked for about three months in constructions, renovating buildings, decorating interiors, and so on. Afterwards, I came home for a while. I moved back to Italy after a month. Now I have been working in a furniture factory for about one and a half years. The plant is ten minutes away from home, but I still have to work under the counter. If there is a control, I have to run. There are still risks. If you get ill, or if the police catch you, and you are expelled, Romanian authorities confiscate your passport for five years. It is not "la vie en rose," a "pink" life, but it is a bit better than in Romania (Vlad).

Motivations to remain in Italy changed. As Radu puts it, migration entered into a sort of normality after 2002 and the organized migration that prevailed before was replaced by shuttle mobility in which migration was no longer seen as a long-term irregular stay. In the opinion of some of my interviewees, migrants' decisions after 2002 did not involve *a priori* decisions to settle in Italy. People could come, see how life in Italy was, and return home. They could learn the language and reflect whether migration might be beneficial to them: "I went after 2002, and I stayed one and a half months. I came back to Borşa to take care of my daughter. The second time I went there for three months and I started to learn the language. The third time I decided to stay" (Sanda).

The ease of traveling and the falling costs of migration enlarged the category of potential migrants. After 2002 economic reasons were not always the only push factors. Raluca was about twenty-five in 2005. In Milan she worked in the fashion industry, a job she found relatively easily, only three years after her arrival in Italy. However, her first move to Italy was made out of curiosity.

> I worked here [in Romania] in a restaurant and "Italians" (Romanian migrants in Italy) would always say: "Goodness, how nice it is in Italy!" I had never heard about Italy and I didn't intend to go there. But I talked to my friends: "Let's go, girls!" We went in the beginning of 2002. I first moved to Bergamo, to some friends. I went with my passport and 500 Euros. Then I went to Milan to one of my cousins (Raluca).

Even fresh high-school graduates now had the choice to remain in Romania or to go to Italy. In many cases they chose Italy out of curiosity, fashion, naivety, or simply for fun. The role of the culture of migration for young people was important here. As Alexandru (2006) and Horváth (2008) show, in Romania migration created a new context of socialization for youngsters in which their transition to adulthood took place. Especially in remote areas such as Borşa, migration organized the youngsters' aspirations in the areas of education and labor incorporation. Migration becomes culturally a desirable life conduct, a stage towards adulthood. Like the cases discussed by Horváth (2008), the passage from youth to adult life was realized during socialism through incorporation in the socialist labor market, which provided youngsters enough certainty to start their families. Once industry collapsed after 1990, the post-socialist economy was too weak to absorb the large pool of potential workers. Besides, the labor market offered very often temporary job contracts and poor salaries, leaving youngsters unable to make ends meet or set up new families. After 2002, the passage to adult life was realized in the context of migration. Teenagers from Borşa who did not aim to continue their education, preferred to migrate. As Constantin recalls, he first went to Italy after finishing high school for a vacation. He had fun there with his brother and traveled around a lot. But as he did not have plans to continue studying, his brother asked him what plans he did have, and if he wasn't interested in going to Italy and working.

Due to the low costs and the increase ease of migration, temporary workers changed their stay strategy. Previously, after obtaining a temporary legal contract in agriculture people had no choice but to overstay. After 2002, they could shuttle between Italy and Romania and opt for temporary labor arrangements if they wanted. This temporary migration was often legal and generally defined by particular time limits.

Dan was one such migrant. He obtained a labor contract from his brother-in-law, for which he had to pay a lump sum at the beginning. He went to Italy every year but had no intention to settle there. Once he arrived in Italy, he worked in the orchards in Trento, in northern Italy. He was noticed by one Italian employer, who, after watching him working, offered him better wages. So Dan changed his employer. He continued going to Italy seasonally to work in agriculture. He was pretty comfortable with this arrangement that offered better pay than in Romania and a safe contract with housing and insurance included besides the actual wages.

Additionally, there were irregular migrants who shuttled between Borşa and Italy. Migrants could now go to Italy, find irregular employment, and come back to Romania every three months, thus managing not to exceed the period of legal residence in the EU (the arrangement in place between 2002 and 2007, when Romania joined the EU). Such was the case with Lucia, who worked irregularly in a factory on the outskirts of Milan. "For me everything was simple because my relatives were already there. I come for one to two months, then I move back for two months, it depends . . . I go when I am in the mood for work. Last time I came back to Borşa after my period of stay expired" (Lucia).

In 2007 Romania became a new EU member state, Romanian citizens becoming European citizens. This change of status did not affect migration from Borşa substantially, as a large part of the young people were already residing in Italy. Migration still continued among the youth and the temporary workers who continued going to work in agriculture in northern Italy. Nor did the current economic crisis produce much change. Despite major effects on the Italian construction sector, and an increasing uncertainty that people complained about, there is no noticeable increase in the return of migrants, as the crisis hit Romania particularly strongly and unemployment was growing.

As a result of the strong migration that has taken place over the last years, the circulation of persons and capital between Borşa and Italy developed and a number of significant changes appeared at the local level, which I will discuss in the following chapters. After 2002, these provided new motivations for migration, different from the causes that triggered migration in the 1990s. In a sense, it was no longer the wage differentials solely that influenced migration now, but the marked difference in consumption patterns and the different status of migrants against the nonmigrants.

NOTES

1. The Moldavian region of Romania is made up of eight counties on the eastern side of Romania.

2. This was actually a process that occurred in many former socialist states. For the Russian case, see Burawoy (1996).

3. This compensation amounted to about 4,000 Euros, but due to inflation they barely received a half of that. It was, however, enough to finance emigration.

4. See also Crăciun, Stan, and Grecu (2002), Horváth (2007).

5. For a more general discussion see Chelcea and Mateescu (2005).

6. Thus according to ISTAT, the Italian Statistical Office, the number of Romanian migrants was: 95,039 on December 31, 2002; 177,812 in 2003; 248,849 in 2004; 297,570 in 2005; 342,200 in 2006; and 625,278 in 2007. However, official figures hide the real number of Romanian migrants in Italy, hence the marked differences between the data of ISTAT and the data of Caritas, which suggest the figures are higher.

7. See ISTAT. Data for the province of Rome (Rome and the surrounding localities).

8. See ISTAT. Same for the province of Turin.

9. See ISTAT. Data available for the province of Milan. According to the same source, there are 56,000 Romanians in the region of Lombardy.

10. 943.

11. 39.

12. These amnesties are called *sanatorie* (Colombo and Sciortino 2003, 197). These *sanatorie* were: Legge 943/1986, legalizing 105,000 migrants; Legge 39/1990 (Martelli), affecting 222,000 migrants; Dl. 489/1995 (Dini) embracing 246,000 migrants; and Dpcm 16.10.1998 (Napolitano), affecting 215,000 migrants. The last *sanatoria* was in 2002, embracing 650,000 migrants.

13. No. 91, 5 February.

14. On the regulation of Immigration and the Legal Status of Foreigners in Italy (no. 40, 6 March; then Consolidated Act no. 286, 25 July).

15. Norms Concerning Immigration and Asylum (no. 189, §0 July).

16. We may add to this that Italy has low levels of asylum seekers (Finotelli 2006).

17. The following figures illustrate the growth in the number of migrants: 630,000 in 1993, 886,000 in 1996, 1,116,000 in 1998, 1,350,000 in 2001, 1,990,000 in 2003, and 2,950,000 in 2007. But the real number of migrants was undoubtedly much higher.

18. Vişeu is a small town in the region which used to have about 3,000 ethnic Germans. Many of them migrated to southern Germany (Ingolstadt, Nuremberg, and Ansbach). During my fieldwork in Nuremberg I interviewed some of them. Their relatedness to Romania was extraordinarily similar to that of the migrants from Timişoara, although their context of migration and socio-professional backgrounds differed.

19. A local group of ethnic Germans.

20. See the first part of the thesis. Information based also on personal interviews in Nuremberg.

21. The main railway station of the city.

22. A city in northern Italy, not far from Milan.

23. The Italian law enforcement agency.

24. I will analyze these aspects in the following chapter, which deals with the migrants' incorporation in Milan.

25. Prior to 1999 one visa cost about 2,000 DM (1,000 Euros).

26. Romanians could travel through Serbia, Hungary, and the Czech Republic, for instance, without visa requirements. From there on they had to cross irregularly.

27. For example, during my fieldwork I found cases where migrants had no less than 100 cousins. In as far as families in Borşa were large this case was not unique. This gives an idea of the potential for the development of migration if resources were mobilized through kinship ties.

28. The visa-free agreement for Romanian citizens was adopted by the EU countries but not by Great Britain.

29. This does not necessarily refer to numbers of migrants.

30. These estimates are relative. No clear statistical data on migration are available. However, in my interviews with local authorities and local statistical offices, as well as with non-migrants and migrants from Borşa, medical doctors, and school teachers, it was generally stated that more than 60 to 70 percent of the labor force migrated. This coincides with the data on employment, namely that 11,000 people lost their jobs. We should also include the younger people who accompanied the adults in migration.

FIVE

Making Milan Their Own

From Precariousness to Adaptation

Migrants from Borşa migrated mostly to northern Italy, especially to Milan. Men were generally employed in the construction sector, while women worked in the care and cleaning industries, and in different plants around the city. All the migrants I interviewed were involved in one of these job categories. In the context of strong irregular migration and little state control, networks from the same place of origin facilitated migration and played a significant role in the incorporation of newcomers into the informal sector.[1]

In the first part of the book I showed how networks of migrants from Timişoara served the purposes of socialization in Germany, but played almost no role in migration and in migrants' labor market incorporation. Migrants from Timişoara encountered an "advantaged context of reception" (Portes and Böröcz 1989, 618) measured in terms of institutional support for their economic and social incorporation. In contrast, migrants from Borşa found a "handicapped context of reception" (idem), which tended, over time, to turn into a "neutral context of reception." A context of reception is described as handicapped when the host society has low receptivity for migrants and "immigrants are negatively typified by employers, either as unsuitable labor or as suitable only for menial jobs" (idem: 619). The context of reception is neutral when "immigration is permitted, but not actively encouraged, and . . . no strong stereotypes exist about the characteristics of immigrants" (idem: 619). In this vein, I consider that Milan offered a handicapped context with regard to the institutional framework for receiving migrants, and a neutral one in respect to jobs.

As emerges clearly from my research, migrant networks proved essential for the migration and incorporation of irregular migrants. The structuring of such networks points towards the crucial importance of the embeddedness of networks and social ties to local social contexts (Vertovec 1999; 2001; Portes and Sensenbrenner 1993), which is one aspect of the creation of migrants' locality (Smith and Guarnizo 1998). Later on, when migrants became legal residents, they could take advantage of insertion into institutions too: registration at financial offices, enrollment at schools for their children, registration with the health system, and so on.

In fact, the migrant community in Milan was divided between legal and irregular migrants, with legal migrants mediating the incorporation of the newcomers into the informal sector. During their social and economic incorporation, migrants maintained continuous relations to Borşa, sending back remittances and waiting for the newcomers to arrive in Milan. In the previous section I analyzed the process of migration from Borşa to Milan. In this chapter I discuss the pathways to migrants' incorporation. I describe the ways in which people adapted in Milan, how migrants organized their housing and found employment, and how relations between migrants changed with the regularization policies of the Italian state. I then document the changes that occurred after 2002, when visa exemption was granted to Romanian citizens traveling to other EU countries. I discuss how Romanian irregular migrants adapted in Milan and actively enhanced their social and economic status, and show how they moved upward on the social ladder from a condition of marginalization to one of incorporation into the Italian labor market.

GETTING TO MILAN

In my first weekend in Milan, I went to *Milano Centrale*, the main train station. In front of the main building some dozens of Romanians were gathered close to a kiosk serving hot coffee, brandy, and sandwiches. The Romanians formed a large group. A few dozen meters behind, on the right side of the station's main building, Ukrainians and Romanian-speaking Moldovans gathered in two other distinct groups. Towards the left side, there were Moroccans and migrants from Sub-Saharan Africa. In the weekend, the large square in front of *Centrale* was the gathering point for migrants from all over Milan. There I encountered Romanians from many parts of the country. People exchanged information on jobs and other opportunities. At the same time, they swapped jokes and shared the latest news from Romania. They told each other their life stories and why and how they arrived in Italy. When I arrived in 2004, many of these migrants were irregular and had left behind families and children waiting for them in Romania. On the left side, close to the Ukrainians and Moldovans, the migrants had organized a flea market where all sorts of things could be bought cheaply. The Italians, too, came to find bargains there. *Centrale* was a meeting place where people got to know each other and learn about life in the city.

One Saturday I met Nicu, a migrant from Borşa. He was working casually and was looking for more stable employment. So he regularly visited places in Milan where migrants used to meet: *Centrale, Molino Dorino*, the Romanian Orthodox Church, or some of the parks in the suburbs of the city. For single migrants without acquaintances these were the only places where job opportunities could be found. He was often successful when he went to these places. Italians and Romanian middle men came by whenever they needed workers, and there were always migrants looking for new flatmates.

We first went to *Centrale*. After spending a few hours over a coffee and a *Vecchia Romagna*—a strong Italian brandy—Nicu made contact with some other migrants. They exchanged phone numbers in case any job offers appeared. We went afterwards to *Molino Dorino*—to have some fun, as Nicu said. *Molino Dorino* was a parking lot near one of Milan's metro stations. Cars, buses, and minibuses arrived there from Eastern Europe, mainly from Romania, Moldova, and Ukraine. It had the atmosphere of a bazaar. Bus drivers were selling cheap Eastern European products including foodstuffs, alcoholic beverages, and music CDs. The music was loud. Romanian Gypsy music covered the noise of the arriving and departing vehicles and people's conversation. There were people selling sausages, and in a corner there was a kiosk offering Romanian beer, meat rolls, coffee, and brandy. Some while later, cars from Romania crowded into the parking lot. Some loaded "Italian" goods into the trunk to take to those back home; others collected the packages sent by relatives from Romania. Christmas was approaching, so relatives at home were sending Romanian foodstuff to parents, brothers, or husbands in Italy. The migrants liked sausages, smoked meat, and cabbage, as well as *palinka*, a strong plum brandy. In exchange, migrants sent back other things, usually cheaper textiles or other products they thought those left home would value. When Nicu and I arrived he decided to make some acquaintances among the Moldovans. As he put it, there were more women than men coming from Moldova, and he was alone and looking for a partner. After half an hour's walk through the bazaar, he attempted to launch a conversation with some of them. In a corner some migrants from Moldova were enjoying Russian music. Nicu joined them eventually. After a few words and some brandy, a small ad-hoc party started in the open space of the parking lot.

* * *

The first people arriving from Borşa had virtually no support relations in Milan, and found accommodation only in the city's parks and in abandoned houses. Food was available from charitable organizations such as Caritas, a Catholic Church organization. Migrants searched for jobs in Milan and the surrounding cities, moving wherever temporary work was available, or trying to secure longer-term employment. For many who were attempting to find jobs and housing in northern Italy, Milan was only a place of short-term residence.

But it was a very important first step for the pioneers of migration, who had no networks in Italy: "The problem was to find work and a home. [We moved to] Milan because in the smaller cities it was [very] difficult. Staying in Milan was important [as there were more opportunities]" (Adrian).

A parking lot on the outskirts of the city became the place where people from Borşa could meet, expand their networks, and make contact with their acquaintances. The tent camp, called *Zama*, was situated in its vicinity. Nevertheless, it was not only migrants from Milan who used *Zama* as a meeting place, but also others coming from Trento, Treviso, and other locations in northern Italy. Migration routes to Italy passed through Milan, and the existence of a growing number of Borşeni gave the newcomers the motivation and opportunities to remain there for at least a certain period of time. *Zama* was like *Molino Dorino*: a place where migrants could meet others and find out about jobs and accommodation. The only difference is that *Zama* was used only by buses coming from Borşa or the Maramureş region. Here all the buses for northern Italy arrived. As Tudor, one of the migrants, mentioned: "They all stopped there. From there everyone was distributed [to a certain destination]. At *Zama* it was like a center for managing migration, but without [a formal] office. Many people used to come to send packages home."

Many still remember their first migration days—the fact that despite the difficulty of accommodation, Milan could always provide plenty of job opportunities. Thus migrants from Borşa were able to settle in large numbers in Milan, creating dense sets of networks. These networks "locked-in" (Guilmoto and Sandron 2001), that is, they got more and more embedded in the social context and facilitated migrants' incorporation, so that over the years they provided them not only with accommodation but also with access to multiple economic opportunities. "Most of the people I know are in Milan. Many people from my neighborhood in Borşa went to Milan and to the surrounding cities. Milan is one of the richest cities in Italy, with many jobs. This is why many people go there. If you go to Rome, for instance, you cannot find as many jobs as there are in Milan" (Vlad).

Romanian migrants were initially very mobile—people were moving from one city to another in a constant search for jobs (Bleahu 2004b; Constantin 2004). Migrants' territorial mobility in Italy has also been underlined by Schuster (2005), who found high rates of mobility among migrants in Italy until the point where they could become settled. In the

Figure 5.1.   Zama, the Borşeni's parking lot, close to the former tent camp.
Source: Author's personal archive

case of the first migrants from Borşa, mobility was a strategy up until the point when migrants received longer-term employment. The first migrants employed exploratory practices in searching for jobs: they moved from one city to another and relied on the support of their peers from the tents in Milan. Mobility between different Italian cities remained high, at least for a certain period of time. This was the case with Dana, a migrant woman who left Romania taking with her phone numbers of friends who had promised her jobs in Italy. She was hosted by one of her neighbors for the first one and a half months. She didn't find work and she didn't know the language. She then moved to Trento, where she started taking care of an old man. After two to three months, her employer died. One of her neighbors found another job for her. She had to go through a trial period [living with an Italian family]. But afterwards she obtained a position. She worked there one and a half years. She went after that to Milan, where she took another job.

Over the years, however, territorial mobility decreased among the Borşeni as networks expanded in Milan and migrants found steady employment. As Eve points out (2008), the evidence suggests that with the development of networks migrants tended to settle in certain locales and they became less peripatetic. Compared to migration to Nuremberg, where institutions such as receiving camps, labor offices, and companies formally mediated the incorporation of migrants by providing housing and support for incorporation into the labor market, the Italian case is strikingly different. Here migrants had to be mobile and to cultivate social ties with other migrants and Italian employers. This was especially the case of irregular migrants who had no opportunity to obtain formal employment or housing contracts.

FINDING HOUSING

> People had difficulties in Italy. Nowadays there is such luxury. Everyone has a place to stay. If someone goes with his wife, they may even have their own room (Ruxandra).

Housing in Milan involved miserable conditions for the pioneers. Compared to the cases presented in the previous chapter, where Dumitru had to sleep in garbage dumpsters in Paris, the conditions Milan offered were no better. Migrants were often in desperate situations: they had to sleep in empty trains, in abandoned houses, on park benches, under bridges, and so on. The migrants I interviewed complained about the precariousness of their living conditions. Making do in tent camps is in fact a strange outcome of Italy's migration policy, or better put, of the flagrant inability of Italy's institutions to deal adequately with newly arriving immigrants.

In fact, such tent camps with their wretched living conditions are a widespread phenomenon in Italy (Bleahu 2007; Todesco 2008), as it came out in the media in recent years, which revealed how many Roma migrants from Romania settled in similar conditions in large numbers. Such improvised lodging developed in Milan, Verona, Rome, and Turin as well, so rather than a marginal phenomenon, they are to be considered a structural outcome of the laissez-faire policy in place throughout Italy. By comparison, Romanian migrants in Spain or Germany were much better received, and in Germany migrants from Romania received organized housing.[2] Even irregular migrants in Spain were able to find better housing, as they were able to register with the municipalities and rent flats (Șerban 2008).

Migrants in Milan generally did not obtain improved housing until their networks managed to access the formal housing market, usually after some migrants legalized their status. As an example, the experiences of a young couple migrating to Milan offer valuable insight into housing strategies and how such situations were perceived by migrants. Dana and Eugen arrived in Italy by irregular means. They had no residence papers and didn't know the language. Dana found a place to stay at some friends, but Eugen was not allowed to stay with them and had to find somewhere to sleep in the open. It was winter and he had only a jacket on.

He remained on the street and went to the manhole of the heating system of the town to warm himself up. He would stay there for five to ten minutes, and then he would move further. He slept on benches, under benches, everywhere he could. He used to tell Dana he had lodgings. In reality he didn't. Eugen had to put up with the situation for some time. He was finally able to find accommodation only after he began to earn some income, mainly from some temporary work he obtained through the mediation of acquaintances.

Migrants from Borşa set up the tent camp at *Zama* in the first years of migration, so new arriving immigrants had a place to stay overnight. Besides the housing problem, irregular migrants encountered other difficulties: they were facing life in a new society, they lacked knowledge of the Italian language, and they were staying on an irregular basis. These risks made them easy targets both for other migrants who could rob them, and the police who could arrest them at any time. In this context, the Borşeni organized their own exclusive camp, close to the *Zama* parking lot, and Romanians from other regions were not welcome. In this way they could better protect one another. Sandu, whom I interviewed during his trip back in Borşa, went to the tent camp once in Milan. He was with another friend at that time, and they had to sleep on a bench at first. They had some money, about 120 DM (60 Euros). As he retold it, he was not able to survive more than a few days on it. Later, they got meals to eat at churches. Until he got a job, he slept in tents at *Zama*, behind some bushes close to the parking lot. Back home, the economy was collapsing, so he had no other option than to stay there together with fifty to sixty persons, all from Borşa.

The charity organization Caritas offered food and clothes to migrants. Migrants without employment were able to live in Milan, stay at *Zama*, and have a daily meal at Caritas. If they found any casual work, they could use this money to buy better food and ease their stay. As in other cases (Bleahu 2007; Colombo 1996; Massey, Goldring, and Durand 1994), migrants from Borşa at first lived in inadequate conditions, migrating and maintaining support relations with each other on the basis of locality of origin and friendship and kinship ties (see also Durand and Massey 1992). Migrants remained at the camp during their initial period of migration while they searched for jobs in different parts of the city. Nicolae, a migrant who crossed the Schengen borders together with ten other colleagues and friends from Borşa, arrived in Italy in a truck that had taken him through Austria in the winter of 1997. Nicolae lived for seven months in a tent at *Zama*. He found work from time to time with the help of other migrants, but he could not leave the tents until he could find longer-term employment. Later he could afford to pay for housing to a legal Romanian migrant who was subletting a place in his flat. The practice of having a long stay in tents was common in the period of early migration. Even if they got work, people were not entitled to rent flats as irregular migrants, and could only stay at other migrants' places, be they Romanians, Moroccans, or Nigerians. These Romanian migrants met regularly in city parks, in *Milano Centrale, Zama*, and *Molino Dorino*. As I have previously shown, the process of place-making in Milan was marked by activities of exchange, the making of new friends, and the sharing of culture. Particularly in parking lots, Romanian goods like beer, spirits, and food were sold and bought along with Romanian music. This pattern, of making new acquaintances in the public places of Italian cities, is also noted by Colombo (1996) and Banfi and Boccagni (2008). Colombo analyzes irregular migration in Milan, observing how migrants seek to make friendships outside their own groups in places where finding new acquaintances is easier. "To find some other migrants to communicate with is the quickest way to access different kinds of resources" (Colombo 1996, 54);[3] Banfi and Boccagni (2008) report the existence of a similar pattern among Ukrainian women in northern Italy, where such places provided migrants with opportunities and new social ties.

In comparison to the situation in Nuremberg, place-making in Milan did not involve a lively network of Romanian ethnic retail businesses. There were no established Romanian shops or restaurants such as came into existence with other ethnic groups like the Turks in Duisburg (Ehrkamp 2005) or the Indians in Auckland (Friesen, Murphy, and Kearns 2005), to name just a few. Ethnic businesses were developed by Asian, Latin American, and African migrants in Milan, who opened a number of shops with ethnic goods such as food and cloths. Internet cafes appeared all over the city. From there, migrants could call back home to friends and relatives and meet with their acquaintances.

After a few years, when migration had developed and the Borşeni started to legalize their residence in Italy, living in tents was replaced by a system of shared housing between irregular and regular migrants. Regular migrants rented flats and sublet rooms to irregular migrants. Newcomers from Borşa could then easily find accommodation and work. The risks associated with migration were minimized when they had the choice to live with their relatives who were already residing in flats. A monetary-based system of migration and support developed, while use was made of shared housing in bringing over new relatives and enlarging kin groups in Milan. This shared housing system was a much better alternative to living in tents, but in most cases the houses were still overcrowded and could offer little more than "a roof above one's head" (Ioana).

Raluca was in her twenties when she first arrived in Italy. When she left Romania she thought she would receive proper accommodation there and had no idea about the difficulties she would need to overcome. Upon first arriving she was hosted in a house she described as being in horrible condition. She wanted to go back, but she couldn't because her boyfriend was already working in a laundry and she herself had to start working the day after her arrival.

These houses were a very important factor in migrants' incorporation. They facilitated migration by providing some sort of living conditions on arrival and lowering the level of insecurity. I regard Sandu's story as a typical one of migration from Borşa to Milan. He and his wife brought at least migrants from Borşa, provided them with housing, and made arrangements for their employment. Ruxandra recalled the facts:

> Initially, you were happy to have a place to sleep. You wouldn't even dare think about renting your own room. We were the first to move here from our neighborhood in Borşa. [Our house in Milan] was a sort of transit place until the other inhabitants of the house got out of poverty, at least to a degree. There were three beds in a room and we were even sleeping three persons on a couch. When you had to go to the toilet, you had to take care not to step on anybody. Others were sleeping in the second room. What was I supposed to do if they had no other place to sleep? You had to host them. Could you let them sleep in the street?

As she went on to relate, the others received money from them so that they were able to come to Italy. Ruxandra and Sandu had their money in Borşa. The newcomers borrowed from them and came to Italy. They did not charge the newcomers for housing or food when they had no jobs. But afterwards, they shared the costs. Ruxandra's brother was the first who arrived. Then she brought her sister-in-law over. They shared the flat with Sandu's cousin.

Then Sandu's brother-in-law arrived, then his sister, and his brother. Sandu and Ruxandra had to find a job for them, host them; then after a few months they had to find lodging somewhere else and had to leave. There was no certainty about jobs for the newcomers, so Sandu and Ruxandra were taking on the risk of accommodating and supporting newcomers for extended periods of time.

The practice of financing migration, housing newcomers, and finding jobs for them continued over the years, and the group expanded. Sandu and his wife, Ruxandra, lived between 1997 and 1998 in their first flat measuring about twenty square meters. Sandu, his wife, six of Sandu's cousins, and one of his nephews lived together in it for most of this time. When Sandu rented out space in this flat, some of his relatives came from the tents to live with him and they shared the costs. About fourteen temporary residents passed through his flat, mostly cousins and siblings of Sandu's relatives. They could not stay long since space was scarce. They were not asked to pay, just to contribute to household expenses if they had a job.

In 1998 Sandu and Ruxandra moved to a second flat. This was a bit larger, forty square meters compared to twenty square meters in the first one. They rented the second flat, which was in the same building as the first flat, between 1998 and 2000. Only Sandu's nephew stayed there for a longer period. All the migrants living in the second flat were brought to Milan by Sandu and Ruxandra. There were five siblings of Ruxandra and a brother and a cousin of Sandu. Apart from these, many other temporary migrants also passed through this second dwelling; sometimes mere acquaintances from Borşa were also hosted. Payment was similar as in the first house: the migrants would only share the common costs.

The third place of residence was no longer rented, but bought by Sandu and Vlad, the brother of Ruxandra. Two other brothers of Ruxandra followed them from the second flat to the new place, but they rented something else afterwards. Over the years other cousins of Ruxandra were also hosted, but they eventually moved to other places, too. Two migrant brothers coming from a different region of Romania were taken in by Sandu together with their partners, but they were asked to pay some rent. They left after a while and two other migrants arrived instead. The migrants whom they took in, and who were neither relatives of Sandu or Ruxandra nor from Borşa, were nevertheless trustworthy and had to pay rent.

In the following I present the scheme of how Sandu's kinship network functioned and the type of residence the migrants had over the years. In Figure 5.2, men are triangles and women are circles. Sandu and his wife Ruxandra are represented as couple 1. Migrants 2 to 7 are Sandu's cousins. Migrants who lived temporarily there were relatives of migrants 2 to 7. Migrant 8 is Sandu's nephew. In the second flat, migrant 9 is Sandu's brother and 10 is a cousin. Migrants 11 to 15 are Ruxandra's siblings. The third flat was bought by Sandu and Vlad,[4] his brother-in-law. Both couples are colored in black in the diagram. Migrants 16 to 22 are Ruxandra's cousins. Most of Sandu's and Ruxandra's relatives would come to the second and third flats, received financial support for migration, and were put up by Sandu and Ruxandra. Migrant 23 was in Borşa the neighbor of migrant 21. The brothers in couples 24 and 25, as well as migrants 26 and 27, are not from Borşa, and had to pay rent. The woman in couple 25 is Italian.

This scheme does not capture the whole process of renting and subletting sleeping places, but it does show its main principle of organization: kinship obligations organized both housing and migration from Borşa. As they provided lodging to a large number of migrants from Borşa, these houses were generally overcrowded. Space was scarce and had to be managed carefully:

> At that time we stayed many in the same flat, living with relatives from Borşa. I was sleeping with my husband in a small bed. I was working at

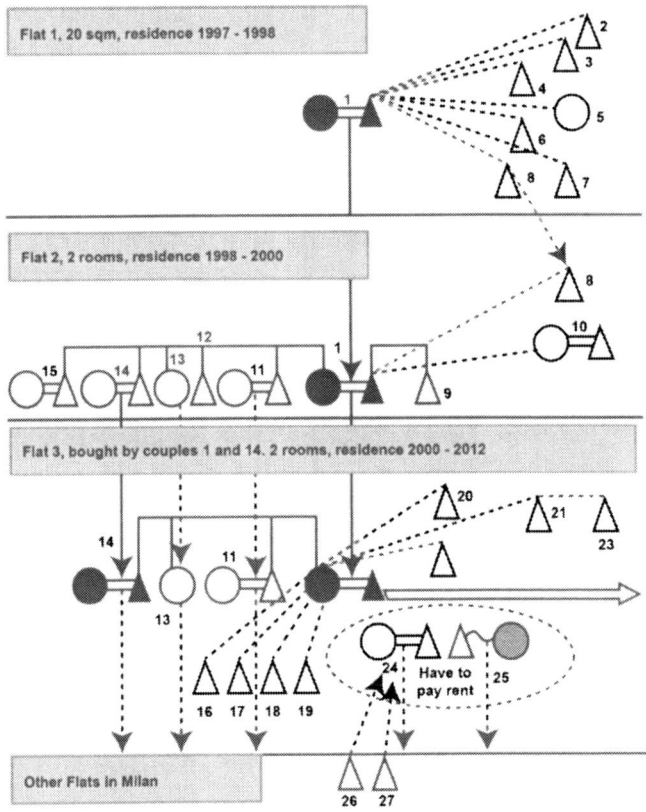

Figure 5.2. Migrant network of Romanians in Milan. Source: Author's personal archive

> that time and I could only come home for weekends. We were around seven or eight persons in a two-room flat. Once we were even ten. We were a couple, and intimate things happened. We were two families in a single room; you could imagine [how it was] (Ruxandra).

I arrived in the third flat in 2010. It was located in a relatively new condominium in one of the new quarters on the outskirts of the city, in the north of Milan pretty close to one of the metro stations. The flat was not big, about sixty square meters. It was composed of two bigger rooms, the lobby, a kitchen, and bathroom. When I arrived, the two large rooms were hosting Sandu and four of his employees. At that time Sandu had already opened a company in Milan, hiring a number of people from Borşa. They were all young and their wives were in Romania. Ruxandra was also in Romania, together with their children. The flat didn't offer proper living conditions for families and it was pretty untidy. One of the rooms was Sandu's; the other was used by his employees. In Sandu's room the window had a hole in it, to allow a better connection for the satellite plate he bought in Romania. "It's better like that," he said, "to get a better connection to the Romanian TV stations." As they were working all day long, they didn't have time to clean the place properly and put it in order. But staying there was very practical, as it was located close to the metro station and the highway.

Because of the limited hosting capacity in these flats and the growing number of relatives from Borșa wishing to come to Milan, migrants were always looking for new places to sleep. Enforceable trust was used when their place was made available to people from Borșa whom the migrants knew. For people outside of Borșa, whose acquaintance they made in Milan, and for whom they managed to find temporary accommodation, contractual relations were set. If they happened to be accepted as flat-mates, as in the cases of brothers 24 and 25 in Sandu's flat, and migrants 26 and 27, they had to gain the trust of the others and to pay rent. The sharing of costs was common practice only between those with kin ties.

The mechanism I have summarized is a part of a kin-based migration strategy, whereby migration was facilitated by earlier migrants in both locales, in Borșa and in Milan. The example of Sandu depicts the process of migration from Borșa and the expansion of the networks in Milan. Sandu and Ruxandra gained prestige within their kin group for facilitating the migrants' trip to Milan and housing them: they had made possible the others' access to migration and to a better life. Social prestige was not constructed primarily by comparison with Italians or with other migrants, but in relation to kin members or other Romanians. Even if they continued to have menial jobs for a couple of years, and even if Sandu had slept at the tents upon his arrival in Milan, they received much appreciation from the newcomers afterwards. During interviews, Sandu and Ruxandra remembered the events in Milan as an episode in the adventures they were finally able to emerge successfully from.

In certain other cases I investigated, such houses were used to put up migrants from Borșa who did not belong to the kin group. Such is the case of Nicolae who started to host Borșeni from the tents at *Zama* after he received legal residence and rented a flat. In the beginning he did not charge migrants for lodging but nor did he support them to find jobs. Afterwards all the newcomers had to share the expenses and later they started to pay rent too.

Nicolae's flat was differently organized than Sandu's. In 2004 when I visited him, Nicolae was renting a three-room flat in San Donato Milanese, a small town of about 30,000 very close to Milan. And Nicolae lived very close to the metro station, so he could get to the city easily. In one of the rooms Nicolae, his wife, Elena, and their ten-year-old daughter, Alexandra, lived; in the second room, Nicolae's second daughter, Oana, and Bogdan, her fiancé. Both rooms were pretty small, so the organization of the two couples was a bit difficult. In the third room, the larger one, there were three couches and a bed. These beds were offered to different people. Despite having less comfort, subletting the bigger room covered a large part of the rent Nicolae and his family had to pay. Nicolae's living conditions in Milan contrasted starkly with those he enjoyed in Romania, where he had a big house of about two hundred square meters.

This example is similar to that of other migrants who hosted migrants "from the bushes"[5] out of compassion for their situation, and also in order to share the costs of their own house. These were mostly cases of people from Borşa helping each other out. Such lodging agreements multiplied after 2002, but nevertheless for a certain period of time insecurity about housing remained latent. The promise of a place to sleep did not always mean that the place was indeed available when they turned up. Even though there was a continuous process of improvement in the housing situation in Milan, there were many newcomers who were receiving misleading promises: "In Borşa they would say: 'Sure, you can stay at my place.' And when you got there: 'Sorry, you cannot stay at my place, I am sharing it with someone else'" (Magdalena).

Over the years the networks of Borşeni multiplied and many of them received legal residence. So the number of rented flats also increased. After 2004–2005, housing was no longer a problem for migrants. Even though they sometimes had to share the same room, their situation was to a degree normalized, and cases of living at the tent camp almost disappeared by 2005–2006. Afterwards, shared housing was still preferred for financial reasons, as it reduced the costs of living substantially. There were other practical reasons as well: living together with other Borşeni not only removed the risks migrants faced staying at tents, but information about employment opportunities was more accessible: "We developed some solidarity there although we paid for everything. But we had a place to stay; we were not sleeping 'in the bushes' anymore" (Octavian).

As far as migration is concerned, much standardization of migrants' practices has been seen over the years, as well as improvement and relief of the hardships of life. The initial risky circumstances were replaced by easier, if more costly procedures. The locality of the Borşeni still remained under a cloud of mistrust, insecurity, and lack of state support. But a different, much more tolerable situation arose when the networks multiplied. The status downgrading which usually occurred during the first years also reversed and migrants' socioeconomic status improved over the years.

In comparison, Romanian Germans in Nuremberg could take advantage of the housing available in the organized camps for *Aussiedler*. As they were allowed to rent flats shortly after arrival and were granted full access to labor markets, housing was not a problem at all. They were never in the position of needing to develop such adaptive strategies as the Borşeni did, or to rely so much on networks and social ties for their accommodation. By and large they had secure living conditions in Nuremberg and were very well received and cared for by the German authorities.

FINDING JOBS

Migrants from Borşa achieved labor incorporation through the Milanese secondary labor market. There they encountered a strong informal economy where they could find jobs due to a strong discrepancy between labor demand in the construction and home-care industries on the one hand and feeble recruitment policies on the other (Colombo and Sciortino 2003). The combination of an aging population in Italy and a welfare regime which put all responsibility on Italian families to take care of their senior members (Banfi and Boccagni 2008) created demands for home-care work (Castagnone and Petrillo 2007; Torre 2008; Vlase 2008). Yet there was no large-scale labor recruitment organized by the state to fulfill the demand. Irregular migration intensified after the mid-1990s fueled by the demands for such labor. New arrivals started coming not only from Romania but also from Africa, Asia, Latin America, and from other East European countries such as Albania, Ukraine, Moldova, and Poland.[6]

Irregular migrants employed in 3D jobs, as in other migration contexts, "[depended] heavily on the structures which they [became] incorporated in, and, in particular, on the character of their own communities" (Portes and Sensenbrenner 1993, 1322). With little knowledge of Italian and no institution to mediate labor market incorporation, irregular migrants from Borşa had to rely on their own networks. I have previously described how migrants managed to come to Italy and how they organized their housing. I now propose to look at how irregular migrants used their ties with other migrants and with Italian citizens in order to become integrated in the labor market.

Migrants' access to the secondary labor market did not depend on specialized training, as they worked in the construction and care industries. By comparison, migrants in Germany had to have completed professional education and training courses in order to obtain jobs, ending up having jobs which corresponded with their training. In Italy, skills and qualifications were acquired at the workplace. Such a lack of formal criteria created flexible opportunities for migrants to take up jobs. This explained their quick incorporation into the labor market and the flexibility that migrants from Borşa demonstrated when they changed their workplace. Such was the situation of Octavian, who was able to take up a decision-making level job without having the relevant specialized education. In Romania Octavian was a waiter. He had no experience whatsoever in construction. But in just a few years he was able to coordinate the work on a construction site and was now in charge of a team of workers.

His employer relied on him very much, only checking the drawings and watching how Octavian was leading the team.

In this context, migrants' initiatives were especially important during the first years of migration when pioneers had to find jobs without having access to a large number of social ties. Such was the case with Dan, the pioneer whose story I presented in the previous chapter. He moved to Italy and tried repeatedly to use his social ties to obtain employment. And yet he failed. Even his cousin tried to avoid him. The labor market was not only informal, what work was available was casual, and migrants were often cheated and exploited, depending on their access to information and labor opportunities. In the previous chapter I showed that it generally took quite a long time before first-wave migrants found some sort of employment. Dan was twice given false addresses, and the strategies he employed to get a job failed him several times. Another migrant, Adrian, looked for jobs, but his attempts were only rarely successful. Migrants were also often misled and sometimes not paid for their work by fellow Romanians, so that for those lacking the right social networks finding employment could indeed be difficult. Codruţ complained about this state of affairs. "When my brother was unemployed, some other Romanians would come and say, 'I can help you; tomorrow we'll meet and I'll take you to work.' He would wake up as early as five o'clock in the morning, but they never showed up. Sometimes they would call later: 'Sorry, I couldn't come today, leave it for some other time.'"

But the Italian economic context was uneven, and in different circumstances migrants could find jobs with ease. Another example, Tudor, shows that even without the advantage of migrant networks and information about the labor market in Italy migrants were all the same able to find jobs quite easily sometimes. Tudor left Borşa in his twenties and moved to Italy, where he found a job in a pizzeria. He was able to extend his stay over several years. Upon arrival he started to look for jobs, asking in restaurants if they needed someone. He found work in one of them. He liked the job and remained there. In the beginning he washed dishes, but after two years he was already baking pizza. He worked at the pizzeria about one year. But it closed down and he moved to a plant producing spare parts for the car industry. He worked there for a while, but went back to working in the hospitality industry. For the rest of the time he was in Italy he worked in a number of different restaurants.

In most cases I analyzed, job-finding was mediated by others. When they looked for jobs, new migrants came into direct contact with Italian employers. They could get help with job information from other migrants, be hired by a Romanian employer in Italy, or could finally pay for a job offer through a job broker. Such opportunities were available in *Centrale*, in city parks, in *Molino Dorino*, or in *Zama*. These places, as well as the churches, were hubs of information for those in search of support, shelter, and jobs. Jobs were informally negotiated, sold, or offered to new migrants on the basis of trust between migrants, job brokers, and employers. The higher the number of social ties migrants had, the greater migrants' ability to adapt to the randomly available labor offers.

In Milan, trust was an important aspect in hiring someone. One day at *Centrale* I was able to observe how irregular migrants looked for new labor opportunities and how their life was influenced by uncertainties. I arrived there together with Gabriel, a migrant from Borşa. He was looking for someone he had an appointment with. As was usual every weekend, Romanian migrants gathered in front of the station, talking to each other, joking, and spending time together. Gabriel met Ana, a migrant woman from southern Romania, whom he knew previously. Ana was with Mariana, another Romanian woman who had come to Italy from Petroşani, a former mining city in southern Transylvania. Mariana had only a few acquaintances in Milan, and Ana was one of them. Mariana had no employment and was desperate to find something soon, as she was short of money. Ana said she might know of something. Meanwhile, the group of Romanians at *Centrale* grew bigger. Ana recognized some of them. There were two Romanian men working in construction. They lived close to Milan. As they had no time to clean their flat, they needed a migrant woman to take care of it and cook for the whole group. Ana was tempted to accept the job, but in the end she didn't. "I don't know them," she said. "How do I know they are trustworthy, serious people?" She needed the job badly, and was in a precarious situation, as she had little money left. Yet she wouldn't take the risk of working for people she didn't fully trust. In the meantime, the *Carabinieri*, the Italian military police, arrived at *Centrale*. Most of the Romanians were irregular. The whole group scattered. Mariana, Ana, and Gabriel fled from the station immediately.

When only a few of the Borşeni lived in Milan, they had to use their new ties with other Romanians which they had fostered in the context of migration, as was the situation with Mariana and Ana. But when relatives and acquaintances from Borşa started to arrive, interaction seemed to be conducted on more certain and solid ground: social relations were now based on kinship obligations and enforceable trust. As a consequence, migrants began to access jobs much faster and were able to find better offers. This is why they considered having acquaintances or relatives in Milan as indispensable. "This is how things are at the beginning; everyone has to have someone here. If you don't have someone, you can't do anything" (Bogdan).

At the same time, migrants entered into a process of constructing new support and trust relations with other migrants, with small entrepreneurs, and with job brokers. As Kindler (2008) points out, "with growing migration experience the migrant can balance the migration risks [by creating new social ties to employers]." In a similar vein, Jordan and

Düvell (2002) describe that irregular migrants survive in destination countries by using resources within their communities and by mingling with groups of citizens and with legal migrants who often live at the margins of society. Finally, irregular migrants "make themselves inconspicuously useful" (Jordan and Düvell 2002, 112). The Borșeni worked in the construction and care industries, where their work was needed. With the arrival of new migrants, they were able to provide job opportunities to the new migrants and organize themselves according to friendship and kinship networks. Jobs were found through weak ties to potential Italian employers, or sometimes to other migrants. Afterwards they were offered to other migrants within migrant networks. The strategy of developing bridging social capital to Italian citizens was employed in securing new opportunities. In many cases long-resident migrants cultivated friendships and acquaintances with Italians, as these persons could provide or facilitate new job offers for them or others.

> Once I used a ruse. I brought my boss [to Borșa]; I offered him accommodation. I arranged it at one of my friends' houses. They got to know each other. My plan was he would have the chance to get acquainted with my friend so that when my friend came [to Italy], I could ask my boss: "That person from Borșa came here. Don't you want to hire him?" When someone recommends you, it is only normal that you receive some sort of work (Dumitru).

To exemplify the process of migrants' adaptation to the informal labor market in Milan, I provide three further examples of migrants with different trajectories. These cases highlight the mechanisms employed by migrants to obtain labor. Two are cases of women working in the caring industry, and one of a man working in the construction sector.

Ruxandra, the wife of Sandu, migrated to Italy in 1997. Her husband had already found a job, moved to a flat, and considered he was able to provide her with decent living conditions. She learned about a job while she was still living in Borșa. The offer was from an Italian family living far away from Milan. After a week working for that family, she came back to Milan, where she found an Italian family to work for. She replaced a Romanian woman who was sick and had to go back to Romania. This second job was also short, as she was already looking for better offers.

In Milan she went to churches to look for other sources of support. A nun recommended her to some Italians looking for a woman for caring and cleaning work. Ruxandra went to meet them outside Milan. She was to take care of an old lady living with her son. She had to cook and clean the house.

> In the meantime, a lady [for whom I had worked] before, called me. She offered me a better wage, 700–750 Euros a month instead of 500–550 Euros. Besides, the job was located in Milan. Apart from mon-

ey, I received housing and food. I had to work 10–14 hours a day. Sundays were free. I moved to Milan. [For my former employers] I brought a niece of my husband's [to replace me]. [The new job] wore me out. That lady had some weird ideas and she always looked down at me. [I was so drained that I started to seriously lose weight.] Later the lady divorced [and moved away from Milan]. I started to work for different clients. My former employer liked me very much and she recommended me to other Italian ladies. [In Italy] everything is just about relations. I maintained [over the years] my relation with that lady and we kept in touch by phone even years after I ceased to work [for her]. Once I worked for a year at a factory, packing detergents, but I didn't like it. It paid badly and was far from where I was living. I finally decided to work in caring (Ruxandra).

Indeed, it was very important to foster weak ties to Italians in order to get jobs. Ruxandra obtained her first job through the Borşeni and later she was able to establish relations with the Italian women. Milan offered more than just poor living conditions to these irregular migrants; it also provided access to labor opportunities. Migrants were able to find better offers and change their employment. This was particularly visible when Ruxandra left for her second job, or when she decided to take care of Italian families instead of working in a factory.

Codruţ had a different but simpler trajectory. He followed his brother to Milan, where one of his acquaintances had opened a small construction company. Codruţ remained there for years and showed no inclination to change his job. Like Ruxandra, he also found his first job through other migrants from Borşa living in Milan.

He spent the first month trying to find work. Afterwards, in September or October he was able to find something through a colleague from Borşa, who was one of his neighbors. They met in Milan and Codruţ asked about a job. Ion, Codruţ's neighbor, said that his cousin Mihai might need some workers. Codruţ started to work for Mihai's company. He received about 40 Euros a day, but he had to work from five o'clock in the morning until late at night, installing windows and doors in newly constructed flats.

Ioana's experience was different from Ruxandra's and Codruţ's. She had a university degree from Romania and had worked as an engineer in Borşa. Because of financial difficulties she decided to go to Italy for a few years. Like Ruxandra and Codruţ, she found easy access to jobs using her ties with acquaintances. In time she developed good relations with her Italian employers, too.

I found work through my cousin. She had already been in Italy for about three months when I arrived there. I did the cleaning for a seventy-nine-year-old Italian woman. In general you had to pay to get a labor contract, but that was not the practice among us [the Borşeni]. I went to another old woman afterwards. She enjoyed terrorizing people. I couldn't stay there for more than three weeks. I had to live all the time with the lady, and I only had two to three free hours a week. I didn't like that job. I said to myself: "In spite of all the debts I have, I would rather simply give it up. If I find another job, fine. If not, I'll go back home and pay off my debts somehow." I went to the Church afterwards and there I met some women involved in charity work. [They facilitated a job for me] with another old lady. It worked out well and I started to learn Italian. When I couldn't understand something, I just called a friend of mine from Borşa who lived nearby and she translated for me what it was all about. I got 1,200 DM (600 Euros) a month. Saturdays and Sundays were free (Ioana).

In the meantime, one of her friends from Borşa had learned about a job taking care of a ninety-two-year-old woman with Alzheimer's disease. It was a better offer. As the woman was paralyzed, taking care of her was physically more difficult than with the others. Ioana received 1,500 DM (750 Euros) for a part-time working schedule. After seven months, she renegotiated the payment to 2,250 DM (1,125 Euros) for extended working hours. She worked there from 1999 until 2001. Nevertheless, she was dissatisfied with her status downgrading—an engineer working as a live-in care worker.

For Ioana migration was a painful experience. She considered she had lost something in migration, and she had never had time to visit Milan or the north of Italy, although she lived there for several years. She was aware that the Italians she worked for appreciated her and expressed sympathy for the fact that she, an educated person, ended up having to work as a care worker. For her, migration was difficult, an alienating experience involving long working hours and social isolation.

> Italy makes you get closer to other persons. You need someone around, to talk to or cry on her shoulder. I was working the whole time; I didn't have many contacts with other Romanians. I only had contacts with persons I already knew, my friends working in the area and my relatives. Working as a live-in care woman, thirty days out of thirty, twenty-two hours out of twenty-four, I couldn't always see them. They would visit me from time to time; that was not a problem. We could go out to a pub, for a coffee, or a walk in a park and have a talk. But my whole life was limited to this (Ioana).

However, Ioana was an exception in this respect. Most migrants did not perceive status downgrading as their main problem. As mentioned before, the majority of migrants came from lower-skilled jobs in mining and forestry, people who supplemented their subsistence consumption with a small-scale agricultural production. When the Borşeni moved to Milan most of them perceived this change as a gain. Despite all obstacles and the living conditions in overcrowded houses, they had the strong feeling of achieving something, as their financial gains were significant in comparison to what they could earn in Romania. These migrants went irregularly to Italy, and they expected no support from the Italian state and institutions. The way they saw it, they chose these risks and difficulties. When they recalled the difficult moments they went through, they did so with a sense of achievement: they had encountered difficulties, but in the end they overcame them.

In the cases presented above, the jobs were initially mediated by other migrants from Borşa, and in two cases they were found through churches. Ruxandra and Ioana were able to adapt to different requirements and even to construct social ties with their Italian employers. Their employers' trust in them was very important for accessing pools of potential new employers. Ruxandra was able to switch to better jobs by using her relationships with other migrants from Borşa and with her Italian employers. Similarly, Codruţ got his job via other migrants. In the case of the men I interviewed they had found jobs through the mediation of migrants who had gained the trust of some Italian entrepreneurs or had been hired by migrant entrepreneurs.

During the first years of migration, migrants from Borşa had some incidental support relations and friendships with other Romanian migrants. Nonetheless, at the time of my fieldwork support relations with other Romanians were infrequent. The multiplication of the groups of migrants from Borşa and the arrival of many more Romanians in Italy led to "closure" among them. "In Italy at the beginning [Romanians sometimes helped] each other, were more united. In time, there were too many coming and envy crept in" (Adrian). The growing number of migrants from Romania, Moldova, Ukraine, and northern Africa made the competition in the labor market tighter. In an attempt to protect their jobs, migrants relied mostly on kin members and on people coming from Borşa. Whenever they learned about new jobs, these migrants preferred to pass the tip among themselves, instead of letting the information flow to other Romanians.

> With time more [migrants] came so that today it is hard to find a place to work. The pay is worse than before. Whenever you demand something from your employers, they say: "There are those from the Republic of Moldova willing to work for half the price, just 500 Euros a month." Such migrants reduce wages, and if you go now and ask [for] 1,000 Euros, employers say: "Let's see how you work first" (Maria).

Migrants' incorporation in the labor market was also influenced by the emergence of Romanian ethnic businesses. Over the years, the number of legal Romanian migrants grew and many started to open their own businesses and companies. In 2008 there were 1,289 self-employed Romanians and businesses run by Romanians in Milan and 3,228 in the province of Lombardy as a whole (Pittau, Ricci, and Silj 2008). In Milan migrants from Borşa opened up companies in the construction sector, where they usually employed other Romanians. "The Borşeni coped well with their situation in Italy, and in Milan many of them now own companies. The ones who have companies bring other Borșeni to work for them and try not to pay them too much" (Vlad). Sandu is one such example. He migrated to Milan together with his wife and in a few years he was able to open his own company in the construction sector:

> After two years of regular work [in construction] I was more experienced. In the meantime I had made some acquaintances among Italians. At a certain point the company where I had worked closed down, and they owed us a lot of money. We didn't get it. Finally I decided to open my own company. With your own company [it is better and] you can make more money.

Despite the increased competition the expansion of networks brought more certainty about jobs compared to the pioneers' period. Not only had migration gotten easier and accommodation better, but there was also steady improvement in ease of finding new jobs in the labor market. Later on, the uncertainty related to accessing jobs in an irregular labor market remained, but other risks were significantly reduced. There was still the risk of losing these jobs, as work was carried out on a non-contractual basis and with no legal protection for workers. Maria, a young migrant woman, complained about the lack of legal protection. In her view, economic risks were not the only ones, and health problems could cause just as much trouble. She mentioned the case of a woman who, after working for years for an Italian family, was fired because she had health problems. "I know someone who worked four, five years for an Italian woman. They had a very good relationship. The Italian woman always spoke highly of her. Then the Romanian woman got a problem with her eyes and she was thinking about having them operated on. When she announced her intention [to the employer], she was immediately fired" (Maria).

Migrants were imaginative in obtaining jobs, and in reality difficulties were not less than in Romania. Studies on the informal economy and on societal transformations in Romania (Chelcea and Mateescu 2005; Crăciun, Stan, and Grecu 2002; Verdery 1996) show Romanian people have been very imaginative in overcoming difficulties and securing their livelihood during the transition from state socialism to capitalism. In Italy, too, these people encountered many difficulties; however, they derived greater benefits. The male migrants I interviewed could earn between 1,700 and 2,000 Euros a month, and the women between 800 and 1,200. These are above-average earnings for Romanian migrants in Italy, which is normally about 1,100 Euros a month (MMT and ASG 2007). Thus, couples living in overcrowded houses were able to save between 1,500 and 2,000 Euros a month. When migrants rented their own flats, their level of savings showed a marked decrease, but their living standards improved significantly.

My analysis of the strategies employed by migrants to obtain jobs revealed both the steady improvement of their situation and the constant relevance of kinship networks. By cultivating new ties with Italians, Ruxandra, Sandu, and Ioana generated new jobs to be distributed among their relatives. Ruxandra offered jobs to other migrants from Borşa too, apart from her relatives, and Sandu hired other migrants in his company. Labor was obtained in the context of strong competition between Romanians and non-Romanians. Kinship obligations and enforceable trust based on locality of origin were just as important in securing jobs as they were in migration and in getting lodging. The Romanian companies which started to appear in the labor market could also provide additional jobs. The position of these migrants improved constantly, yet their lives would continue to be beset by uncertainty.

By comparison, in other contexts of Romanian migration, success in the labor market was sometimes based on gender or religion. This was the case with some Romanian migrants in Rome (Vlase 2008), where the women were better incorporated than their husbands into the labor market. In Turin, the Romanian migrant networks show similarities with those in Milan. The members of the Pentecostal Church were better incorporated into the labor market than Orthodox believers due to their greater solidarity with each other based on religious ties (Cingolani 2008; 2009). In certain other cases, Romanian networks were subject to change in the process of migrants' incorporation, as was the case in Madrid, where migrants started to sever their ties to their fellow Romanians a few years after their arrival, once they adapted to the Spanish society and economy (Şerban 2008; Şerban and Voicu 2010). In Milan, the Borşeni maintained their kinship relations, using them with success. Despite uncertainties, these migrants were able to protect their jobs, negotiate their employment conditions, and change jobs when better offers came along.

LEGALIZATION

The number of legal migrants in Italy increased dramatically due to regularization campaigns. Mass amnesties (*sanatoria*) were in the end the most effective policies to manage irregular migration. Italian authorities regularized the irregular stay of a large number of migrants residing in Italy who could prove they had proper employment. The number of migrants legalized by the *sanatoria* kept rising in proportion: in 1986, 105,000 immigrants; in 1990, 220,000; in 1995, 246,000; in 1998, 215,000; in 2002, 650,000 (Colombo and Sciortino 2003, 197). In 2009 another *sanatoria* legalized 297,744 care workers (Colombo 2012).

By legalizing their status and winning the right to reside longer in the country, the lives of irregular migrants and their future perspectives in Italy changed fundamentally. In addition, legal migration also grew because of family reunions and the policies of legal recruitment of migrants which started to gain some traction. The number of migrants grew accordingly over the years: in 2002 there were 1,549,373 migrants altogether; in 2003—1,990,159; in 2004—2,402,157; in 2005—2,670,514; in 2006— 2,938,922; in 2007—3,432,651; in 2008—3,891,295; in 2009—4,235,059; in 2010—4,570,317.[7]

In contrast to irregular migrants, legal migrants were able to work legally, open bank accounts, take advantage of social benefits, rent and buy properties, and start their own businesses. The change of status, from irregular to legal, was deeply felt by Romanian migrants.

> [As an illegal migrant] you don't have an identity. I don't know what to say. For me it was very difficult to live four years without any document. I could not buy a TV, a phone card [for my mobile phone]. I always had to ask someone else to buy it for me. [I kept my money in the account of] my cousin; everything I saved in Italy [I put there]. After I got the papers, I did all these things by myself (Octavian).

One of the main difficulties irregular migrants complained about was that they could not come back to Romania to visit their families. Initially migrants could see their families only after obtaining legal status, for which they generally had to wait several years. This state of affairs led to emotional distress. Rarely, though, as in the case of Dan in the previous chapter, would migrants return to Romania, as they ran the risk of being denied entry upon returning. Their remaining in Italy was necessary for the success of their migration. In such cases, migrants' children grew up in the absence of at least one of the parents, a situation that was painfully felt by many migrants.

Moreover, as stated at the beginning of this chapter, irregular migrants faced various risks. Apart from living in very poor conditions, they could be prey to thieves and organized gangs, robbed by other migrants, and exploited by employers. Migrants also feared apprehension by the police or other authorities:[8] "You could be caught without papers and sent back to Romania. Your employment was informal, and if you were caught you could lose your money" (Alin). However, irregularity was perceived differently by migrants from Borşa, and the risks I list here rarely caused the migrants to suffer difficulties once their networks matured.

Besides, authorities were *de facto* tolerant with migrants. Even if migrants were caught without residency papers, the authorities did not proceed to their expulsion. Vlad remembers that he was stopped once by the *Carabinieri*. He was with some other migrants going to work at five o'clock in the morning. They were asked where they were going. Vlad and his colleagues said they were going to work, but had no legal documents with them, as the Italian employer just started their regularization. *The Carabinieri* saw their working equipment and let them go.

Companies hiring irregular migrants also risked being inspected by the *Guardia di Finanza*, the Italian law enforcement agency. Alin was an irregular when he was caught working for a construction company. He had no residence papers or labor permit. He received expulsion letters during the check-up, but he remained in Italy. "I used to commute to a construction site where I worked. One day, the inspectors arrived. [They caught me] and I received the expulsion letter. [I had to leave Italy within the next fifteen days.] If they had caught me again after these fifteen days, I would have risked imprisonment from two to six years. [But I stayed]" (Alin).

Trade unions, who wanted to limit informal work and protect legal workers in the labor market, were also entitled to check on Italian employers. This was a more effective mechanism of control, since migrants caught without papers could end up being fired by the company where they worked. This was the case with Alin, even though being caught did not result in his expulsion from Italy.

> Once I got a contract with a Sicilian who had hired about fifty people. I worked there about four months. One day the guys from the trade unions arrived. They caught me without papers and asked me to pay them a visit and to bring my residence permits. I didn't go, obviously. After a month they returned and recognized me. They called my employer, but he didn't answer the phone. They said they would come again. They were entitled to issue penalties, about 2,000 Euros for my employer, a penalty for the engineer, and one for me. They [could even] close down the company. My boss fired me, as it was too risky for him to be caught again (Alex).

In these three instances, I describe situations where irregular migrants came face-to-face with the authorities. Migrants lived in fear of expulsion, but these examples show that actually irregular migrants did not face severe control, and expulsion was easily avoided. This situation is rather general in Italy, where despite the high number of irregular migrants and official declarations about fighting informal labor and restricting irregular migration, migrants could easily cope with the difficult moments when they encountered the authorities. Control was in practice ineffective. The police, financial guards, and trade unions were entitled to limit the work of the irregular migrants, but as these examples clearly suggest, irregular migration and informal labor were tolerated, as in practice they were badly needed. The most effective way to cope with the large number of irregular migrants was, again, mass legalization.

Regularization was oriented towards labor migrants already in the country and did not involve the state in the question of the pre-selection of workers. The process grew more structured over time, from a more laissez-faire, to a stricter and clearer setting of criteria for granting residency to irregular migrants. To fulfill the eligibility criteria and to obtain residency, migrants would often use false papers in the amnesty campaigns prior to 2002. Afterwards, this was no longer possible, and they had to produce documents relating to housing and their informal workplace in connection with an application made by their employers. But by legalizing their stay, migrants' status improved. Their families were able to come to Italy and to obtain legal residency too, and migrants could travel freely between their countries of origin and destination. They could also enjoy the benefits of the Italian welfare system. Access to the health system and to unemployment benefits was the most important entitlement. If initially irregular migrants had to rely on their acquaintances and informal arrangements to find work, once they received legal status they could use intermediary companies, just as was usually the case for the Romanian Germans in Nuremberg. Ruxandra considered that "with residency papers you could go anywhere to look for jobs. I found a job through some labor force recruitment agencies. These agencies worked with some of the bigger employers. If you are lucky, you can work for years through these agencies."

Legalization also led to the changing of relationships between migrants. Legal migrants could now offer housing to newcomers, and collect rent or a share of house costs from the others. Moreover, legal migrants could open companies and work independently. Consequently the number of Romanian companies and of self-employed Romanians grew, providing an additional source of jobs for irregular migrants. Migrants from Borşa who opened up construction companies in Milan employed Romanian migrants and brought new migrants from Borşa when they needed more workers: "When I need four or five persons, for instance, I just make a call to Borşa and some boys will come" (Adrian).

Legal migrants also maintained their relations with Borşa, made investments there, and traveled back and forth between Italy and Romania. But they tended more and more to settle in Italy and started to buy flats in Milan. For such migrants, a process of settlement was in progress: "Once you got the papers, you started thinking about whether to remain in Italy or not to remain. They brought their families and their children too" (Tudor).

FREEDOM TO TRAVEL AND ITS EFFECTS IN MILAN

In accordance with the accession agreement between the EU and Romania, from 2002 Romanian citizens were exempted from visa requirements for traveling to the EU. Accordingly, Romanian migration to Italy has increased steadily ever since, as the following numbers indicate: 95,039 (in 2002), 177,812 (2003), 248,849 (2004), 297,570 (2005), 342,200 (2006), 625,278 (2007), 796,477 (2008), 887,763 (2009), and 968,576 in 2011,[9] the last official data.

The migration and socioeconomic incorporation of migrants from Borşa changed dramatically from this date. There was almost a mass migration of Romanians from Borşa and from many other parts of the country. Yet, compared to the Borşeni who already had networks in Milan, many of the Romanian migrants had nothing awaiting them when they arrived at the beginning of 2002. The informal housing market inflated because of the mass migration. Railroads, parks, and deserted houses around Milan were overcrowded with irregular migrants who had no proper sleeping arrangements. Many interviewees still remembered very vividly the first months of 2002, when large numbers of Romanian migrants arrived with no prearranged housing or labor offers.

The shift from 2002 meant for the Borşeni increased competition for jobs, but also the multiplication of support relations, as many newcomers from Borşa arrived over a very short period of time, rapidly expanding migrant networks. Since many had already managed to legalize their stay and rent apartments, housing opportunities for the newcomers were plentiful by 2004–2005. Migrants arriving after the year 2002 often perceived their migration and stay in Italy differently than the first arrivers. In the beginning, the possibility of access to Italy made migrants mobilize huge efforts and large amounts of money. In most cases migrants stayed irregularly. Afterwards, the Borşeni would often choose shorter stays and safer migrations. An example is Nicolae's brother, who would come to Italy only for secure short-term contracts. He did not have to remain in Milan for a longer time, as used to be the case before when people had no option but to remain in Italy until they received legal residency.

> Today they don't go if they don't have work in Italy. Before, you had to take risks, you had no relations in Milan. But you had to migrate. . . . Now, my brother wants to come to me, and I say: "You can come for three months after I find a job for you." He earns 3,000–4,000 Euros and then he goes back. It is easier to find jobs now; before it was more difficult (Ruxandra).

One may conclude that initially the incorporation of the Borşeni in the Milanese economy was structured along the lines of kinship and friendship ties from Borşa, with occasional support relations with other Romanians. At the beginning migrants slept in tents on the outskirts of the city and worked randomly. In time they were able to find longer-term contracts, rent or buy flats, and establish new ties with Italians to better access job offers for the whole kin group. Public spaces in Milan were important places where migrants could obtain new jobs, housing, and new social ties. Competition among Romanians increased after 2002 and the locality of the Borşeni changed again as an array of individual migration practices emerged along with the diminishing role of kinship.

In Milan, people were forced to undergo many difficulties in order to bring security to their lives and to get jobs. But the migrants' economic status improved. Due to the development of networks, information and resources became more available. Freedom of movement lowered the costs and the risks of migration. Regularizations (amnesties) in Italy opened up new opportunities for migrants, including formal access to the labor market and to the Italian welfare system. However, these migrants from Borşa remained a "close circle" among the Romanians. This is particularly visible when looking at their housing strategies and labor market incorporation. Labor opportunities were created by making use of weak ties to Italians or other migrants, but were distributed within the kin network. The shared housing was also organized with relatives and people from Borşa. In a few years through the use of extensive networks in a strong irregular context they were able to adapt successfully to an adverse context of reception caused by the lack of institutional support. These people faced socioeconomic downgrading at the beginning of their migration, as they had to accommodate to very poor conditions. But they obtained legal status after a few years, and by relying on their peers their economic circumstances improved greatly. The laissez-faire migration policy in Italy generated no high expectations among these migrants, so that migrants' improvement in status was felt as a well-deserved reward. The life of these migrants was initially difficult, pretty similar to how the Italian media portrayed the promiscuous life of Romanian irregular migrants in Rome or elsewhere. But these migrants were not disempowered. They applied themselves to finding jobs and improving their lives, and in the end they turned into successful migrants.

NOTES

1. See, for instance, Eve (2008) and Cingolani (2009).
2. See the first part of this study.
3. My translation.
4. The man in couple number 14.
5. That is, living in tents or in deserted houses.
6. According to ISTAT (2013), there were in 2008 officially 400,000 Albanians, 365,000 Moroccans, 156,000 Chinese, and 132,000 Ukrainians. This undoubtedly underestimates the real number of migrants.
7. The number of legal migrants on December 31 of each year (see www.istat.it).
8. Such as *Guardia di Finanza*, for instance.
9. Number of legal Romanian migrants (ISTAT 2013) on December 31 of each year.

SIX

Back Home

Prestige Gain, Remittances, and Social Change

During the summer, Borşa looked very different from November, when I was there for the first time, visiting Dragoş's father. The center of the city was crowded with new cars trying to get through the traffic jam. Most of them were bearing Italian plate numbers. The center was full of people hanging around, shopping and enjoying their free time, and it was pretty difficult to find a free place on a terrace or at a café, as everything was full. Between 2004 when I was first there and the summer of 2007, a series of new pubs, shops, and restaurants had been built, and a new supermarket appeared. People's colorful dress and their new cars contrasted with the grim atmosphere I encountered there in November.

In August the city came back to life as many of the migrants in Western Europe returned to spend their holidays at home. People met up with friends they hadn't seen for a year or more. Pubs and restaurants kept going until two o'clock in the morning. Shops extended their working hours. From among the people I knew in Milan I met Nicolae in the center. He had come by car with his wife and daughter and parked in the city center. He greeted everybody on the street. In his words, he was somebody in town, and people knew about him. He had also helped many people in Milan with accommodation and jobs, so he knew that many thought highly of him. Similar to many immigrants in Italy, Nicolae sprinkled his Romanian with Italian words. "Let's go, *faciamo un giro*[1] in the center. *Andiamo!*[2]" he said. I went with them, to see what was new in the town and learn about local news. After walking through the center and meeting many of Nicolae's acquaintances, we headed towards his place. He had just completed the construction of his house. It was a big two-hundred-square-meter construction, much more than what he and

Elena, his wife, actually needed. But he was sold on it, as in his view, it resulted from his work in Italy.

"You will see," he said, "when all the Borșeni come back from abroad, this town will flourish!" Nicolae and many like him genuinely believed there would be a time when they would all come back to Borșa for good. Their migration projects were conducted with the aim of return, as they saw migration to Milan as a temporary strategy to overcome economic difficulties. But time went by and their stay was prolonged indefinitely. Nevertheless, they continued to come back and send remittances, and they considered their stakes were in Romania and not in Italy.

* * *

The migration of so many people from this town produced considerable social and economic changes. In what follows, I analyze these changes and how they led to the reconstruction of locality (Vertovec 1999). Having previously investigated the migrants' incorporation in Milan, I will now turn to their transnational involvement back home. In the process, I will also attempt to shed light on the redefinition of migrants' social status and prestige. In the first part of the book I showed how migrants in Nuremberg reacted to prestige loss by becoming "Romanianized." In this part I will show how migrants gain social status and prestige at home and become differentiated from non-migrants.

Over the past ten years the literature on transnationalism has turned the focus of migration studies towards a reconsideration of the contexts of origin of migrants within a broader theoretical and methodological approach. Migration is no longer regarded as a unidirectional process from origin to destination followed by migrants' incorporation ending up with assimilation (Basch, Glick-Schiller, and Szanton Blanc 1994; Kivisto 2001; 2003). Rather, students of transnationalism have raised the question of migrants' double embeddedness in social relations, both in the origin and destination societies, and also of the active roles they play in changing their origin locales. I consider three theoretical debates useful for my analysis on the effects of migration and migrants' roles in their societies of origin. These are the theory of culture of migration, the relationship between migration and development, and migration and social change. The theory of culture of migration (Cohen 2004; Horváth 2008; Massey, Goldring, and Durand 1994) argues that by transferring remittances, goods, and ideas to origin communities, migrants alter the motivations for the out-migration of the home-stayers. Migration further generates relative deprivation and a relative frustration within non-migrant households vis-à-vis migrant households, as there is more that the latter are able to afford. On this basis, migration becomes socially and culturally a desirable social conduct. As the culture of migration becomes stronger, the motivations for out-migration grow. This theory stresses that once migration starts, it generates a process of social change that develops in such a way that makes further migration more likely.

A second theoretical line of inquiry framing my approach is on the relationship between migration and economic development, where development is understood in economic terms and as an improvement in living standards. Due to the steady growth of migrants' remittances over the past decade (Vertovec 2009), there is growing interest in researching the role of remittances in changing migrants' communities of origin (Levitt and Lamba-Nieves 2011). Thus migrants and migrant associations are often studied as developing actors (Østergaard Nielsen 2011; Gerharz forthcoming), a perspective used only to a relatively limited extent in past decades (de Haas 2008). Empirical evidence has shown that migration substantially changes migrants' locales of origin economically and socially, the whole world over (Black and Sward 2008; Delgado Wise and Covarrubias 2007; Rescher 2008; Vertovec 2000). However, a positive relationship between migration and development is not generally assumed as universally valid. The financial remittances that migration generates do not simply improve people's living standards. They may also generate economic dependency on these remittances and on migration, leading to massive depopulation and economic stagnation once migration intensifies (Delgado-Wise and Covarrubias 2007; Portes 2009). In Romania, too, a group of researchers has looked at the developmental effects of migration on origin communities[3] (Grigoraş 2006; Horváth and Anghel 2009; Oţeanu 2005; Stan 2005b) measured in terms of changing lifestyles and improving local economies. In this chapter I deal mainly with why people remitted and how these remittances changed migrant households. I will inquire into the relationship between migration and development only to a limited extent when I analyze migrant entrepreneurship.

Finally, research from the perspective of social change stresses that migration produces multifaceted social change in both origin and destination societies (Castles 2010). Although some authors are skeptical whether migration produces social change in the destination countries, arguing that ultimately migrants adapt to the basic values and institutional practices of their societies of reception (Portes 2010), others argue that such social changes do indeed occur (Castles 2010). However, there is more consensus over the consequences of migration in the societies of origin. Empirical evidence from origin countries reveals how new ideas, values, and schemes for social action are transmitted to and change migrants' origin communities (Levitt 2001b). Unlike the concept of culture of migration, which was applied in order to explain how migration is a force for perpetuating further migration, the focus on social change looks at the effects of migration and the new ideas, values, and expectations that are transmitted to migrants' origin communities. The effects of these transfers are not necessarily limited simply to the continuation of migration but extend to a wider transformation of the migrants' communities of origin.

In this chapter I depict how such a process of social change occurred in a Romanian town. I look at social change not only in terms of changing behaviors and values, but also in terms of the re-stratification of the origin community, where migrants' households tended to occupy a higher socioeconomic status vis-à-vis non-migrant households. In Borşa, intense migration to Milan brought about a series of changes at the local level which influenced people's behavior, at least in respect to power relations and consumption patterns. As previously described, the collapse of the former socialist industry led to economic decay and the impoverishment of the population after communism. In this context, international migration was the most viable solution for households to cope with increasing economic risks. Migration did not simply fulfill certain needs of migrants' households; it rather set in motion a complex process of economic, social, and cultural change, which intensified with the booming of migration after 2002.

Thousands of Borşeni used to return every year during the month of August, when holidays are taken in Italy. Even though the return effects of migration were visible throughout the whole year (for example in the modern villas that started to mushroom in the town or close to it), the ostentatious display of success and wealth during August was in fact the most visible part of a very intense transnational space that altered social relations in Borşa. In what follows, I summarize the main transnational practices that migrants sustain back home and indicate their effects. Then, I explain how these practices changed with the regularization of irregular migrants in Italy and the granting of freedom of movement to Romanians after 2002. I conclude by explaining how migration was culturally regarded as a process of social emancipation and prestige gain for migrants and their families.

REMITTANCES FOR SUSTAINING HOUSEHOLDS

After 1989 people moved to Western Europe in order to minimize households' risks and sustain their consumption during economic transition. Remittances involved several forms of arrangement. First, there were those in the form of money gained during the first years of irregularity, when savings were sent back to the households in Borşa. Second, there were remittances sent by legal migrants to support their relatives back home financially. In these cases, migrants continued remitting to sustain households and relatives even when these migrants had taken residence in Italy or intended to settle there long term. Third and finally, remittances were sent back when migrants had a clear intention not to settle in Italy. Migrants whose families were in Borşa, most of them middle-aged or with no plans to settle in Italy, used their remittances to cover house-hold costs, such as consumption and educational expenses for children, or to improve living standards and to build new houses. In other cases, migrants deposited their remittances in Romanian banks.

Research on Romanian migration stresses that Romanian migrants initially regarded their destinations of migration as countries where money could be earned and not as countries of settlement (Diminescu 2003; Diminescu, Ohlinger, and Rey 2003; Sandu 2005; Stan 2005b). With the migrants from Borşa, this was the case during the period when migrants lacked a specific legal status. Migration to Milan was an irregular enter-prise and for a few years only legal migrants were able to settle in Italy. This period of irregular stay represented for many a time frame during which they had to find appropriate housing and jobs in Italy, while sav-ings were sent back home. "There were risks, when I managed to gather some money I couldn't use it; I would send it home. I started to work for a company where they paid me three Euros an hour. I used some of the money for eating and sleeping. [The rest] I would send home" (George).

As they lived an insecure life in the first years of migration and did not have the possibility to hold bank accounts in Italy, migrants used to send their money back home. This was considered one of the safest strat-egies to protect their savings. In other words, migrants sent money home because they had no other choice, not because this was their purposeful intention. Different from investments in households and small-scale com-panies, this pattern of remitting had no other utility than securing the savings. Remitting was partially an act of supporting households but mainly a safety measure against potential risks, for example, situations when migrants could not find further employment and believed they had enough savings back home in order to return. Irregular migrants did not have clear plans to settle in Italy. They might save significant amounts of money but they rarely kept it in Milan. In such cases money was sent back home to parents or families, who safeguarded it or invested it: "They sent their money to their parents. They were illegal in Italy, didn't have any papers, so money was sent to their parents" (Pavel).

The strategies for sending money home were different over the years, from informal and risky practices to more institutionalized forms. In the cases I analyzed, during the first years of migration irregular migrants would send their remittances through the mediation of legal migrants going back to Borşa. Ruxandra remembered that in the beginning none of her relatives went home, as they were staying irregularly. They all had to send money through their acquaintances who were legal in Italy and who were able to travel home.

When a significant number of Borşeni had legalized their stay in Italy, they used to transport other migrants' savings back home. During the first years of migration, when legal migrants had on them large amounts of money, risks were understandably high.

> After I got my residency, I once brought about 6,000 DM (3,000 Euros) [of my money]. I was with a friend of mine who had 6,000 DM (3,000 Euros) too. In total, we had 42,000 DM (21,000 Euros), money taken from other migrants [to be carried to their families]. There were risks as it was [too much cash]. At the border crossing points we were supposed to declare it. We didn't think it was sensible [to fill in the financial declaration]; you never knew what could happen. [By then] you had to organize these journeys in groups, at least two persons in a car. It was safer to do so (George).

With the increase in the number of legal migrants, opportunities for money transfer multiplied. The development of the banking system and transfer agencies such as Western Union, but also of transport companies from Borşa offering money transfer services, facilitated the process of remitting. Finally, when freedom of movement was granted to Romanians, irregular migrants were able to come to Romania and carry their savings with them. It became easier and safer than before when irregular migrants were not able to travel back. Remittances were no longer brought by others. Currently this pattern of remitting has disappeared, although it was the preferred method of sending money in the first years after 2002, when the number of irregular migrants was quite high. By and large this procedure of remitting during migrants' irregular stay was important for migrants. It meant if something went wrong in Italy, migrants would have a second chance in their community of origin.

In contrast to irregular migrants, legal migrants were able to deposit their money in banks. Their savings were secure, and whatever their transnational practices, above all remittances, they were no longer related to protecting their money. For migrants residing legally in Italy the amounts sent back were meant to improve household economies back home until the migrants' families moved to Milan. If migrants' families continued living in Romania, the level of remittances remained high. Money was invested in improving living standards, consumption, better health services, and their children's education.

There were also temporary migrants who invested their savings in Romania. Legal temporary migrants worked legally for three to four months a year, mostly in agriculture. When this time was up, many migrants came back to Romania where they had regular employment. A typical example is Dumitru, who paid an intermediary to obtain a legal labor contract in Italy in agriculture. For the last few years he has worked for only three months a year. The rest of the time he worked in Borşa in construction, earning a few hundred Euros a month. His legal status in Italy was convenient for him, since his employer covered health and social insurance costs. With the money he earned in Italy Dumitru completed the construction of his house and was able to afford the costs of his household's consumption. He had two young children, whose care and education required more money than he was able to earn in Borşa; temporary labor contracts in the Italian agriculture sector helped him realize his goal to provide for his children's education.

Similarly, after 2002 there appeared irregular temporary workers who moved to Italy whenever they found job offers from migrants residing in Milan. Their stay was not limited to contracted seasonal labor, and they were involved in all kinds of activities. In the new context where Romanians were able to travel freely in the EU, migrants were able to reside for three months at a time in Italy, which led many migrants to decide to shuttle between Italy and Romania without overstaying the legal limit. Lucia said: "I come home during every holiday. I stay for one and a half months, then I go back to Italy. I stay there for two months whenever I want to. When my legal stay is over, I [always] come home. When I go back to Italy, I always find work."

Like Lucia, Vlad worked in Italy for short periods only and managed to keep his job there: "I stay there for three months and then I come back [to Romania] for a month, and so on . . . they keep the job for me. I plan to work there for a while and then come back." In such cases both the entry and the stay in Italy were legal, but work was irregular. After 2002 this became a possible and very convenient solution for migrants which allowed them to be in both locations, in Italy and in Borşa. It helped fill the demand for short-term labor on the Italian labor market, as migrants in Italy persuaded their employers to bring others in as well for such short labor contracts.

> [The Borşeni] come to work for five Euros an hour, and they help each other [when there is demand of labor]. They say [to their relatives back home]: "Come here to work one week." [After finishing the job] you go back home. This is convenient for everyone. [If these arrangements are] profitable for the employer too, they can stay there longer. One person can go for three months, come back home, and so on (Magdalena).

After 2007 Romanians were no longer limited in their residence in Western Europe, as they became European citizens. Their access to the labor market was restricted for a certain number of years after accession, but their residence was no longer limited to three months. Romania's access to the EU did not in fact change migration from Borşa significantly, as migration had already developed enormously after 2002. But people had increasingly more rights in Italy, which would increase their future opportunities in Milan even further.

Another important factor that influenced people's migration practices was the economic crisis that started after 2009 and affected both Romania and Italy. In Italy migrants complained about weaker labor opportunities and increasing uncertainties. They started to remit and invest less at home, trying to preserve their savings in Italy. This affected the labor market in Borşa, as migrants did not build as many houses as before. In Romania the effects of the economic crisis were particularly strong, so the negative effects of a deteriorating situation in Italy was not balanced by the development of the local or national economy. For a certain number of people, temporary labor migration to Italy remained a very important economic strategy, and they used their savings in Italy to cover their households' expenses in Romania.

Overall, migration, whether long-term or temporary, had marked effects on households' economic status. I already stated that in socialist Romania, rural households in general, but to a large extent in Borşa as well, sustained their consumption from two main sources: employment in socialist industry, which provided jobs for urban dwellers and commuters, and small-scale agriculture, which included cultivating the plots of nearby peasants' houses and breeding cattle and poultry (Horváth 2008; Mihăilescu 2001; Sampson 1995; Verdery 1996). After 1989 these households were strongly affected by the dismantling of socialist industry. For large segments of the population small-scale agricultural production based on farming the land and raising cattle and poultry remained the main provider of food and resources for households. In addition, due to the shrinking economy in towns and the inability of urban households to adapt to the new economic conditions, a process of urban–rural migration occurred. People were no longer able to afford the costs of urban living, so they returned to the villages from where they had first migrated to the cities during the period of socialist urbanization (Kupiszewski et al. 1997). Households in many Romanian regions lost their capacity to adapt to change due to a lack of resources. In a complex process of property restitution (Verdery 2003), land lost its value while agriculture on plots was simply inefficient (Dorondel 2004). The town of Borşa witnessed a dual residential structure. On the one hand, there were blocks of flats constructed during communism to accommodate migrants from other Romanian regions settling in Borşa as well as some of the older residents. On the other hand, there were houses with small plots where poultry, pigs, and cattle could be raised. This was a widespread pattern during communism, which took off again during the transition period. People built improvised cottages, even next to blocks of flats, so that they could breed chickens, or even pigs. During communism, this economic practice was justified by the absence of basic food products from the market. Afterwards it remained a much-practiced activity due to the impoverishment of the population.

Migration emerged as a new context that reoriented the economic activities of households in Borşa. The financial resources migration provided affected households to such an extent that they stopped breeding cattle, cultivating their plots, or using horses for transportation and agricultural work. This substantial change signaled a major shift in the local economy and in people's material culture. This process of change in the Romanian rural economy and the disappearance of subsistence agriculture nowadays have been documented in other Romanian contexts, too

(Voiculescu 2008). In Borşa such changes were generated by the high level of remittances.

Living conditions in Borşa were poor during communism and the transition period. The apartment buildings constructed during communism provided low living standards,[4] while houses were often small, usually made of wood, and inadequately equipped with sanitation. Once they started receiving money from abroad, people invested in improving their living standards.[5] With the development of migration, households were better protected in the face of economic risks, and people's consumption behavior changed significantly. They renovated their interiors, bought electrical appliances, and upgraded the furniture. People's level of comfort increased as well as their expectations of earnings. In consequence, remittances led to strong pressure on the wages employers paid in Borşa. Migrants' relatives were no longer interested in working for wages only marginally higher than the funds they received from their relatives abroad. This further increased the earning expectations in all households.

TRANSNATIONAL STRATEGIES OF INVESTMENT

Remittances sent to Borşa in recent years were privately invested, either in constructing new houses, or in small businesses opened up by migrants such as restaurants and small hotels. House construction has been the most visible and dynamic trend over the last ten years. It demonstrated a change of lifestyle and consumption, and it was also regarded as one of the safest investments. According to official data there were 1,166 new houses built in Borşa between 2001 and 2005, although the real number is in fact much higher. In 2002 there were 6,000 houses in Borşa, so that new houses made up about 20 percent of all houses.

There were many reasons that led migrants to invest in new houses. People started to build new houses in the first years of migration when irregular migrants remitted in order to secure their savings. In many cases these savings were invested in constructing houses because they were seen as a safety net. "We built a house because we thought: 'You can't stay all your life [in Italy], who knows [what can happen]?' You could be expelled, or they don't extend your residency, [you never know]" (Ruxandra). For the migrants who did intend to come back to Borşa, the construction of a house had practical uses. They were still fearful about their jobs in Milan with the increasing competition in the labor market. This uncertainty was one more reason to invest their money in something whose value would not decrease, and a house thus became a good option at least in the case of those migrants who thought about returning. "Some returned and wanted to construct houses here. In the last three years it has been difficult [in Italy]" (Bogdan). In other cases migrants' parents exerted social pressure on their children, thinking that building houses enabled young people to set up a family. The pressure for early marriage was very strong in Borşa,[6] and ownership of a house was often seen as a precondition. Consequently, when the parents of migrants received remittances, they made all the arrangements for them and supervised the construction work for the house. "I financed the construction of the house because that was what my parents wanted; I couldn't stand up to them any longer. They kept saying: 'Build a house, build a house'" (Alin).

A pattern was created: since most migrants did build houses in Borşa, it was understood that if someone was a respected and successful person, he had to build a house. Therefore, high expectations from relatives and friends generated a strong motivation if migrants were to show their worth and success in migration. Migrants' eagerness to construct new and big houses can thus be seen as the mark of competition fueled by locals' rapid enrichment through migration: "They built such big houses [to show they are no longer poor]. If one builds a house, the neighbor wants to have a bigger house too" (Tudor). Investments in houses made migrants' achievement very tangible; they could show off the wealth they accumulated in Italy and attest the success of migration: "They think that by having bigger houses, [they show] they are richer. It is a kind of self-esteem. They didn't think to invest their money somewhere else. They say: 'I have money, let's make a house, I won't lose'" (Vlad).

Initially the Borşeni moved to Italy as irregular migrants, ran risks, and lived in unsafe and inadequate conditions for years. Their socioeconomic status in Italy was low, as they mostly had jobs in the secondary labor market. But meanwhile they were able to gain higher prestige and achieve a higher socioeconomic status in their locality of origin. Migrants' multiple belonging at home and abroad thus resulted in a puzzling situation. On the one hand, they had a low socioeconomic profile in the destination countries because of the menial jobs and the marginal position they had to accept initially. On the other hand, the big houses they built in their origin community rendered them successful in the eyes of their fellow townsfolk and consequently they increased their social prestige.

We may conclude that investing remittances in building houses was caused by a multitude of factors: financial insecurity in Italy, the intention to found a family, the logic of competition among migrants, the struggle to attain new and better living standards, or simply strategic investment. It marked the new status migrants gained at home. Certainly constructing houses proved to be a good investment for many migrants a few years ago. Due to Romania's economic growth the real estate market boomed and prices multiplied several times between 2000 and 2007. In Borşa the market was inflated because much of the remittance investment went into construction. Labor became more expensive and land prices skyrocketed. According to my interviewees, these houses are now worth

Figure 6.1. Effects of remittances: constructing new houses. Source: Author's personal archive

far more than they cost when they were built.[7] Whereas initially migrants were able to construct a house with the money they could earn in less than two years, nowadays this would take much longer. The subsequent arrival of the economic crisis in Romania dampened real estate prices, which dropped by more than 60 percent in less than four years, between 2008 and 2012. But the construction of a house was still an economic proposition even in these circumstances, as it is still much cheaper to build than to buy, even at reduced house prices. Studies on migration throughout Romania have shown that migrants usually undertake house construction in their origin localities, especially in rural areas (Cingolani and Piperno 2006; Grigoraş 2006; Nagy 2008; Sandu 2006; Stan 2005b; Şerban and Grigoraş 2000). In Borşa a similar process took place.

Another important phenomenon is the growth in investment and entrepreneurship on the part of migrants, which reached its peak between 2005 and 2009. Some migrants started businesses locally, some invested their money elsewhere in Romania by purchasing land and flats in cities at high profit, whereas others preferred to open businesses in Borşa while maintaining work or business contacts in Italy. In these cases migrants had simultaneous involvements in business and investment.[8] Studies on different Romanian locales conclude that migrants developed small businesses in construction, trade, and even in the tourism industry (Grigoraş 2006; Oţeanu 2005; Stan 2005b), though, in truth, in most cases remittances went into consumption. At the Romanian national level, migrants' households evidenced a higher rate of entrepreneurial activity (10 percent) in comparison to the overall Romanian population (5 percent).[9] In Borşa there were cases of migrants with long migration experience and legal status in Italy who invested their money in the real estate sector both in Italy and Romania, buying flats in Italy and acquiring land and flats in different places in Romania. George, a fifty-year-old migrant, thought that he would stay in Italy a few more years and then return to Romania. He and his wife had two children, Anca and Sorin. Anca had completed her studies when I was in Borşa in 2005 but lived in Timişoara, where she had a job and a boyfriend. Anca had also lived for a few years in Italy but thought it made no sense to go there to work as a nanny when she could find a better job in Romania, even if it paid less. George and his wife decided from the beginning it made no sense thinking of staying in Italy for good, as they were in their forties when they left Romania. But both realized that sound investments would matter, helping them upon return and offering their children better prospects in life. The land George bought was for agriculture, as he thought of starting a business in agriculture after coming back from Italy.

> I bought 32 hectares of land in Timiş county using loans from Italian banks. Yet I want to take out another loan. I don't think I will stay long there; in less than five years I plan to come back. I talked to my brother in Timişoara about buying land. I also tried to buy a flat in Timişoara or Cluj, but finally I bought one in Timişoara for 21,000 DM (10,500 Euros). This flat is worth 40,000 Euros. Now I meant to buy another one in Cluj, but they are too expensive at the moment (George).

This type of investment was practiced by many Borşeni, such as Ruxandra, for instance, who "put about 80 to 90 percent of her savings into building a house and buying a large plot of land at Satu Mare"[10] (Ruxandra). The land was considered a good investment: as she herself explained her strategy for me, "I bought land not for agriculture, but to have [a good investment]."

With this piece of land, Ruxandra and Sandu tried to convince one of Sandu's Italian business partners in Milan to invest with them in a real estate condominium, as the land in question was located in the suburbs of the city and had good investment potential. In the end the plan did not materialize, as the crisis in 2009 had an enormous impact on real estate prices, which fell significantly. But for both of them, investment still has a great potential, as they think prices will resume growing in the foreseeable future. So what they did instead was to postpone their investment plans and await better times. Ruxandra and Sandu had some personal reasons to develop their investments in Romania. Sandu had a profitable business in Italy, but his four children did not all adapt well in Milan so Sandu preferred to keep his family in Borşa instead. He commuted between Milan and Borşa, but all the time he kept trying to open a profitable business in Romania in order to be closer to his family.

Migrants who did not follow this strategy and chose to invest only in Borşa expressed regret, as they thought they could have turned a bigger profit had they invested somewhere else in Romania: "If I had invested my money in a different city, my life could be much, much better. With this money [I put in Borşa], I could have got a good plot in Bucharest, Cluj, or Timişoara"[11] (Adrian). In Romania they faced no restrictions on how to invest their remittances, but in Italy only legal migrants were able to buy flats and sublet rooms to other migrants. Investments in Italy were made on different grounds than in Romania: the system of shared housing described in the previous chapter, designed to reduce rents, made these investments very profitable. In the long run legal migrants had the opportunity to become small-scale but successful entrepreneurs, especially those who could benefit from subletting housing space to other migrants; moreover, they acquired properties in a favorable context. "I know some [Borşeni] who bought houses in Italy. When Italy adopted the Euro, the value of these houses doubled. These [acquisitions] were good investments" (George).

In addition to investments in real estate, small-scale businesses were set up both in Italy and in Romania. In Italy Romanians started companies in the construction sector, while in Borşa migrants invested in the service industry, restaurants, and the construction sector. In one of these cases, a young migrant, who worked seven years in a pizzeria in Italy, opened a restaurant which became extremely profitable during the months when migrants, nicknamed "Italians," returned home for holidays in August–September. "With the money I saved I opened a pizzeria in Borşa. I started in 1997. I had bought the land in 1995 or 1996. When I came home with 10,000 DM (5,000 Euros), 20,000 DM (10,000 Euros), I could start building something. In what else could I have invested this money? Just let it waste? I bought some land and opened up this pizzeria" (Tudor).

Tudor is a young man who had a job in Italy. But he preferred the status of a small entrepreneur back home to that of a labor migrant in Italy. Because most of his clients were migrants from Italy, his business went well when "the Italians" were back in town. He thought about going back to Italy to work in a restaurant for the other less profitable months. In another case, a migrant started a construction company in Borşa but also had occasional contracts in Italy. Adrian was hopeful that the country would develop once in the EU and his business would grow in the future. He kept up some of his business relations in Italy, but he decided to return and brought his family with him.

> I was [in Italy] for nine years. Afterwards we said . . . [do we want] to
> stay our whole life [there]? I could stay till I reach pension age in
> Italy . . . I have permanent residency. I said: "I am going to come home
> and do something." I came back to Romania with my brothers. We
> opened up a plumbing and interior decorating company. We intend to
> open a pizzeria as well. Besides, this year I had a contract in Italy; I am
> going there right now. I don't have my company there any longer, but
> the architect with whom I used to work calls me from time to time. I go
> there for one or two months. I take my boys from Borşa, stay there for a
> while, fulfill the contracts, and then we come back (Adrian).

Migrants also started or planned to start their own transportation companies or small businesses in commerce or the tourism industry. The size of Borşa and its weak economy seriously limited the prospects for business, so that new companies were created only in certain economic sectors, and almost exclusively with the inflow of capital from remittances: "Many want to [start a business] in Borşa with the money from Italy. For instance, my ex-husband is in Romania already and he has a company in international transportation services" (Gina).

Finally, migrants like Ruxandra and Sandu have also attempted to attract Italian investors to Borşa, but their plans have not materialized so far. The tourism industry seemed very appealing to most migrants who considered using their newly constructed houses as tourism facilities. Borşa does have some tourism potential, as it is situated at the foot of the Carpathians, in the vicinity of a mountain resort with ski slopes and hiking routes. But tourism requires large investments in infrastructure, including better roads, and for that, a more active local administration (which has been bitterly criticized by many migrants for its lack of efficiency).

The investment enthusiasm that characterized the first years after Romania's accession to the EU did not continue afterwards once the current economic crisis struck. Migrants did not cease thinking about investing or developing some businesses in Romania, but they now postponed their plans.[12] Furthermore, some who had already invested did not see much profit from it when the real estate market collapsed in 2009–2010. In Western Europe also, migrants experienced increased precariousness. As the construction markets shrank in Italy and Spain, labor offers were no longer as rewarding as before, putting a lot of strain on Romanian migrants. In Spain, for instance, Marcu (2011) found out that plans to return among Romanians in the Madrid region doubled from 30 percent to 60 percent in the wake of the Spanish economic crisis. In Italy the labor market did not suffer as much as in Spain, but migrants similarly complained about the dearth of labor offers (Stănculescu and Stoiciu 2012). In such a context, the most profitable investments for people from Borşa were in real estate in Italy and Romania, and land acquisition in Romania, investments that would not lose too much of their value.

In sum, migrants' transnational investments materialized mainly in the form of new houses. Migrants with long residency histories in Italy diversified their investments in real estate: in Romania, in Borşa, or other locations in Romania and in Italy. Migrants who planned to return permanently had already opened up small-scale businesses at home. Some of them postponed their investment plans. Confronted with an unpredictable local market, migrants tried to maintain their business or work relations in Italy at least until their businesses in Borşa could get off the ground and attain a certain level of stability. Thus migrants developed business involvements in multiple locations and relied on different markets and opportunities, making use of local, national, or transnational ties.

MIGRANT TRANSNATIONALISM, SOCIAL CHANGE, AND PRESTIGE GAIN

Migration produced social change in regard to marriage patterns and consumption behaviors, and to the ways in which migrants' prestige changed. Research on the transnational family has recently started to focus on investigating the ways in which gender and family relations change in the course of migration. Empirical findings from different regions of the world (Jansen 2008; Morokvasic 1984; 1999; Parreñas 2005; 2008; Phizacklea 1998), Romania included (Şerban 2008; Vlase 2008), point to the reorganization of gender relations and family carework (Torre 2008). Borşa is no exception; indeed, many of these changes are noticeable to the naked eye. In what follows I focus on the ways in which marriage patterns have been redefined through migration. I will deal with the changes of consumption and social prestige later.

During the first years of migration, men outnumbered women among those leaving the country. This unevenness had consequences in Borşa in respect to marital practices. Initially, migration involved mainly young men who were away for long periods of time, and who encountered difficulties in finding partners in Italy. After obtaining legal status there, many took out loans from banks, bought cars, and went back to Romania for the summer and winter holidays to look for partners.

> There are some without education, and they go a few years to Italy and come here with some money. This is what many do. For instance, I come back from Italy, in a BMW X5, or a Jeep, and in a Versace suit. I say to my friends: "Can you introduce me to that girl?" If I like her, I can say: "Miss, let's buy you a leather jacket, let's go for a juice." The girl may be seventeen years old. And you can imagine: she may be poor, she might not have been in a car before. When she sees the money, what could she think? "He has money, I'll have a nice life." After a few years, she realizes they don't belong together, maybe (Codruţ).

Young migrants thus spent their savings to "show off how they made it big in Italy" (Magdalena), pretending to be successful persons in order to smooth their way into some love affair in Romania. "These men migrated from remote valleys where they had seen nothing at all before but mud and mountain roads. Suddenly they find themselves in the position to afford cars, and these cars become their life dream. [Here], they go out drinking and buying drinks for the girls" (Radu).

The negotiation of a new relationship and even a marriage was generally a quick matter; in many cases a relationship was set up within a month after a migrant got to know the young woman: "There are some who come with the clear plan to get married, and after two weeks they marry any available girl. Girls, too, want to escape from home and get married. In August, from Monday to Friday it is full with marriage ceremonies so that if you want to have a wedding you have to make reservations and announcements a year before the event" (Maria).

The couples often marry in the following year, and afterwards they move to Italy. Continuing their education is regarded as pointless by many youngsters, and often young girls marry before or immediately after graduating from high school. Early marriages and the minimum worth attached to the role of education in personal achievement accord with the locally defined gender role of women as housewives and mothers: education and professional careers are downplayed in comparison to household duties. Ruxandra said: "Here, they are quick to marry. From what we observed, in two months girls can be married if the boys are doing well financially. Girls here go to high school but all they dream about is Italy. There are just a few youngsters today who take school and education seriously" (Ruxandra).

Because of the local understanding of family and gender roles, there is social pressure to marry young and have children. As Lucia, a twenty-year-old woman, disclosed: "My mother always says: 'Hey, old women ask me when you will get married. You have to let me know in advance where and when, so that I can buy a proper outfit.' If I were to play by her wishes, I would have had children by now." She was very critical of her parents' attitudes. But she also married young. When I met her in Borşa in 2005 she had just finished high school. In 2006 she was already married and living in Milan. The social pressure to marry young, the short supply of young men in Borşa—as most of them had already gone abroad—and the mirage of Italy as Wonderland for many of the young people have markedly influenced love and marital choices. August was the month of making acquaintances, expediting love affairs, and partying out: "During the year you cannot find a girl on the street, and in August all of them are outside. The whole city is full of [young people getting to know each other]. And in September or October, the city is empty again" (Alexandra).

The image of migrants as successful in Italy played an important role in the selection of partners. In this context, "the Italians" were able to make a show of their wealth and were often preferred to those who chose to remain in Borşa. This state of affairs caused tensions between migrant and non-migrant men, since the latter felt the unfair competition of "the Italians." The pattern changed rapidly after 2002. Before that, only a small number of the migrants, those who were legal, could come back to Borşa for holidays, while the irregular migrants were not able to return for long periods of time. After 2002, they could all come back freely and their partners could visit them in Milan without restrictions. As a consequence, the rate of marriages has intensified over the past few years. Officials at the local registry office extended their working hours in August in order to process all the marriage requests.

Consumption was another important aspect of life that underwent a rapid change due to remittances and migrants' transnational practices. As noted above, it was clear from people's attitudes that "Italy" had become a model for consumption and had rearranged the local hierarchy of worth and prestige. Initially the local notion of prestige was organized around the concept of work: to be hardworking and conscientious was a highly appreciated attribute. With the onset of migration, this hierarchy started to change. Migration became culturally valued and a stay in Italy even for a short period endowed migrants with an aura of emancipation and prestige. New consumption patterns emerging in the city, and the image of Italy played an important role in this reshaping of prestige. Food, styles of fashion, and house design and decoration often imitated what migrants saw in Italy. Houses are probably the most telling example: on the one hand they were safe investments, but at the same time they emulated a type of lifestyle and level of comfort. As Dan, a young migrant man, put it, "I want to make my house like in Italy, with wall and floor tiles, not the way it looked before. 'The Italians' come back home, they don't like how [their houses look: if they have] wooden floors, they change them for tiles."

The migrants' emergent replication of "Italy" reshaped the framework of goods consumption—yet another change in the much longer and dynamic history of consumption patterns. During the socialist times, in the 1970s and especially in the 1980s, the great scarcity of goods in Romania led to a dramatic shrinking in consumption. Especially in the 1980s the socialist state imposed severe economic restrictions on the Romanian population. Western goods like clothes, music, and electronic appliances could be purchased only with great difficulty. A range of consumption goods as simple as chewing gum, pens, or pencils were stored by people in their houses. Things which were broken or used up were fixed or refurbished (Chelcea 2002b). Consumption had an added political meaning as well. In Romania, Western goods were seen as symbols of a prosperous and free Western Europe and people strove to procure them.

After the fall of communism, goods became available on the free market, but people were thrown into poverty and could not afford them. In Borşa, this was the context in which migrants could finally aspire to the type of consumption behavior they dreamed of and that they only saw in the West. Consumption was interpreted not only as a proof of financial well-being but also as a realization of the possibility, after decades of restriction, to at last consume as they do in Western Europe.

Nevertheless, through migration, consumption gained new attributes related to changes in the city and to migrants' newly acquired status. One of these new meanings of consumption is connected to the ways in which migrants associated their holidays in Borşa with leisure time: a stay in Romania was regarded as the deserved reward for their hard work in Italy, and migrants were willing to overspend their savings while they were there. To return home was considered a moral obligation towards the family, a time when migrants visited relatives and spent time together. It was also a tourist trip, leisure time, and an occasion for new love affairs after the hard work in Italy.

> When you are in Italy you don't go to a restaurant even once in a month, you don't have fun. When [people] come to Borşa in August, this is when they have fun and enjoy themselves! They have three such periods a year: in August, over Christmas, and during Easter (Călin). . . . [They come especially] in August during the holidays in Italy. They also come to see their brothers, mothers, sisters (Codruţ).

Second, consumption derived from migration became instrumental in new forms of social differentiation: it served to highlight the difference between migrants and their households on the one hand, and non-migrants on the other. Thanks to migration, migrants' families were now able to spend more than the remainder of the population. The disparity was visible throughout the whole year as constant consumption became an indicator of higher social status and prestige. But during the summers consumption was at its most ostentatious and many migrants spent large amounts of money in pubs and with their friends and relatives.

> When "the Italians" come home they are carefree and they forget [about their life in Italy]. They were poor [when they left], used to earn their money by working with a shovel, and now they are big shots and don't greet you any longer [on the street]. Today, they think highly of themselves and they drive four wheel drives (Dan). . . . Everything is busy in August: commerce, pubs, everything. And the streets are crowded and it is difficult to drive here, there are so many cars (Tudor).

Consumption was also interpreted as a form of competition among migrants, each trying to outclass the others. The almost universally shared impression was that "everyone wants to be perceived as higher and mightier in comparison to the others" (Magdalena), and that a kind of symbolic competition was operating. If someone had a grand house, the others felt the urge to build theirs even grander; the same logic applied in the acquisition of new and expensive cars. Conspicuous consumption and the display of one's wealth was flaunted by many migrants not simply by spending their incomes in Borşa; they would also borrow gold bracelets, fashionable clothes, or even cars from other Romanians in Italy and give them back upon their return to Italy.

> There are some guys who say: "Give me your necklace, I want to go home." Or: "Give me your car, please, I want to show off, to pick up some girls." There are many who do such things. And when they come to Borşa, [many girls] say: "Goodness, how much gold they have!" And those who didn't go to Italy think: "Wow! They came from Italy, [they have] money" (Alexandra).

Thus, consumption was deeply bound up in the processes of redefining prestige and social status difference between migrants and non-migrants. On the one hand, it played a role in fulfilling the needs of households; but it also contributed to satisfying desires, as people were able to access goods they had only been able to dream about during communism and afterwards. On the other hand, the goods migrants brought and the remittances they sent back created new tensions in Borşa, which was displayed in the competition among migrants themselves, who strove for status and prestige in their home town. After 2002 consumption did not change substantially, except in intensity as the number of migrants visiting Borşa grew and consumption increased. Even poorer irregular migrants were able to come home and emulate the consumption of their better-off counterparts.

TRANSNATIONAL MIGRATION AND SOCIAL TRANSFORMATION

Migrants' transnational practices were not without dramatic consequences for the social and economic life of the town. The local economy came to depend almost entirely on migrants' remittances. Employment changed as well: if before 1989 most people in Borşa were employed in socialist industry,[13] now they worked in commerce, construction, and services, all associated with the consumption generated by migrants' households. Through migration and migrants' remittances, the local economy was tightly connected to the Milanese economy. There was no other source of income that could compete successfully with migrants' incomes. The new investments in the city were started up by migrants primarily, and especially after they obtained longer-term contracts in Italy, or managed to open up businesses there.

Several other changes complete the canvas of economic and social shifts brought about by migration. Borşa was and still is a relatively isolated place. It is a small town in terms of its population, spread over hills and steep mountain slopes. No longer than thirty years ago many people lived without basic modern facilities such as electricity, a sewage system, or paved roads. This was not an exceptional situation in Romania, where such towns were but a conglomeration of shabby blocks of flats, appended to socialist industrial sites. Migration could therefore be regarded as social emancipation mainly in the shape of rapid change in the living standards of migrants' households: "Migration was the salvation of this region. These people were poor, and had quite large families. When they migrated, their first goal was to build new houses. If before they lived in poverty, now they could afford new houses and good cars" (Tudor).

Many did consider that migration had "civilized" the Borșeni and that access to a different culture and language had been nothing but beneficial to them. Whenever this opinion was verbalized, it was clearly framed in a "before," described in terms like "isolated," "impoverished," and "uneducated," and an "afterwards," defined as "civilized." Elements of the latter included a "better life" or knowledge of a foreign language. "They come back a bit more civilized, and are able to speak foreign languages" (Ionel).

Furthermore, the high level of remittances and migrants' transnational practices led to the restructuring of the local community into two strata: migrants and non-migrants. Thanks to migration, migrants and their households were now able to improve their material circumstances significantly, and in a short time they became richer in comparison to the rest of the population. Their social relations changed as well. As they became richer, the others were put out and considered the migrants' attitudes ostentatious and excessively aggressive towards the others.

> These people were poor, they lived somewhere in the hills. They didn't have electricity, they had nothing. Suddenly, they woke up in the West, with money "on" them. Now they want to show to the peasants remaining at home that they are no longer peasants. It is an emotional issue here, and they invest emotionally [in constructing houses and buying cars]. This is not an investment with a certain utilitarian purpose behind it. . . . They come home to show that they have cars (Sorin). . . . For some it doesn't matter if they earned money or not, if they slept on streets or even starved. It is important that they were in Italy (Dan).

Other qualitative studies analyzing the impact of migration on Romania (Alexandru 2006; Grigoraș 2006; Horváth 2008; Oțeanu 2005; Stan 2005b) point to a similar social differentiation between migrants and non-migrants in locales with a big incidence of migration outflows. At the national level, migrants' families were able to invest more in consumption (Grigoraș 2006), house construction, and the opening of businesses (idem). And in consequence of the economic betterment experienced by migrants' households, migration became the norm which organized the social and economic life in migrants' origin locales, at least in the poorer and rural areas of Romania (Horváth 2008). Accordingly, migrants' transnational practices in Borşa contributed to the increasing social "heterogeneity and struggles between conflicting identities and groups that [were] (re-)negotiated in the local places" (Ehrkamp 2005). Here this reorganization of social relations can be described as the rise in migrants' prestige and social status as well as the changing relations between "the Italians" and the rest of the population. The visible changes and this cleavage evolving around migrants' enrichment, which was seen by non-migrants as marks of ostentatious consumption, came to beat all records in August.

> When "the Italians" come back, they know they have more money in their pockets. So they say: "I do [here what I want]." Those who stayed home think that they want to show off, that they speak Italian now, and that they have forgotten to speak Romanian (Bogdan). . . . They want to show they're emancipated. For instance you cannot find ice cream with biscuits, nobody buys that here. [But] once I heard an "Italian" asking: "Do you have ice cream with *biscotti* (biscuits)?" Another time another one asked, "Do you have *coniglietto* (bunny meat)?" It is so obvious that it's only to show off. It makes you angry because if you have been [in Italy] you know how they live there. And here in Borşa you see them [overdoing it] (Magdalena).

These comments expressed the irritation of those left behind in face of the rapid changes in migrants' socioeconomic status and the redefinition of power relations. Migration was displayed in terms of emancipation and cultural and economic gain, and is in stark contrast to the living conditions that previously existed there. This was accompanied by changes in lifestyle and wealth associated with the prestige gain. But migrants developed a different attitude not only towards their non-migrant fellow citizens, but also towards national and local authorities in Romania, often raising critical voices against the way they handle public matters. People were aware that in Borşa the local economy depended on their incomes. They demanded better roads, and better mobilization of the local authorities towards improving the quality of public services.

> [The authorities] don't care about us. For instance here in Borşa, this town exists on the money [that we send]. Mining is almost closed. I send money every month to five persons here. Every month I send about 200 Euros at least. Only the "Italians" sustain Borşa economically. But we don't receive anything in exchange. These roads need repairing, at least two kilometers need to be laid. And tourism here doesn't function. Without us, this town would collapse. And when we come here, we damage our cars [on these roads] (Octavian).

In conclusion, migration was the main recourse for improving standards of life in the context of the collapsing post-socialist economy. It had the effect of improving income and led to the emergence of small-scale businesses, partly owned by migrants. Migrant remittances contribute essentially to the local economy. In the context of post-socialism de-industrialization and economic downturn, remittances saved many small businesses. Migrant households greatly benefited from migration, as they reached financial prosperity in a short period of time. Migration to Western Europe, particularly to Milan, became a desired life strategy. What is indeed striking is to observe the degree of change in the status these migrants experienced. In Italy they had lived a precarious life, often struggling to survive at the margins of the Italian society. Thanks to Italy's regularization programs and then to the accession of Romania to the EU, these migrants occupied a better socioeconomic position there than they had before. In Borșa in a couple of years they were transformed into successful investors. They competed over prestige and social status and became part of a privileged social category at home, eager to exhibit their rapid financial progress. Migration produced far-reaching social change: it reoriented people's life expectations, marriage behavior, and consumption, and it became a sought-after strategy for improving the course of one's life. Social hierarchy was reset on new grounds. As "Italy" became the model of social and economic success, migrants competed with the non-migrants in gaining reputation and social status.

NOTES

1. To have a walk.
2. Let's go!
3. For the levels of remittances in Romania and the macro and micro-economical factors, see Horváth and Anghel (2009).
4. See also Turnock 1991 and Ronnas 1982 for a more general consideration of the situation in Romania.
5. See also Nagy (2008), Stan (2005b), and Oțeanu (2005) for similar cases.
6. As in many Romanian rural areas (Stahl 2000).
7. For instance in 2001 a house could be constructed for 20,000 Euros, whereas in 2007 the same house would be worth 80,000 Euros.
8. See for instance the discussion of Smith (2001) on simultaneity, when he saw migrants involved simultaneously at multiple sites.
9. See Grigoraș (2006).
10. A largish city on the western side of Romania, by the border with Hungary.
11. Three of the largest Romanian cities.
12. The research was completed by 2008, when the economic crisis struck Romania. Although it led to significant changes, I do not aim to deal here in depth with the effect of the current economic crisis.
13. See table 4.2.

Conclusions

In the course of this book I have endeavored to show how certain groups of migrants constructed social status transnationally and how important prestige was in shaping migrants' life expectances and social action. So far there have been few attempts in the research on migrant transnationalism to analyze migrants' social status (Nieswand 2011), even though migrants' social status and social prestige are essential factors for understanding migrants' transnational subjectivities and their construction of selfhood. The issue that bewildered me throughout the course of my investigation was the following: how was it possible to explain that migrants receiving fewer rights perceived themselves as winners in terms of status and prestige, whereas those receiving a greater range of rights perceived that they had suffered a loss of prestige? Ethnic Germans from Timişoara who migrated legally to Germany after 1990 encountered a privileged reception: they acquired citizenship soon after their arrival and received relatively good jobs. In stark contrast to them, ethnic Romanians from Borşa had to face innumerable difficulties in order to migrate to Italy and first lived in poor conditions. And yet, over the years ethnic Germans came to feel they had suffered a downgrading of their previous social prestige, whereas Romanians from Borşa experienced a gain in status and prestige. This paradox reveals of the ambivalences and fractures existing in migrants' lives, which through various practices, connections, and symbols are connected to very different social realities *abroad* and *at home*.

The present analysis shows that in the long run migrants' status perceptions, their understandings of success or failure, are outcomes of social interactions generated in specific social contexts at home and abroad rather than by policies and ideologies of migration and integration. Romanian Germans in Nuremberg had high status and integration aspirations when they migrated, but felt social exclusion in Germany. Migrants in Italy, in contrast, did not aspire to higher social status abroad, as they moved there *as irregular migrants* with a clear aim of returning *home*. In spite of their low-skill jobs, they succeeded in gaining decently paid jobs over the years. Migrants' social status in their origin society dramatically influenced their status perception in the West. The ethnic Germans came from Timişoara, a developed Romanian city, where they had a very high symbolic status constructed historically in the regions they inhabited in Romania. Recognized as industrious, diligent, and modernizing individuals, they were able to secure a position of high social prestige in the ethnic hierarchy of Romania. In the first chapter I showed how ethnic Germans in Banat, previously composed of a well-off peasantry and urban dwellers, were the richest ethnic group there prior to the Second World War. With the arrival of socialism they lost much of their possessions. But despite the regime change and their lost property, they turned towards technical professions and managed to regain a position of high prestige in Romanian society. Their mass migration during the last years of socialism and the first years after the regime change, and consequently the almost entire extinction of centuries-old German communities, was regarded as a great economic and cultural loss. Migrants I interviewed had diverse occupations in Timișoara; some even came from well-positioned families there. This would in part explain the ethnic Germans' higher status aspirations upon their arrival in Nuremberg.

In contrast, the Romanians in Italy came from a remote and poor Romanian region. The town of Borșa developed and industrialized during socialism when the mining and forestry industries developed. Most migrants in Milan had previously been employed in one of these two domains, although there were also people who had been involved in administrative jobs. With the collapse of state socialism, people started to lose their jobs and became poor. In that context, migration was conceived of as something they had to do in order to avoid stark impoverishment and economic risks. Henceforth, migrants from Timișoara and Borșa had different social statuses in their origin society. This had great relevance for how they would perceive their social status abroad, as well as their success or failure in migration.

Second, and related to the first argument, policies played a role in the ways in which migration was carried out and migrants accommodated to the new societies, and on how they attained a particular social status after arrival. They also shaped migrants' expectations and how they understood their roles in the new contexts. But as the present research has shown, such policies carried significantly less weight over the years, once migrants received rights and adapted to their new contexts.

The destination states' migration policies, once adopted and implemented, provided migrants defined structures of opportunities for migration and incorporation. They created social ideologies for both migrants and locals, shaping the future framework of interactions between migrants, institutions, and the local population. When Germany adopted a policy for ethnic Germans' migration in the 1950s, migration was fiercely restricted by the Romanian communist state. Only after 1977, when the Romanian state came to an agreement with West Germany, were ethnic Germans able to migrate. In Romania, ethnic Germans had the sense they were *going home*. Their previous high prestige based on their German ethnicity, and the information on migration coming from other ethnic Germans already in Germany, had created high expectations among Romania's Germans. In a context where Germany's migration policy was extremely supportive for the arriving ethnic Germans, migrants from Romania went to Germany as *entitled* to receive a preferential treatment. Germany's migration policy towards ethnic Germans explains why and how these people migrated to Germany using the institutional channels that were offered them by the German state. Due to the very supportive framework of that policy, after 1989 entire German communities, including pensioners, moved to Germany overnight. This fact accounts for the weak transnationalism German migrants sustained to Romania later on. As there were no more friends, relatives, and acquaintances left in Romania, migrants ceased at least for the time being to maintain their relation to their country of origin. By providing extensive rights and opportunities, Germany's policy towards ethnic Germans also helped in explaining their successful adaptation to the labor market upon their arrival.

In contrast, Italy employed a laissez-faire policy. That Romanian irregular migrants arrived there can be accounted for by the weak state control and the recruitment campaigns to attract migrants in a context where labor was badly needed. Moving to Italy as irregular migrants, and encountering difficulties and risks all along their migrant careers, Romanians had no high expectations regarding Italy. But as Romania entered a critical economic downturn they were pressured to find ways to improve their economic stance at home. Migrants had to accept the fact that they were irregular, easy to be exploited and employed in 3D jobs, and had to climb the social ladder when new opportunities would come. Initially, migrants from Borşa encountered very difficult situations and high risks. They crossed borders on foot, underwent huge struggles to reach their destinations, were at times caught by the police, ran off risking capture again, and so on. They had to adapt to precarious living and working conditions. Their travel back and forth between Borşa and Western Europe was also irregular. Compared to the initial stages of migration, the process later on became more orderly: migrants' destinations were clearer and migration strategies were simpler and more efficient. Migration was still mainly driven by wage differentials between Romania and Italy and continued to be greatly facilitated by the existence of extended social networks among Romanians in Italy. One may also say that having large families helped the migrants throughout the process in financing and facilitating their migration as well as helped the migrating members to cope with the uncertainties they found in Italy. With the subsequent development of networks, newcomers did not face the same miserable conditions as the first movers. Despite having to live in overcrowded houses, they still had better conditions than the pioneers who went before them. Those who had moved first helped people recently arrived. Even if the role of kinship decreased when people's travel became unrestricted, the use of networks in the migration context remained important.

Enforceable trust and kinship obligations were also mobilized in this migration process. Before 2002 migration was realized mostly through the use of ties of kinship. But in 2002 Romanians received the right to travel freely within the EU. Thereafter, trust played an ever greater role, as kinship obligations were no longer required to finance and support migration to the same extent as before. Finally, new forms of mobility emerged after 2002 with the development of shuttle migration. The social costs of migration lowered further, as migrants and their families were able to see each other periodically by traveling between Romania and Italy. The socioeconomic status and the situation of migrants improved steadily due to the increasing rights migrants won over the years once Romania joined the EU. Even though they continued to work in 3D jobs, in time they did not perceive this to involve a status loss. But the destination states' migration and integration policies had unintended consequences. In contrast to the Germans, who settled in Germany and constructed their social status in Germany, Romanians retained their stakes in Romania and could claim no privileged status for themselves in Italy. Ethnic Germans in Germany were meant to arrive and live "as Germans among Germans," and their cultural and ethnic belonging was taken as a strong presumption of smooth integration (or better put, assimilation). Ironically, it was precisely this cultural and ethnic affinity that caused these migrants *not* to adapt to German society. They arrived as migrants, claiming the status of the locals, but it was precisely this status that was denied to them, and this became a source of social frustration.

Migrants' experience of incorporation was realized in terms of social and economic status attainment and as the construction of selfhood. Here migrants' understanding of the relationship between their expectations and the reality of incorporation was basic. Migrants could reasonably complain of status downgrading when their socioeconomic background was higher than their current employment opportunities. In other situations they could well become "middlemen minorities" (Portes and Böröcz 1989) if they had enough capital and stock of social resources. But as, for instance, in the case of highly educated East Europeans working as nurses in West European households, they were often unable to enhance their economic and social status. Conversely, migrants felt they succeeded when their expectations were met during incorporation. As my research suggests, what mattered was not the migrants' socioeconomic status *per se*, but how migrants valorized it. Ethnic Germans from Romania succeeded in attaining a good economic status, as they received state support for their incorporation in the labor market and access to the school system. In contrast, Romanians in Italy had to adapt to a pretty rough context. But by using their ties with relatives and friends coming from Borşa, they finally ended up successful. Although they worked overwhelmingly in the construction and caring industries, some gradually began to take up other jobs: in industry, transportation, and restaurants. Unlike the situation of the Germans, the networks of Romanians in Italy were structured along the lines of kinship and friendship ties from Borşa, and were enabled by kinship obligations and enforceable trust, yet with occasional support from their relations with Romanians from other parts of Romania. At the beginning migrants had a very low socioeconomic status, sleeping in tents on the outskirts of the city and finding work as best they could. Initially they used weak ties to obtain labor, but when networks of migrants multiplied, close ties were used to distribute jobs within these networks. By using networks, migrants were able to find longer-term contracts, rent and buy flats, and establish new ties with Italians to better access job offers for the whole kin group. Thus, these migrants' socioeconomic status improved steadily. Here status attainment was not realized through education and further specialization, as in the German case, but by access to jobs and intensive labor. Due to the development of networks, information and resources became more available to migrants in Milan. Amnesties in Italy also opened up new opportunities for migrants, including formal access to the labor market and to the Italian welfare system. Labor opportunities emerged through exploitation of weak ties to Italians or other migrants. Shared housing was also organized together with relatives and people from Borşa. Within a few years the migrants were able to adapt adequately to the adverse context of reception (Portes and Böröcz 1989) caused by the lack of institutional support. Their *closure* helped them in becoming successful. Despite the Germans' successful incorporation into the labor market, they continued to complain about their lack of social incorporation in Nuremberg and preferred to remain among themselves. The Romanians in Milan adapted well to the labor market in spite of Italy's laissez-faire approach. They, too, remained a close circle, but over the years they also started to develop friendships with Italians, notwithstanding negative public discourses on Romanian migration. Consequently, despite the huge difference in how migrants from the two groups were received and accommodated, they both adapted well to the labor markets over the years, succeeding eventually in earning decent wages.

Third, prestige was constructed as *respectability* by migrants in Germany and as *reputation* by migrants in Italy. Whereas migrants in Nuremberg constructed their social status *abroad* (i.e., in Germany) and wanted to be recognized and respected *as equals* by the local Germans, migrants in Italy constructed their status *at home* and wanted to be considered *as different* from those they left behind at home. The main difference between these migrants was how they conceived of their incorporation. Germans complained of non-integration, that they were considered Romanians by the local Germans and that their German ethnicity was not socially recognized. They were also inclined to construct an idealized image of Romanian women. The marriages of ethnic German migrants to Romanian women completed a paradoxical process. Although in Romania they had been Germans, some of these migrants "Romanianized," not in Romania but in Germany, and eventually reconnected with Romania. They differentiated themselves markedly from the local German popula-tion, socializing among themselves, using the Romanian language, and marrying Romanian women. Thus they ethnicized in Germany, ending up as "Romanians" in Germany. Romanians in Milan, in contrast, consid-ered their migration as successful when they obtained jobs and improved the economies of their households. In as far as Romanians had no high incorporation expectations upon arriving in Italy, this big leap forward was considered a real achievement for most of them.

These different attitudes towards social prestige also point towards two different understandings of migrant transnationalism. Whereas mi-grants in Germany developed only *transnational linkages* back home and simply traveled there from time to time, migrants in Italy maintained continuous *transnational practices and activities* with their origin commu-nity. In the latter case, migrant transnationalism provided an avenue for gaining social status at home and for accessing symbolic resources that migrants lacked in the societies of reception. The Germans had *no home community* against which to gain prestige. While a very large number of studies argue that migrants maintain sustained relations between the so-cieties of origin and destination, this case shows this assertion is not always true. By contrast, Romanians in Italy maintained strong transna-tional ties to their place of origin, where migration had wrought a deep process of social and economic change. Thus, if the Germans had fewer opportunities to claim prestige in their place of origin, the Romanians had plenty of them. Migrants sent their remittances from Italy to Roma-nia, sustaining their families, erecting new and big houses, and investing in small companies and real estate in Borşa and in other parts of Roma-nia. They also flaunted the success of their migration, wearing gold bracelets, renting and buying cars, wearing new clothes, and showing all of them off in the public spaces of the city. This ostentatious consumption arrived in a context where access to Western goods had been desired by people for decades. Migrants differentiated themselves markedly from non-migrants. Non-migrants complained that migrants showed off their newly acquired status. But even more, migration became a desired pat-tern of life. In a context where the passage from youth to adulthood could hardly be realized in the weak and unstable local economy, migration offered opportunities for young people to obtain decent and regular wages that they felt they needed in order to marry and start a family.

In this context, migration was perceived as access not only to econom-ic resources, but also to a different lifestyle, to West European culture and a life of new horizons and personal emancipation. Despite the hardship of migration and the hard work they put in in Italy, migrants perceived their life as successful, and the travel to and from between Italy and Romania, with progressively longer periods spent in Italy, was indeed rewarding. "People interpret status claims in a historical and community context" (Goldring, 1998, 173), and my analysis highlights the changes of migrants' socioeconomic statuses, capturing their perceptions over the years. In Italy the migrants led a precarious life, often struggling to survive on the margins of Italian society. But in the course of several years they turned into successful investors in the town of origin. They competed for prestige and became part of a privileged social category *at home*.

Accordingly, I have tried to show that when analyzing migrants' status and social prestige, attention must be paid to the often ambivalent or contradictory positions migrants have in relation to their societies of origin and reception. Instead of looking only at practices, connections, and ties that migrants sustain between their societies of origin and destination, I have preferred to pay attention to the migrants' ambivalent status and their attitudes in different societies and communities. As this book has illustrated, transnational spaces are social spaces where new fractures, contradictions, frustrations, and power relations emerge. Instead of the continuation of social relations and a simple direct transfer of capital, goods and money from, say, the core to the semi-periphery or periphery, I saw processes where people were trying to find new meanings and purposes to their lives.

In the first place, migrants' social status at home impacted on their status perceptions abroad, even when migrants did not maintain constant transnational practices back home. Second, the analysis showed the need for a multi-dimensional research perspective. A closer look needs to be taken at how migration policies impact comparatively on migrants' lives. It is not irrelevant if migrants receive fewer or more rights, if they can make use of institutions, if they have to face positive or negative public stereotypes. At the same time, policies impact on migrants' lives just for a certain period of time. Afterwards, their incorporation is more influenced by the social contexts of reception and labor market participation. Finally, my analysis looks at migrants' status attainment and social prestige in relation to longer experiences of incorporation and transnationalism (Itzigsohn and Saucedo 2002; Portes, Guarnizo, and Landolt 1999; Soehl and Waldinger 2010; Nieswand 2011). In short, I looked at migrants' status attainment in the context of the major changes taking place in migrants' lives over the years. I thus underlined the importance of a long-term perspective, according to which migrants construct their social status and prestige over a prolonged period of migration. The answer to the riddle I set out to solve in this book, and which guided my research efforts, emerged from this longer-term view.

References

Alba, Richard, and Victor Nee. 1997. "Rethinking assimilation theory for a new era of immigration." *International Migration Review* 4: 826-74.

Alexandru, Monica. 2006. "Migranți de migranți. Minori neînsoțiți în Italia." *Societatea Reală* (4) (Între România și Italia. Traiectorii migratorii): 144-66.

Allasino, Enrico, Emilio Reynieri, Alessandra Venturini, and Giovanna Zincone. 2004. "Labour market discrimination against migrant workers in Italy." *International Migration Papers 67*. Accessed July 26, 2012, http://ilo.org/public/english/protection/migrant/download/imp/imp67.pdf.

Alt, Jörg. 2003. *Leben in der Schattenwelt: Problemkomplex illegale Migration*. Karsruhe: Von-Loeper Literaturverlag.

Andreescu, Gabriel. 2005. *Schimbări în harta etnică a României*. Cluj- Napoca: Edit. CRDE.

Anghel, Remus G. 2005. "Economie informală în comunism și postcomunism: mere și țuică într-un sat din Maramureș." In *Economia informală după 1989: Piețe, practici sociale și transformări ale statului,* edited by Liviu Chelcea and Oana Mateescu, 787-802. București: Paideia.

———. 2008. "Changing statuses: Freedom of movement, locality and transnationality of irregular Romanian migrants in Milan." *Journal of Ethnic and Migration Studies* 34(5): 787-802.

———. 2010. "La migration internationale: Panacée ou entrave au développement local? Etude du changement social récent dans une ville roumaine de forte émigration," *Revue d'Études Comparatives Est-Ouest*, 41(4), 73-96.

———. 2011. "From irregular migrants to fellow Europeans: Changes in the Romanian migration flows?" In *Foggy social structures. Irregular migration, European labour markets and the welfare state*, edited by Michael Bommes and Giuseppe. Sciortino Amsterdam: Amsterdam University Press, 23-43.

———. 2012a. "On successfulness. How national models of integration policies shape migrants' incorporation." *Journal of Immigrant & Refugee Studies* 10(3): 319-337.

———. 2012b. "The migration of Romanian Croats: Between ethnic and labour migration." *Studia Sociologia* 57(2): 9-26.

Appadurai, Arjun. 1995. "The production of locality." In *Counterworks: Managing the diversity of knowledge,* edited by Richard Fardon, 204-23. London: Routledge.

———. 1997. "Discussion. Fieldwork in the era of globalization." *Anthropology of Humanism* 22(1): 115-18.

Bader, Veit. 2007. "The governance of Islam in Europe: The perils of modelling." *Journal of Ethnic and Migration Studies* 33(6): 871-86.

Baldwin-Edwards, Martin. 2007. "Navigating between Scylla and Charybdis: Migration policies for a Romania within the European Union." *Southeast European and Black Sea Studies* 7(1): 5–35.

BAMF (Bundesamt für Migration und Flüchtlinge) *Migrationstatistik Herkunftsländer 1974-2000*.

Ban, Cornel. 2009. "Economic transnationalism and its ambiguities: The case of Romanian migration to Italy." *International Migration*. Accessed June 2012. doi: 10.1111/j.1468-2435.2009.00556.x.

Banfi, Ludovica, and Paulo Boccagni. 2008. "Transnational family life: One pattern or many, and why?" In *Gender, generations and the family in international migration,* edited by Albert Kraler, Eleonore Kofman, Martin Kohli, Camille Schmoll, 287–313. Amsterdam: Amsterdam University Press.

Basch, Linda, Nina Glick-Schiller, and Cristina Szanton Blanc. 1994. *Nations unbound: Transnational projects, postcolonial predicaments, and deterritorialized nation-states.* Basel: Gordon and Breach.

Bauböck, Rainer. 2003. "Towards a political theory of migrant transnationalism." *International Migration Review* 37(3): 700-23.

Bauer, Thomas, and Klaus F. Zimmermann. 1997. "Network migration of ethnic Germans." *International Migration Review* 31(1): 143-49.

Beaverstock, Jonathan. 2005. "Transnational elites in the City: British highly-skilled inter-company transferees in New York City's financial district." *Journal of Ethnic and Migration Studies* 31(2): 245-68.

Black, Richard, and Jon Sward. 2008. "Measuring the migration-development nexus: An overview of available data." *Briefing no 13*: 1–4.

Bleahu, Ana. 2004a. "Fenomenul migrației externe în rândul tinerilor din România." *Revista ICCV* 3-4.

———. 2004b. "Romanian migration to Spain: Motivations, networks and strategies." In *New patterns of labour migration in CEE*, edited by Daniel Pop. Cluj: AMM.

———. 2006. "Între informal și ilegal, tolerați, dar nelegalizați!" In *Locuirea temporară în străinătate. Migrația economică a românilor: 1990-2006*, edited by Dumitru Sandu, 85-92. Bucharest: Fundația pentru o Societate Deschisă.

———. 2007. "With calluses on your palms they don't bother you: Illegal Romanian migrants in Italy." *Focaal* 49: 101-9.

Bommes, Michael, and Veronika Tacke. 2010. *Netzwerke in der funktional differenzierten Gesellschaft* Wiesbaden: VS Verlag für Sozialwissenschaften.

Bourdieu, Pierre. 1984. *Language and symbolic power.* Cambridge, MA: Harvard University Press.

Brubaker, Rogers. 1992. *Citizenship and nationhood in France and Germany.* Cambridge, MA: Harvard University Press.

———. 1998. "Migrations of ethnic unmixing in the 'New Europe.'" *International Migration Review* 32(4): 1047-66.

———. 2001. "The return of assimilation? Changing perspectives on immigration and its sequels in France, Germany, and the United States." *Ethnic and Racial Studies* 24(4): 531-48.

Bundesvewaltungsamt, *Aussiedlerstatistik.* Accessed July 25, 2006, www.bmi.de.

Burawoy, Michael. 1996. "Industrial involution: The Russian road to capitalism." In *A la recherche des certitudes perdues... Anthropologie du travail et des affaires dans une Europe en mutation*, edited by Müller Birgit,11-58. Berlin: Centre Marc Bloch.

———. 2000. *Global ethnography: Forces, connections, and imaginations in a postmodern world.* Berkeley: University of California Press.

Burawoy, Michael, and Katherine Verdery. 1999. *Uncertain transition: Ethnographies of change in the postsocialist world.* Lanham, MD: Rowman & Littlefield Publishers.

Çağlar, Ayse. 2001. "Constraining metaphors and the transnationalisation of spaces in Berlin." *Journal of Ethnic and Migration Studies* 27(4): 601-13.

Câmpeanu, Claudia. 2011. "Migration and changing ethnic relationships in a rural community in Transylvania, Romania." 8th annual conference, IMSCOE Research Network: Dynamics of European migration space: Economy, politics and development, September, 7-9, 2011, Warsaw, Poland

Carsten, Janet. 1995. "The politics of forgetting: Migration, kinship and memory on the periphery of the southeast Asian State." *Journal of the Royal Anthropological Institute* 1(2): 317-35.

Castagnone, Eleonora, and Roberta E. Petrillo. 2007. *Ukrainian and Romanian care workers in Italy: Two different migration models and strategies.* Manuscript.

Castellan, Georges. 1971. "The Germans of Rumania." *Journal of Contemporary History* 6(1): 52-75.

Castells, Manuel. 1996. *The Information Age: Economy, society, and culture. Vol. 1: The rise of the Network Society.* Oxford: Blackwell Publishers.
———. 1997. *The Information Age: Economy, society, and culture. Vol. 2: The power of identity.* Oxford: Blackwell Publishers.
Castles, Stephen. 1995. "How nation states respond to immigration and ethnic diversity." *New Community* 21(3): 293-308.
———. 2004. "Why migration policies fail." *Ethnic and Racial Studies* 27(2): 205-27.
———. 2010. "Understanding human migration: A social transformation perspective." *Journal of Ethnic and Migration Studies* 36(10): 1565-86.
Chelcea, Liviu. 1999. "Why did Banat become "multicultural?" Social transformation and collective memory in a pluriethnic region during communism." Paper presented at Socrates Kokkalis student workshop "New approaches to Southeastern Europe," Harvard University, February 12-13.
———. 2002a. "Informal credit, money and time in the Romanian countryside." Paper presented at the Fourth Nordic conference on the anthropology of post-socialism.
———. 2002b. "The culture of shortage during state-socialism: Consumption practices in a Romanian village in the 1980s." *Cultural Studies* 16(1): 16-43.
Chelcea, Liviu, and Oana Mateescu. 2005. *Economia informală după 1989: Piețe, practici sociale și transformări ale statului.* București : Paideia.
Chelcea, Liviu, and Puiu Lățea. 2000. *România profundă în comunism.* București: Nemira.
Chirot, Daniel. 1978. "Social change in communist Romania." *Social Forces* 57(2): 457-99.
Cingolani, Pietro. 2008. "Prin forțe proprii. Vieți transnaționale ale migranților români în Italia." In *Sociologia migrației. Teorii și studii de caz românești,* edited by Remus Anghel and István Horváth, 176-94. Iași: Paideia.
———. 2009. *Romani d'Italia. Migrazioni, vita quotidiana e legami transnazionali.* Bologna: Il Mulino.
———, ed. 2011. "Rom(eni) tra Torino e territori di partenza. Vita quotidiana, rapresentazioni mediatiche e politiche pubbliche." FIERI research report. Accessed January 30, 2013, athttp://www.fieri.it/rapporto_di_ricerca_romeni_tra_italia_e_territori_di_ partenza.php.
Cingolani, Pietro, and Flavia Piperno. 2006. "Migrazioni, legami transnazionali e sviluppo nei contesti locali. Il caso di Marginea e di Focșani." In *Intre România and Italia. Traiectorii migratoare,* edited by Vintilă Mihăilescu, 54-76. Bucharest: Paideia.
Cohen, Jeffrey H. 2004. *The culture of migration in Southern Mexico.* Austin: University of Texas Press.
Cohen, Robin. 1995. *The Cambridge survey of world migration,* Cambridge: Cambridge University Press.
———. 1997. *Global diaspora: An introduction.* London: UCL Press.
Coleman, James S. 1988. "Social capital in the creation of human capital." *The American Journal of Sociology* 94: 95-120.
Collyer, Michael. Myriam Cherti, Thomas Lacroix, and Anja van Heelsum. 2009. "Migration and development: The Euro-Moroccan experience." *Journal of Ethnic and Migration Studies* 35(10): 1555-70.
Colombo, Asher. 1996. "Amici, clienti, polizzioti." *Quaderni di Sociologia* 11: 51-77.
———. 2012. *Fuori controlo? Miti e realtà dell'immigrazione in Italia.* Bologna: Il Mulino.
Colombo, Asher, and Giuseppe Sciortino. 2003. "La Legge Bossi-Fini: estremismi gridati, moderazioni implicite e frutti avvelenati." In *Politica in Italia. I fatti dell'anno e le interpretazioni,* edited by Jean Blondel and Paolo Segatti, 195-215. Bologna: Il Mulino.
CNS (Comisia națională pentru statistică). 1993. *Anuarul statistic al României.* Bucharest : CNS.
———. 1994. *Anuarul statistic al României.* Bucharest : CNS.
———. 1995. *Anuarul statistic al României.* Bucharest : CNS.

Constantin, Florentina. 2004. "Migrating or commuting? The case of Romanian workers in Italy: Niches for labor commuting in the EU." In *(Un)Freedom of movement: migration issues in Europe. Part I.* Accessed July 26, 2012, http://www.soros.org/sites/default/files/romanian-workers-italy-20040101.pdf.

Crăciun, Magda, Răzvan S. Stan, and Maria Grecu. 2002. *Lumea văii. Unitatea minei, diversitatea minerilor.* Bucharest: Paideia.

Csedö, Krisztina. 2005. "Negotiating skills in global cities: Hungarian and Romanian professionals and graduates in London." *Journal of Ethnic and Migration Studies* 34(5): 803-23.

———. 2008. "Routes leading to London, negotiating skills in the Global City." Paper presented at ICOSS, The University of Sheffield, UK December 2-3.

Culic, Irina. 2010. "State of immagination: Embodiments of immigration Canada." *The Sociological Review* 58(3): 343-60.

Cvajner, Martina, and Giuseppe Sciortino. 2009. "A tale of networks and policies: Prolegomena to an analysis of irregular migration careers and their developmental paths." *Population Space and Place* 16(3): 213-25.

De Haas, Hein. 2008. "Migration and development: A theoretical perspective." Working Paper 9, Center on Migration, Citizenship and Development. Accessed July 26, 2012, http://www.imi.ox.ac.uk/pdfs/imi-working-papers/WP9%20Migration%20and%20development%20theory%20HdH.pdf.

Delgado Wise, Raúl, and Humberto M. Covarrubias. 2007. "The migration and development mantra in Mexico: Toward a new analytical approach." Paper presented at the conference Transnationalisation and development(s): Towards a North-South perspective, Center for Interdisciplinary Research, Bielefeld, Germany, May 31-June 01.

Dietz, Barbara. 1999. "Ethnic German immigration from Eastern Europe and the former Soviet Union to Germany: The effects of migrant networks." *IZA discussion paper no. 68.*

———. 2003. "East is West: The German experience of people flow." Accessed October 17, 2007,www.opendemocracy.net/people-migrationeurope/article_1417.jsp.

———. 2006. *Die Integration von mittel- und osteuropäischen Zuwanderern in den deutschen Arbeitsmarkt.* München: Osteuropa-Institut München.

Diminescu, Dana. 1998. "Installation dans la mobilité: The Migration to France of Romanian Peasants from the Oas Region." Paper presented at the conference *Social usage of an economic handicap or economic usage of a social handicap?* SSHA, Chicago, November 19-22.

———, ed. 2003. *Visible mais peu nombreux. Les circulations migratoires roumaines.* Paris: Éditions de la Maison de Science des L'Homme.

Diminescu, Dana, and Rose Marie Lagrave. 1999. "Faire une saison. Pour une anthropologie des migrations roumaines en France. Le cas du pays d'Oaş." *Migrations Études* 91: 1-16.

Diminescu, Dana, Rainer Ohlinger, and Violette Rey. 2003. "Les circulations migratoires roumaines: une intégration européenne par le bas?" *Cahiers de recherche de la MiRe* 15 : 61-69.

Dorondel, Ştefan. 2004. "Property, land use and the new rural elite in postsocialist Romania. A comparative study." In *Between East and West. Studies in anthropology and social history,* edited by S. Serban, 268-307. Bucharest: The Romanian Cultural Institute Publishing House.

Dowling, William C. 1991. "Germanissimi Germanorum: Romania's vanishing German culture." *East European Politics and Societies* 5(2): 341-55.

Durand, José, and Douglas S. Massey. 1992. "Mexican migration to the United States: A critical review." *Latin American Research Review* 27(20): 3-42.

Düvell, Franck. 2004. "Globalization, migration and policy response." Lecture held at the University of Koc, Istanbul, November 6.

————. 2005. "Networks, social capital and decision making in (irregular) migrations from the Eastern Europe: A comparative perspective." Paper presented at the conference: *New patterns of East-West migration*, Hamburg, November.

Ehrkamp, Patricia. 2005. "Placing identities: Transnational practices and local attachments of Turkish immigrants in Germany." *Journal of Ethnic and Migration Studies* 31(2): 345-64.

Elrick, Tim. 2009. *Transnational migration networks of Eastern European labour migrants.* PhD thesis, Freie Universität Berlin.

Elrick, Tim, and Emilia Lewandowska. 2008. "Matching and making labour demand and supply: Agents in Polish migrant networks of domestic elderly care in Germany and Italy." *Journal of Ethnic and Migration Studies* 34(5): 717–34.

Elrick, Tim, and Oana Ciobanu. 2009. "Migration networks and policy impacts: Insights from Romanian-Spanish migrations." *Global Networks* 9(1): 100-16.

Engbersen, Godfried. 2001. "The unanticipated consequences of Panopticon Europe. Residence strategies of illegal immigrants." In *Controlling a new migration world,* edited by Virginie Guiraudon and Christian Joppke, 222-45. New York: Routledge.

Epstein, Arnold L. 1967. "Urbanization and social change in Africa." *Current anthropology* 8(4): 275-284.

Eve, Michael. 2008. "Comparative notes. Some sociological roots of transnational practices in Italy." *Revue Européenne des Migrations Internationales* 27(3): 67-90.

————. 2010. "Integrating via networks: Foreigners and others." *Ethnic and Racial Studies* 33(7): 1231-48.

Faist, Thomas. 1994. "Immigration, integration and the ethnicization of politics." *European Journal of Political Research* 25: 439-59.

————. 1999. "Developing transnational social spaces: The Turkish-German example." In *Migration and transnational social spaces,* edited by Ludger Pries, 36-72. Aldershot: Ashgate.

————. 2000a. *The volume and dynamics of transnational social spaces.* Oxford: Oxford University Press.

————. 2000b. "Transnationalization in international migration: Implications for the study of citizenship and culture." *Ethnic and Racial Studies* 23(2): 189-222.

————. 2004. "Social space." In *Encyclopedia of social theory,* edited by George Ritzer, 760-63. Beverly Hills, CA: Sage.

————. 2007. "Transstate social spaces and development: Exploring the changing balance between communities, states and markets." Discussion Paper DP/169/2007. Accessed July 26, 2012, http://www.ilo.org/public/english/bureau/inst/publications/discussion/dp16907.pdf.

Faist, Thomas, and Andreas Ette. 2007. *The Europeanization of national policies and politics of immigration. Between autonomy and the European Union.* New York: Palgrave Macmillan.

Fassmann, Heintz, and Rainer Münz. 1994. "European East-West migration, 1945–1992." *International Migration Review* 28(3): 520-38.

Favell, Adrian. 2001. *Philosophies of integration. Immigration and the idea of citizenship in France and Britain. 2ⁿᵈ Edition.* New York: Palgrave Macmillan.

————. 2003. "Integrating nations: The nation state and the research on immigrants in Western Europe." *Comparative Social Research, Vol. 22-Multicultural Challenge*: 13-42.

————. 2008. "The new face of East-West migration in Europe." *Journal of Ethnic and Migration Studies* 34(5): 701-16.

Favell, Adrian, and Randall Hansen. 2002. "Markets against politics: Migration, EU enlargement and the idea of Europe." *Journal of Ethnic and Migration Studies* 24(4): 581-601.

Ferro, Anna. 2004a. "Romanians abroad: A snapshot of highly skilled migration." *Higher Education in Europe* 29(3): 381-92.

————. 2004b. "Romanians' email from abroad. A picture of the highly skilled labour migrations from Romania." Paper presented at *International roundtable on brain drain and the academic and the intellectual labour market in South East Europe, UNESCO-CEPES*, Bucharest.

Fijalkowski, Jürgen. 1993. "Aggressive nationalism, immigration pressure and asylum policy disputes in contemporary Germany." *International Migration Review* 27(4): 850-69.

Finotelli, Claudia. 2006. "Accolti o sanati? L'asilo e la protezione umanitaria in 'nuovi' e 'vecchi' paesi d'immigrazione. Il caso italiano in prospettiva comparata." In *Stranieri in Italia: Reti migranti 4th volume,* edited by Giuseppe Sciortino and Francesca Decimo, 211-45. Bologna: Il Mulino.

Flick, Uwe. 2004. *Triangulation. Eine Einführung.* Wiesbaden: VS Verlag.

Fox, Jon. 2007. "From national inclusion to economic exclusion: Ethnic Hungarian labour migration to Hungary." *Nations and Nationalism* 13(1): 77-96.

Friesen, Wardlow, Laurence Murphy, and Robin Kearns. 2005. "Spiced-up Sandringham: Indian transnationalism and new suburban spaces in Auckland, New Zealand." *Journal of Ethnic and Migration Studies* 31(2): 385-401.

Gamlen, Alan. 2008. "The emigration state and the modern geopolitical imagination." *Political Geography* 27(8): 840-56.

Garapich, Michal. 2008. "The migration industry and civil society: Polish immigrants in the United Kingdom before and after EU enlargement." *Journal of Ethnic and Migration Studies* 34(5): 735–54.

Gerharz, E. (forthcoming). *The politics of reconstruction and development in Sri Lanka.* New York: Routledge.

Ghosh, Bhimal. 1998. *Huddled masses and uncertain shores. Insights into irregular migration.* The Hague: Kluwer Law International.

Gieseck, Arne, Ullrich Heilemann, and Hans von Loeffelholz. 1995. "Economic implications of migration into the Federal Republic of Germany 1988-1992." *International Migration Review* 29(3): 693-709.

Glazer, Nathan, and Daniel P. Moynihan. 1963. *Beyond the melting pot: The negroes, Puerto Ricans, Jews, Italians and Irish of New York City.* Cambridge, MA: MIT Press.

Glick-Schiller, Nina. 2003. "The centrality of ethnography in the study of transnational migration: Seeing the wetlands instead of the swamp." In *American arrivals: Anthropology engages the new immigration,* edited by Nancy Foner, 99-128. Santa Fe, NM: School of American Research.

Glick-Schiller, Nina, and Georges E. Fouron. 1999. "Terrains of blood and nation: Haitian transnational social fields." *Ethnic and Racial Studies* 22(2): 340-66.

Glick-Schiller, Nina, Ayşe Çağlar, and Thaddeus Buldbrandsen. 2008. "Beyond the ethnic lens. Locality, globality and born-again incorporation." *American Ethnologist* 33(4): 612-33.

Glick-Schiller, Nina, Boris Nieswand, Günther Schlee, Tsypylma Darieva, Lale Yalcin-Heckmann, and Fosztó László. 2005. "Pathways of migrant incorporation in Germany." *Transit* 1(1): 1-18.

Glick-Schiller, Nina, Linda Basch, and Cristina Szanton Blanc. 1995. "From immigrant to transmigrant: Theorizing transnational migration." *Anthropological Quarterly* 68: 48-63.

Goldring, Luin. 1998. "The power of status in transnational fields." In *Transnationalism from below,* edited by Michael P. Smith and Luis E. Guarnizo, 165-95. New Brunswick, NJ: Transaction Publishers.

Gordon, Milton. 1964. *Assimilation in American life.* New York: Oxford University Press.

Goss, Jon, and Bruce Lindquist. 1995. "Conceptualizing international migration: A structuration perspective." *International Migration Review* 29(2): 317-51.

Gräf, Rudolf, and Mihai Grigoraş. 2003. "The emigration of the ethnic Germans of Romania under communist rule." In *Tolerance and intolerance in historical perspective,* edited by Csaba Lévai and Vasile Vese, 53-71. Pisa: Edizioni Plus, Università di Pisa.

Granovetter, Mark S. 1973. "The strength of weak ties." *The American Journal of Sociology* 78(6): 1360-80.

Grigoraș, Vlad. 2006. "Consecințe și proiecte. Venituri și investiții din migrație." In *Locuirea temporară în străinătate. Migrația economică a românilor: 1990-2006*, edited by Dumitru Sandu, 40-45. Bucharest: Fundația Pentru o Societate Deschisă.

Groenendijk, Kees. 1997. "Regulating ethnic immigration: The case of the Aussiedler." *New Community* 23(4): 461-82.

Guilmoto, Christophe Z., and Frederic Sandron. 2001. "The internal dynamics of migration networks in developing countries." *Population: An English Selection* 13(2): 135-64.

Hann, Chris. 1995. *The skeleton at the feast: Contributions to East European anthropology*. Canterbury: University of Kent.

———. 2002. *Postsocialism: Ideals, ideologies and practices in Eurasia*. London: Routledge.

Hannerz, Ulf. 2000. *Transnational connections: Culture, people, places*. London: Routledge.

Hart, Keith. 2000. "Kinship, contract, and trust: The economic organization of migrants in an African city slum." In *Trust: Making and breaking cooperative relations*, edited by Diego Gambetta, 176-93. Oxford: Oxford University Press.

Horváth, István. 2007. "Focus migration." *Country Profile* No. 9: 1-10.

———. 2008. "The culture of migration of the rural Romanian youth." *Journal of Ethnic and Migration Studies* 34(5): 771-86.

Horváth, István, and Remus G. Anghel. 2009. "Migration and its consequences for Romania." *Südosteuropa. Zeitschrift für Politik und Gesellschaft* 57(4): 386-403.

Hubert, Michel. 1998. *Deutschland im Wandel. Geschichte der deutschen Bevölkerung seit 1815*. Stuttgart: Franz Steier Verlag.

Isajiw, Wsewolod. 1997. "On the concept and theory of social incorporation." In *Multiculturalism in North America and Europe: Comparative perspectives on interethnic relations and social incorporation*, edited by Isajiw Wsewolod, 79-102. Toronto: Canadian Scholars Publisher.

ISTAT. 2013. *Popolazione straniera residente al 1° gennaio-focus sulla cittadinanz*. Accessed January 28, 2013, http://dati.istat.it/Index.aspx?DataSetCode= DCIS_POPSTRCIT1& Lang=.

Itzigsohn, José, and Giorguli S. Saucedo. 2002. "Immigrant incorporation and sociocultural transnationalism." *International Migration Review* 36(3): 766-98.

Janoschka, Michael. 2008. "Identity politics as an expression of European citizenship practice: Participation of transnational migrants in local political conflicts." In *The making of the world society: Perspectives from the transnational research*, edited by Remus G. Anghel, Eva Gerharz, Gilberto Rescher, and Monika Salzbrunn, 133-52. Bielefeld: Transcript Verlag.

Jansen, Stef. 2008. "Misplaced masculinities: Status loss and the location of gendered subjectivities amongst 'non-transnational' Bosnian refugees." *Anthropological Theory* 8(2): 181-200.

Joppke, Christian. 1998. "Why liberal states accept unwanted immigration." *World Politics. A Quarterly Journal of International Relations* 50(2): 266-93.

———. 2007. "Beyond national models: Civic integration policies for immigrants in Western Europe." *West European Politics* 30(1): 1-22.

———. 2010. *Citizenship and immigration*. Malden, MA: Polity Press.

Jordan, Bill, and Franck Düvell. 2002. *Irregular migration: The dilemmas of the transnational mobility*. Cheltenham and North Northampton: Edward Elgar Publishing.

Kaczmarczyk, Paweł, and Marek Okólski. 2005. "International migration in Central and Eastern Europe—Current and future trends." Paper presented at *United Nations Expert Group meeting on International migration and development*, New York, 6-8 July.

Karner, Tracy. 2000. "Social capital." In *Encyclopedia of sociology. Second Edition*, edited by Edgar F. Borgatta and Rhonda J. V. Montgomery, 2637-41. New York: Macmillan.

Kearney, Michael. 1995. "The local and the global: The anthropology of globalization and transnationalism." *Annual Review of Anthropology* 24: 547-66.

Kennedy, Paul T., and Victor Roudometof. 2002. *Communities across borders: New immigrants and transnational cultures.* London: Routledge.

Kindler, Marta. 2008. "Risk and risk strategies in migration: Ukrainian domestic workers in Poland." In *Migration and domestic work: A European perspective on a global theme,* edited by Helma Lutz, 145-160. Aldershot: Ashgate.

Kivisto, Peter. 2001. "Theorizing transnational immigration: A critical review of current efforts." *Ethnic and Racial Studies* 24: 549-77.

———. 2003. "Social spaces, transnational immigrant communities, and the politics of incorporation." *Ethnicities* 3(1): 5–28.

Kligman, Gail. 1988. *The politics of duplicity: Controlling reproduction in Ceausescu's Romania.* Los Angeles: University of California Press.

Koller, Barbara. 1997. "Aussiedler der großen Zuwanderungswellen–was ist aus ihnen geworden? Die Eingliederungssituation von AussiedlerInnen und Aussiedlern auf dem Arbeitsmarkt in Deutschland." In *Mitteilung aus der Arbeitsmarkt- und Berufsforschung,* edited by J. Allmendinger, W. Kohlhammer GmbH. Accessed March 17, 2008, www.iab.de.

Koopmans, Ruud, Paul Stratham, Marco Giugni, and Florene Passy, eds. 2005. *Contested citizenship: Immigration and cultural diversity in Europe.* Minneapolis: University of Minesota Press.

Krissman, Fred. 2005. "Sin coyote ni patrón: Why the "migrant network" fails to explain international migration." *International Migration Review* 39(1): 4-44.

Kupiszewski, Marek, Diana Berinde, Virginia Teodorescu, Helen Durham, and Philip Rees. 1997. *Internal migration and regional population dynamics in Europe: Romanian case study.* Working Paper 97/07. Accessed July 26, 2012, http://eprints.whiterose.ac.uk/5042/1/97-7.pdf.

Kurthen, Hermann. 1995. "Germany at the crossroads: National identity and the challenges of immigration." *International Migration Review* 29(4): 914-38.

Lăzăroiu, Sebastian. 2000. "Trafic de femei—o perspectivă sociologică." *Sociologie Românească* 2/2000: 55-79.

Levitt, Peggy. 2001a. "Transnational migration: Taking stock and future Directions." *Global Networks* 1(3): 195-216.

———. 2001b. *Transnational villagers.* Los Angeles: University of California Press.

Levitt, Peggy, and Deepak Lamba-Nieves. 2011. "Social remittances revisited." *Journal of Ethnic and Migration Studies* 37(1): 1-22.

Levitt, Peggy, and Nina Glick-Schiller. 2006. "Conceptualizing simultaneity: A transnational social field perspective on society." *International Migration Review* 38(3): 1002–39.

Levitt, Peggy, and Rafael de la Dehesa. 2003. "Transnational migration and the redefinition of the state: Variations and explanations." *Ethnic and Racial Studies* 26(4): 578-611.

Lin, Nan. 1999. "Social networks and status attainment." *Annual Review of Sociology* 25: 467-87.

Livezeanu, Irina. 1995. *Cultural politics in greater Romania: Regionalism, nation building and ethnic struggle, 1918-1930.* Ithaca, NY: Cornell University Press.

Luhmann, Niklas. 1997. "Globalization or world society: How to conceive of modern society?" *International Review of Sociology—Revue Internationale de Sociologie* 7(1): 67-79.

Marcu, Oana. 2010. "Health, life conditions and services access: Roma Youth in Gendered Street-work." Proceedings of the 24th *EHPS International Conference, in Psychology and Health* 25 (6):137–376.

———. 2011. "Donne rom e lavoro di strada in Civita, Massaro." In *Disuguaglianza e devianza femminile.* Milano: Franco Angeli.

Marcu, Silvia. 2011. "Romanian migration to the community of Madrid, Spain: Patterns of mobility and return." *International Journal of Population Research* 2011. Hindawi Publishing Corporation. Accessed January 30, 2013, doi:10.1155/2011/258646.

———. 2012. "Emotions on the move: Belonging, sense of place and feelings identities among young Romanian immigrants in Spain." *Journal of Youth Studies* 15(2): 207-23.

Marcus, George E. 1995. "Ethnography of the world system: The emergence of the multi-sited ethnography." *Annual Review of Anthropology* 24: 95-117.

Mardsen, Peter V. 2000. "Social networks." In *Encyclopedia of sociology. Second Edition,* edited by Edgar F Borgatta and Rhonda J. V. Montgomery, 2727-35. New York: Macmillan.

Massey, Douglas S. 1987. "Understanding Mexican migration to the United States." *The American Journal of Sociology* 92(6): 1372-403.

Massey, Douglas S., Joaquin Arango, Graeme Hugo, Ali Kouaouci, Adela Pellegrino, and Edward J. Taylor. 1993. "Theories of international migration: A review and appraisal." *Population and Development Review* 19(3): 431-66.

Massey, Douglas S., Luin Goldring, and Jorge Durand. 1994. "Continuities in transnational migration: An analysis of nineteen Mexican communities." *The American Journal of Sociology* 99(6): 1492-533.

Mazzucato, Valentina. 2008a. "Operationalizing transnational migrant networks through a simultaneous matched sample methodology." In *Diaspora and transnationalism: Concepts, theories and methods,* edited by Rainer Bauböck and Thomas Faist, 205-26. Amsterdam: Amsterdam University Press.

———. 2008b. "The double engagement: Transnationalism and integration—Ghanaian migrants' lives between Ghana and the Netherlands." *Journal of Ethnic and Migration Studies* 34(2): 196-216.

McMahon, Simon. 2012. "Assessing the impact of European Union citizenship: The status and rights of Romanian nationals in Italy." *Journal of Contemporary European Studies* 20(2): 199-214.

Meeus, Bruno. 2012. "How to 'catch' floating populations? Research and the fixing of migration in space and time." *Ethnic and Racial Studies* 35(10), 1775-93.

Meyer, John. 2005. "Weltkultur. Wie die westlichen Prinzipien die Welt durchdringen." Frankfurt am Main: Suhrkamp Taschenbuch Verlag.

MMT (Metro Media Transilvania) and ASG (Agenţia pentru Strategii Guvernamentale), 2007. *Comunitatea românească în Italia: condiţii sociale, valori, aşteptări—studiu sociologic.*

Michalon, Bénédicte. 2003a. "Circuler entre Roumanie et Allemagne. Les Saxons de Transylvanie, de l'emigration ethnique au va-et-vient." *Balkanologie* 7(1): 19-42.

———. 2003b. "Migrations des Saxons de Roumanie en Allemagne. Mythe, interdependence et alterité dans le 'retour.'" PhD thesis, Université de Poitiers.

———. 2004. "Migrations internationales et recompositions territoriales en Roumanie. La propriété immobilière, enjeu des relations des migrants saxons aux acteurs locaux en Transylvanie." *Méditerranée* 3(4): 1-8.

Michalowski, Ines, and Claudia Finotelli. 2012. "The heuristic potential of citizenship and integration models reviewed." *Journal of Immigrant and Refugee Studies* 10(3): 231-48.

Mihăilescu, Vintilă. 2001. "Householding, structure and culture in the Romanian rural society." *Romanian Journal of Sociology* 12: 1-2.

Morokvasic, Mirjana. 1984. "Birds of passage are also women..." *International Migration Review* 18(4) Special Issue: Women in Migration: 886-907.

———. 1999. "La mobilité transnationale comme resource: Le cas des migrants de l'Europe de l'Est." *Cultures et conflits* 33-34:105-22.

Moroşanu, Laura. 2011. "From the 'uprooted' to the 'rootless.' Transnational social ties of Romanians in London." Paper presented at Oxford Graduate migration research seminar series, Compas, Oxford.

Münz, Rainer, and Rainer Ohlinger. 1997. "Deutsche Minderheiten in Ostmittel—und Osteuropa, Aussiedler in Deutschland, Eine Analyse ethnisch privilegierter Migration." In *Diskurse und Entwicklungspfade. Der Gesellschaftsvergleich in den Geschichts- und Sozialwissenschaften,* edited by Hartmut Kaelble and Jürgen Schriewer, 217-70. Auflage. Frankfurt, New York: Campus Verlag.

————, eds. 2003. *Diasporas and ethnic migrants : Germany, Israel and Russia in comparative perspectives.* New York: Routledge.

Münz, Rainer, Wolfgang Seifert, and Ralf E. Ulrich. 1999. *Zuwanderung nach Deutschland. Strukturen, Wirkungen, Perspektiven.* Frankfurt am Main: Campus Verlag.

Nagy, Raluca. 2008. "Le Maramureş et ses mobilités. Cinq points d'articulation entre tourisme et migration." *Archive Martor* 13: 87–100.

Nedelcu, Mihaela F. 2000. "Instrumentalizarea spaţiilor virtuale. Noi strategii de reproducere şi conversie a capitalurilor în situaţie migratorie." *Sociologie Românească* 2: 80-96.

Neef, Rainer, and Manuela Stănculescu Manuela. 2002. *The social impact of informal economies in Eastern Europe.* Aldershot, UK: Ashgate.

Nieswand, Boris. 2006. "Methodological transnationalism and the paradox of migration." Paper presented at EASA Biennial conference, plenary session 3 *Transnationalism, diaspora and the crisis of multiculturalism in Europe,* September 20.

————. 2011. *Theorizing transnational migration: The status paradox of migration.* London: Routledge.

Okólski, Marek. 1996. "Poland's population and population in movements: An interview." In *Causes and consequences of migration in Central and Eastern Europe,* edited by Ewa Jazwinska, and Marek Okolski, 19-50. Warsaw: Migration Research Centre.

Oltmer, Jochen. 2006. "To live as Germans among Germans: Immigration and integration of 'Ethnic Germans' in the German Empire and the Weimar Republic." In *Paths of integration: Migrants in Western Europe,* edited by Leo Lucassen, David Feldman and Jochen Oltmer, 1880-2004. Amsterdam: Amsterdam University Press.

OSB (Oficiul de Statistică Baia Mare). 1967. *Recensământul judeţului Maramureş 1966.* Baia Mare.

————. 1978. *Recensământul judeţului Maramureş 1977.* Baia Mare.

————. 1993. *Recensământul judeţului Maramureş 1992.* Baia Mare.

Østergaard Nielsen, Eva. 2011. "Codevelopment and citizenship: The nexus between local and transnational engagement in migrant incorporation in Catalunya." *Ethnic and Racial Studies,* 34(1): 20-39.

Oţeanu, Ana M.I. 2005. "What do Romanian migrants invest money in? The undertaking of a life strategy for migrants from Vulturu, Vrancea County." In *A Tarkaság Dicsérete. Az Erasmus Kollégium Diákjainak Tanulmányai,* edited by Tibor Bárányi, Gergő Pulay, and Ildikó Zakariás, 366-77. Budapest: Erasmus Kollégium Alapítvány.

Palloni, Alberto, Douglas S. Massey, Miguel Ceballos, Kristin Espinoza, and Michael Spitter. 2001. "Social capital and international migration: A test using information on family networks." *American Journal of Sociology* 106(5): 1261-98.

Parreñas, Rachel S. 2005. *Children of global migration: Transnational families and gendered woes.* Stanford, CA: Stanford University Press.

————. 2008. *The force of domesticity: Filipina migrants and globalization.* New York: New York University Press.

Peleikis, Anja. 2000. "The emergence of a translocal community: The case of a South Lebanese village and its migrant connections to Ivory Coast." *Cahiers d'études sur la Méditerranée orientale et le monde turco-iranian* 30: 297-317.

Penninx, Rinus. 2006. "Recherches européenes sur les migrations internationales." Paper presented at *Conference Migrinter, 1985-2005: 20 ans de recherche sur les migrations internationales,* July 5-7.

Pfaff-Czarnecka, Joanna. 2005. "Das Lokale als Ressource im entgrenzen Wettbewerb: Das Verhandeln kollektiver Represäntationen in Nepal-Himalaya." *Zeitschrift für Soziologie, Sonderheft Weltgesellschaft* 479-99.

Phizacklea, Annie. 1998. "Migration and globalization: A feminist perspective." In *The new migration in Europe: Social constructions and social realities*, edited by Helma Lutz and Khalid Koser, 21-37. London: Macmillan.

Piore, Michael. 1979. *Birds of passage: Migrant labor in industrial societies*. Cambridge: Cambridge University Press.

Pittau, Franco, Antonio Ricci, and Alessandro Silj. 2008. *Romania. Immigrazione e lavoro in Italia. Statitiche, problemi e prospettive*. Roma: Caritas/ Migrantes.

Poledna, Rudolf I. 1998. *Transformări sociale la sașii Ardeleni după 1945*. Phd thesis, Universitatea Babeș-Bolyai, Cluj Napoca. 0

Portes, Alejandro. 1996. "Globalization from below: The rise of the transnational communities." In *Latin America in the world economy*, edited by William C. Smith and Roberto P. Korczenwicz, 151-68. Westport, CT: Greenwood Press.

———. 1998. "Social capital: Its origins and applications in modern sociology." *Annual Review of Sociology* 24: 1-24.

———. 2003. "Theoretical convergencies and empirical evidence in the study of immigrant transnationalism." *International Migration Review* 37(3): 874-92.

———. 2009. "Migration and development: Reconciling opposite views." *Ethnic and Racial Studies* 32(1): 5-22.

———. 2010. "Migration and social change. Some conceptual reflections." *Journal of Ethnic and Migration Studies* 36(10): 1537-63.

Portes, Alejandro, and Jozsef Böröcz. 1989. "Contemporary immigration: Theoretical perspectives and its determinants and modes of incorporation." *International Migration Review* 23(3): 606-30.

Portes, Alejandro, and Julia Sensenbrenner. 1993. "Embededness and immigration: Notes on the social determinants of economic action." *The American Journal of Sociology* 98(6): 1320–50.

Portes, Alejandro, and Patricia Landolt. 1996. "The downside of social capital." *The American Prospect Online* 7: 18-21.

Portes, Alejandro, Luis E. Guarnizo, and Patricia Landolt. 1999. "The study of transnationalism: Pitfalls and promise of an emergent research field." *Ethnic and Racial Studies* 22(2): 217-37.

Portes, Alejandro, William Haller and Luis E. Guarnizo. 2003. *Transnational entrepreneurs: The emergence and determinants of an alternative form of immigrant economic adaptation*. Transnational communities programme, Working Paper Series, Oxford: COMPAS. Accessed July 26, 2012, http://www.transcomm.ox.ac.uk/working%20papers/WPTC-01-05%20Portes.pdf.

Potot, Swanie. 2000. "Étude de deux réseaux migratoires roumains." *Sociologie Românească* 2: 97-115.

———. 2003. *Circulation et reseaux de migrants Roumains: une contribution à l'etude des nouvelles mobilites en Europe*. Phd thesis, Université de Nice-Sophia Antipolis.

Putnam, Robert, Robert Leonardi, and Raffaella Y Nanetti. 1994. *Making democracy work: Civic traditions in modern Italy*. Princeton, NJ: Princeton University Press.

Radu, Cosmin. 2001. "De la Crângeni—Teleorman spre Spania: antreprenoriat, adventism și migrație circulatorie." *Sociologie Românească* 1-4: 215-31.

Rescher, Gilberto. 2008. "Transnationality, translocal citizenship and gender relations: Transformation of rural community organisation, local politics and development." In *The making of the world society: Perspectives from the transnational research*, edited by Remus G. Anghel, Eva Gerharz, Gilberto Rescher and Monika Salzbrunn, 195-219. Bielefeld: Transcript Verlag.

Reyniers, Alain. 2003. "Migrations tsiganes de Roumanie." In *Visible mais peu nombreux. Les circulations migratoires roumaines*, edited by Dana Diminescu, 51-63. Paris: Éditions de la Maison de Science des L'Homme.

Rogers, Alisdair. 2005. "Observations on transnational urbanism: Broadening and narrowing the field." *Journal of Ethnic and Migration Studies* 31(2): 403-7.

Ronnas, Per. 1982. "Centrally planned urbanization: The case of Romania." *Geografiska Annaler. Series B, Human Geography* 64(2): 143–51.

———. 1995. "Romania: Transition to underdevelopment?" In *Problems of economic and political transformation in the Balkans*, edited by Jan Jeffries, 13-32. London: Pinter.

Salih, Ruba. 2002. "Reformulating tradition and modernity: Moroccan migrant women and the transnational division of ritual space." *Global Networks* 2(3): 219–31.

———. 2003. *Gender in transnationalism. Home, longing and belonging among Moroccan migrant women*. London: Routledge.

Sampson, Steven L. 1984. "Elites and mobilization in Romanian villages." *Sociologia Ruralis* 24: 30-51.

———. 1995. "All is possible, nothing is certain: The horizons of transition in a Romanian village." In *East European communities: The struggle for balance in turbulent times*, edited by David Kideckel, 159-76. Oxford: Westview Press.

Sandu, Dumitru. 2005. "Emerging transnational migration from Romanian villages." *Current Sociology* 53 (4): 555-82.

———. 2006. *Locuirea temporară în străinătate. Migraţia economică a românilor: 1990-2006*. Bucharest: Fundaţia pentru o Societate Deschisă.

Sandu, Dumitru, Cosmin Radu, Monica Constantinescu, and Oana Ciobanu. 2004. *A country report on Romanian migration abroad: Stocks and flows after 1989*. Prague: Multicultural center Prague. Accessed July, 26, 2012, http://aa.ecn.cz/img_upload/f76c21488a048c95bc0a5f12deece153/Romanian_Migration_Abroad.pdf.

Sassen, Saskia. 1991. *The global city: New York, London, Tokyo*. Princeton, NJ: Princeton University Press.

———. 1998. *The mobility of labor and capital: A study in international investment and labor flow*. Cambridge: Cambridge University Press, 1998.

Schmidt, Donatella. 2006. "La presenza romena a Padova: Quotidianità, lavoro, reti amicabli e centri di aggregazione." *Societatea Reală* 4: 79-99.

Schönwälder, Karen. 2004. "Why Germany's guestworkers were largely Europeans: The selective principles of post-war labour recruitment policy." *Ethnic and Racial Studies* 27(2): 248-65.

Schuck, Peter, and Rainer Münz. 1998. *Paths to inclusion: The integration of immigrants in the United States and Germany*. Oxford: Berghahn Books.

Schuster, Lisa. 2005. "The continuing mobility of migrants in Italy: Shifting between places and statuses." *Journal of Ethnic and Migration Studies* 31(4): 757-74.

Şerban, Monica. 2008. "Romanians to Spain—the road towards outside." Paper presented at the conference *The effects of international labor migration on political learning*, Cluj Napoca 6-7 June.

Şerban, Monica, and Bogdan Voicu. 2010. "Romanian migrants to Spain: In- or outside the migration networks—a matter of time?" *Revue d'Études Comparatives Est-Ouest* 41(04) : 97–124.

Şerban, Monica, and Vlad Grigoras. 2000. "Dogenii din Teleormani în ţară şi în străinătate." *Sociologie romanească* 2: 30-54.

Smith, Michael P. 2001. *Transnational urbanism: Locating globalization*. Oxford: Blackwell.

Smith, Michael P., and Luis Guarnizo. 1998. *Transnationalism from below*. New Brunswick: Transaction Publishers.

Smith, Raymond T. 1956. *The negro family in British Guyana: Family structure and social status in the villages*. London: Routledge and Paul Kegan.

Soehl, Tomas, and Roger Waldinger. 2010. "Making the connections: Latino immigrants and their cross-border ties." *Ethnic and Racial Studies* 33(9): 1489-510.

Stahl, Paul H. 2000. *Triburi şi sate din sud-estul Europei*. Bucharest: Paideia.

Stan, Răzvan S. 2005a. "Migraţia în România. O provocare sau o soluţie în procesul de integrare europeană?" *Raport asupra Guvernării*: 5-14. Bucharest: Societatea Academică Română.

———. 2005b. "Patterns and socio-economic consequences of international labour migration on Catholic and Orthodox villages from Eastern Romania (Neamt County)." In *A Tarkaság Dicsérete. Az Erasmus Kollégium Diákjainak Tanulmányai*, edited by

Tibor Bárány, Gergő Pulay, and Ildikó Zakariás, 379-93. Budapest: Erasmus Kollégium Alapítvány.

Stănculescu, Sofia M., and Victoria Stoiciu. 2012. *Impactul crizei economice asupra migratiei fortei de munca din Romania*. Bucuresti: Paideia.

Steiner, John, and Doina Magheți. 2009. *Mormintele tac*. Iași: Polirom.

Stoller, Paul. 1996. "Spaces, places, and fields: The politics of West African trade in New York City's informal economy." *American Anthropologist* 98(4): 776-88.

———. 1997. "Globalizing method: The problems of doing ethnography in transnational spaces." *Anthropology and Humanism* 22(1): 81-94.

Tesar, Cătălina. 2011. "Țigan bun tradițional în România, cerșetor de-etnicizat în străinătate. Politici ale re-prezentării publice și etica muncii la romii Cortorari." In *Spectrum. Cercetări sociale despre romi*, edited by Stefania Toma and László Fosztó, 281-313. Cluj Napoca: ISPMN- Kriterion.

Todesco, Daniele. 2008. "Rifiuto e acolienza: i rom romeni tra i gagé in Italia." Paper presented at the conference *In cerca di casa. Rom romeni in Italia e in Romania*, Torino, November 25-26.

Torre, Andreea. 2008. *Migrazioni femminili verso l'Italia: tre collettività a confronto*. Cespi Working Papers 41. Accessed July, 26, 2012, http://www.cespi.it/WP/WP41-TORRE. pdf.

Totok, William. 2003. "Germanii din România între nazism și stalinism." Paper presented at the conference *Minorități, moșteniri culturale, civilizație românească contemporană*, Bucharest, October 21-2.

Tränhardt, Dieter. 1995. "Germany: An undeclared immigration country." *New Community* 21(1): 14-36.

———. 1996. "European migration from East to West: Present patterns and future directions." *New Community* 22(2): 227-42.

Treiman, Donald J. 2000. "Status attainment." In *Encyclopedia of sociology. Second edition*, edited by Edgar Borgatta and Rhonda Montgomery, 3042-49. New York: Macmillan.

Troc, Gabriel. 2012. "Transnational migration and Roma self-identity: Two case studies." *Studia Sociologia* 57(2): 77-100.

Turnock, David. 1970. "The pattern of industrialization in Romania." *Annals of the Association of American Geographers* 60(3): 540-59.

———. 1991. "The planning of rural settlement in Romania." *The Geographical Journal* 157(3): 251-64.

Varga, Árpád E. 2002. *Statistică recensăminte după limba maternă, respectiv naționalitate, jud. Timiș 1880-1992*. Accessed July 26, 2012, http://www.kia.hu/konyvtar/erdely/erdstat/aretn.pdf.

Verdery, Katherine. 1985. "The unmaking of an ethnic collectivity: Transylvania's Germans." *American Ethnologist* 12(1): 62-83.

———. 1991. *National ideology under socialism: Identity and cultural politics in Ceausescu's Romania*. Berkeley: University of California Press.

———. 1996. *What was socialism, and what comes next?* Princeton, NJ: Princeton University Press.

———. 2003. *The vanishing hectare: Property and value in postsocialist Transylvania*. London: Cornell University Press.

Vertovec, Steven. 1999. "Conceiving and researching transnationalism." *Ethnic and Racial Studies* (22)2: 447-62.

———. 2000. "Rethinking Remittances." Plenary lecture at the 5th International Metropolis conference, Vancouver WPTC-2K-15. Accessed at July 26, 2012, http://www.transcomm.ox.ac.uk/wwwroot/drsteve.htm.

———. 2001. "Transnational social formations: Towards conceptual cross-fertilization." Paper presented at the workshop *Transnational migration: Comparative perspectives*, June 30-July 1, Princeton University.

———. 2009. *Transnationalism. Key Ideas*. New York: Routledge.

Vlase, Ionela. 2004. "L'insertion des femmes roumaines sur le marché du travail à Rome: un moyen de développement personnel et collectif." In *Femmes en mouvement. Genre, migrations et nouvelle division du travail*, edited by Fenneke Reysoo and Christine Verschuur, 115-26. Genève: IUED.

———. 2008. *Le genre dans la structuration du processus migratoire. Le cas d'une population rurale roumaine à Rome*. Unpublished PHD thesis, Université de Neuchâtel.

———. 2013. "'My husband is a patriot!' Gender and Romanian family return migration from Italy." *Journal of Ethnic and Migration Studies*. Accessed January 30, 2013, DOI:10.1080/1369183X.2013.756661.

Voiculescu, Cerasela. 2008. "Disappearing peasants? On land, rent, and revenue in post-1989 Romania." *Focaal: European Journal of Anthropology* 52: 77-91.

Voigt-Graf, Carmen. 2004. "Towards a geography of transnational spaces: Indian transnational communities in Australia." *Global Networks* 4(1): 25-49.

———. 2005. "The construction of transnational spaces by Indian migrants in Australia." *Journal of Ethnic and Migration Studies* 31(2): 365-84.

Vultur, Smaranda. 2000. *Germanii din Banat prin povestirile lor*. Bucharest: Paideia.

Wagner, Richard. 1991. *Ausreiseantrag. Begrüßungsgeld. Zwei Erzählungen*. Frankfurt am Main: Luchterhand Literaturverlag.

Waldinger, Roger. 2008. "Between 'here' and 'there': Immigrant cross-border activities and loyalties." *International Migration Review* 42(1): 3-29.

Weber, Georg, Armin Nassehi, Renate Weber-Schlenther, Oliver Sill, Georg Kneer, Gerd Nollmann, and Irmhild Saake. 2003. Emigration der Siebenbürgen Sachsen. Studien zu Ost-West Wanderungen im 20. Jahrhundert. Wiesbaden: VS Verlag.

Weber, Georg, Renate Weber-Schlenther, Armin Nassehi, Oliver Sill, and Georg Kneer. 1996. *Die Deportation der Siebenbürger Sachsen in die Sowjetunion 1945-1949*. Köln: Böhlau Verlag.

Weber, Max. 1964. *The theory of social and economic organization*. New York: The Free Press.

Wilson, Peter J. 1969. "Reputation and respectability: A suggestion for Caribbean anthropology." *Man* 4(1): 70-84.

Wimmer, Andreas. 2004. "Does ethnicity matter? Everyday group formation in three Swiss immigrant neighbourhoods." *Ethnic and Racial Studies* 27(1): 1–36.

Wimmer, Andreas, and Nina Glick-Schiller. 2002. "Methodological nationalism and beyond: Nation state building, migration and the social sciences." *Global Networks* 2(4): 301-34.

Zimmermann, Klaus F. 1999. *Ethnic German migration since 1989—Results and perspectives*. IZA discussion paper Nr. 50. Accessed at July 26, 2012, http://www.iza.org/en/webcontent/publications/papers/viewAbstract?dp_id=50.

Zincone, Giovanna. 2000. "A model of 'reasonable integration': Summary of the first report on the integration of immigrants in Italy." *International Migration Review* 34(3): 956-68.

———. 2006a. *Italian immigrants and immigration policy-making: Structures, actors and practices*. IMISCOE working paper, accessed July 26, 2012, http://library.imiscoe.org/en/record/208535.

———. 2006b. "Main features of Italian immigration flows and stock." Paper presented at *FIERI: Forum internazionale ed Europeo di ricerche sull'immigrazione*, May 31.

Index

About the Author

Remus Gabriel Anghel is a researcher at the Romanian Institute of Research on National Minorities, Cluj, Romania, and recurrent visiting professor at the Political Sciences Department, Babeş-Bolyai University, Cluj, Romania. He obtained his PhD in sociology at the University of Bielefeld, Germany. The areas of his research include Romanian migration in Italy and Germany, as well as the migration of ethnic minorities. He has published on the topics of migrant transnationalism, irregular migration, migration, development, and social change. He is currently involved in researching the effects of migration among Romanian and Roma migrants in Romania.

Lightning Source UK Ltd.
Milton Keynes UK
UKOW05n0815080913

216700UK00002B/32/P